WHAT DOES THIS LOOK LIKE IN THE CLASSROOM?

Bridging the Gap Between Research and Practice

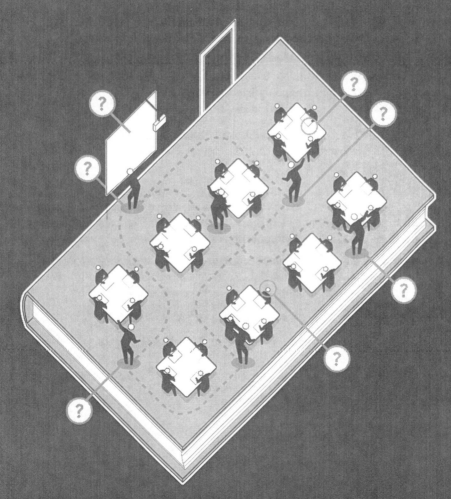

CARL HENDRICK AND ROBIN MACPHERSON

ILLUSTRATIONS BY OLIVER CAVIGLIOLI

First Published 2017

by John Catt Educational Ltd,
12 Deben Mill Business Centre, Old Maltings Approach,
Melton, Woodbridge IP12 1BL

Tel: +44 (0) 1394 389850 Fax: +44 (0) 1394 386893
Email: enquiries@johncatt.com
Website: www.johncatt.com

© 2017 Carl Hendrick and Robin Macpherson
Illustrations © 2017 Oliver Caviglioli

ISBN: 978 1 911382 379

Set and designed by John Catt Educational Limited

"Teachers are eager to use education research, but no one wants to wade through dense academic prose. Happily, this book takes a different approach and provides the 'human voice' of leading education thinkers on key issues, and shares their insights in ways that teachers will find relevant to their practice."

Benjamin Riley, executive director of Deans for Impact

"The pairings of interviewees are brilliant and, through answering teachers' questions in a discursive style, each chapter provides a fascinating insight that is often absent from formal papers. Wiliam and Christodoulou, Lemov and Robinson, Weinstein and Kirschner and all the others explore the territory of their expert fields in a way that will encourage all teachers and schools leaders at every career stage to engage with contemporary research and reflect on their own practice at a deep level. A great idea, executed brilliantly."

Tom Sherrington, author, consultant, trainer, former Head

"If you are a teacher or school leader, imagine having the opportunity to ask questions about what could work in your classroom, to some leading researchers and practitioners, based on their critical engagement with research? Carl and Robin have pulled all that together for you in one book. Engagement with research and evidence is the only thing that can protect teachers from fads and trends, the myths of education. This book demonstrates how you can do that, and reduce your workload at the same time."

George Gilchrist, board member, Scottish Parent Teacher Council, former Headteacher

CONTENTS

FOREWORD

By David Laws, Executive Chairman, Education
Policy Institute; Schools Minister 2012-2015

Most people would assume that education policy and practice is always – at least in richer countries – informed by rigorous evidence and testing. It seems obvious that a teaching profession would also be a learning profession – one informed by evidence of what works, and constantly evolving in the light of new evidence.

Sadly, in our country, and indeed across the world, too much that happens in education is based on hunch, assumption and ideology.

Governments are surprisingly reticent to base their policy actions on pilots, evidence and evaluation. They want to be seen to be 'doing something', rather than waiting before scaling new ideas. And an ever-critical media, which is more interested in bad news stories than in success, provides little incentive for elected politicians to commission genuinely independent evaluations of their most ambitious and expensive policy programmes.

Meanwhile, what research there is in education must often feel to teachers as if it isn't relevant or helpful in meeting the daily challenges which they face. Much analysis focuses on system level issues – school funding, debates over school structures, the impact of funding changes – rather than teaching practice.

And where research does begin to seem more relevant to teachers – for example in relation to continuous professional development – this often relates to arguments about aggregate amounts of activity rather than distinguishing between good and bad practice. In England, all too little time is made available for professional development, and much of this seems to be of limited real value.

For practitioners looking for a book that seeks to bridge the gap between research and practice, this short volume is like an oasis in the desert. In place of the model of 'top down school improvement', this book offers practical advice that is recognisable and useful to the classroom teacher. And instead of research that is presented in obscure and inaccessible form, this book presents the views of some of our leading educationalists in a straightforward and practical manner.

But this book is not just about imparting a bit of good, practical advice. It invites us to reflect on core principles for teacher development and improvement. And it shows how good professional learning can not only improve pupil outcomes but reduce the current very high levels of teacher workload.

The book advises that any intervention, policy change or new strategy must follow the asking and answering of seven key questions:

1. What is the need for change?

2. What are the potential benefits?

3. What is the evidence base for it?

4. What impact will it have on teacher workload?

5. What effect will it have on pupil learning?

6. Can a pilot be done before the initiative goes whole school?

7. Who needs to be consulted to ensure successful implementation?

These are excellent research and practice principles, not only for schools and for groups of teachers, but for all education policy-makers, from government level downwards.

In the meantime, the authors have done a fine service by gathering into one readable volume the reflections of some of our most impressive education thinkers and researchers. This is a book which will be treasured by school leaders and classroom teachers – a rare volume that provides not just immediate practical advice, but a new way of thinking about the development of research-based education in our schools.

David Laws, September 2017

ACKNOWLEDGEMENTS

This book is a collective effort. Many of the schools in the Wellington College Teaching School Alliance responded positively to our call for help, and dedicated time to holding meetings to develop questions. Professional Learning leaders, like Andrea Petri, are worth their weight in gold. Other teachers sent questions directly, which was fantastic. We can't list them individually but we would like to thank all the contributing teachers in the WCTSP who made this book possible:

WCTSP Member schools

Blessed Hugh Faringdon School

Bulmershe School

Carwarden House Community School

Collingwood College

Court Moor School

Edgbarrow School

King's International College

Oakbank School

Sandhurst School

St. Crispin's School

Tomlinscote School & Sixth Form College

The Emmbrook School

The Forest School

The Holt school

The Piggott School

The Wellington Academy

Waingels College

Wellington College

Winston Churchill School

We would also like to thank Iain Henderson, our line-manager. Hendo has been a great supporter of this project and, with Matt Oakman, he awarded the Teaching Fellowship that created much-needed time and financial support for us to complete the research and interviews.

Alex Sharratt deserves the highest praise for responding so enthusiastically when we pitched the idea, and backing us to the hilt with every twist and turn of the creative process. His efficiency and positivity kept things moving at a healthy pace and he has been a pleasure to work for. Jonathan Woolgar has a razor-sharp eye for detail and his editing skills made the text a lot tighter. Janet Aldred managed to keep track of our various emails and queries without ever losing patience, which was pretty remarkable.

Whilst all of this was going on, Hossa and Lu showed wonderful stoicism in putting up with all our enthusiastic updates about 'the book'. We're not quite sure what we've done to deserve their love and support, and we don't dare to ask.

Finally, we'd also like to thank Oliver Caviglioli, the Quentin Blake of education, for making this book come alive in such a vibrant way. When we asked him to help out we had no idea he would make such a massive contribution and he managed to bring our ideas to life in ways that we could never have imagined ourselves.

 I CAN TRACE the idea for this book back to a single event. Some years ago I was at an education conference listening to an accomplished speaker present research on how learning occurs. The presentation was cogent, well evidenced and engaging but I was nagged by a single thought: "this is all fascinating but what does it actually look like in the classroom?" At the time I was a full time teacher in a challenging inner city school, half way through a part-time PhD in education and began to experience a curious phenomenon — the more research I read about what actually happens in the classroom, the more confused I became. How we learn is not only counterintuitive but often contradictory. As Niels Bohr reminds us, the opposite of a true statement is a false one. But the opposite of a profound truth may well be another profound truth.

As an English teacher, I was probably more comfortable with more theoretical, abstract descriptions of the classroom but as I began to read research from other fields such as cognitive psychology, I found that many of my assumptions were being challenged in a way that warranted further exploration. I was discovering that many of the things I took for granted were not standing up to scrutiny. For example, how could it be that students were engaged and focused and yet unable to remember material we had covered so enthusiastically only a week ago? Why did certain lessons go so well and yet others descend into chaos? Why was I spending more time cutting up poems and putting them in envelopes than knowing them inside out?

Some years later, I was afforded some incredible opportunities though work and became a research lead at my school where I was fortunate enough to come into contact with a circle of people both at work and through the Festival of Education who really challenged me to reflect on my practice. From that, the nascent idea of a book that would take questions from the frontier of the classroom and put them to experts in the field began to form. One of the people with whom it was my great fortune to work with was Robin and his vision and organisational skills have been decisive in making this book happen.

If you had told me ten years ago when I started teaching that I would be writing a book like this, I would likely have recoiled in horror. My plan back then was to teach in order to support myself writing a novel and then move to New York to be one of those pretentious aesthetes sitting in cafes tapping away at a laptop, bearing witness to what I felt at the time was the centre of the universe. (Like John Lennon, I profoundly resented not being born in Greenwich Village.) But when I walked into a classroom that first time, something happened. Talking about Shakespeare in a room to a bunch of teenagers proved to be a humbling, zoetic experience from whose bewitchment I am yet to recover.

My view is that there is an ethical imperative to provide the best possible classroom conditions in which the students in our charge can flourish. This means rejecting what wastes time and embracing that which makes the most use of it. It's difficult to think of another serious profession that has so wilfully discarded evidence and embraced the transient and the facile as much as education has, and while evidence cannot give us all the answers, it can at least provide us with a roadmap to avoid the dead-ends and backroads of faddism and misinformation, however well-intentioned they may be. What actually happens in a classroom is in many ways inaccessible to us but good evidence can shed light on, and bring into focus to, what once seemed uninterpretable. As the blind Gloucester says to King Lear when asked how he sees the world, "I see it feelingly."

@C_Hendrick

AUTHOR PROFILE

 MY EARLY CAREER was about as typical as you can get. I studied History, I became a teacher of History and branched out to add Politics, Modern Studies and EAL at summer schools. So far, so normal. My second job was in an international school in the UAE and this piqued my interest in a few things. Firstly, teaching children from across the world was intriguing as cultural differences to learning made me think more deeply about my pedagogy and pupil motivation. I had colleagues from all continents and this opened my eyes to the diversity of our profession. I also taught the International Baccalaureate, and had my first head of department roles in History and Theory of Knowledge. Leadership was also high on my professional learning agenda.

When I moved back to the UK my new head, Sir Anthony Seldon, asked me at interview 'what book are you working on?' I thought he was mad. I'm a teacher, what time do I have to write a book?! However, the thought lingered as it was something I always wanted to do. I also started following a lot of blogs and expanded my reading from being mainly about subject knowledge to more on teaching and research. The only thing I'd ever really read about teaching since I began my career was Jonathan Smith's The Learning Game. Now I was trying to read at least one good book every term. I also joined Twitter thanks to Jill Berry's good guidance (one of many bits of sage advice she's given me) and this exposed me to the range of debate about research and pedagogy, warts and all. I didn't tweet very much (I'm a bit more 'head below the parapet' to be honest), but I did read avidly.

The second thing that made a difference was again a bit of prodding from Anthony Seldon; get involved in initial teacher training. Through this I mentored for PGCE and NQT and then became the overall co-ordinator at my school, and when we started a Teaching School Partnership I had the chance to visit a lot of schools and see a much wider range of teaching issues. This was a brilliant experience, and I think visiting other schools remains one of the most powerful – and cost effective – ways to advance your professional learning.

So here I am, juggling the writing and editing of this work. Why? I've lost track of the days and hours I've spent arguing the toss with Carl Hendrick about marking, feedback, behaviour, cognitive psychology and so on. We agree about a lot, but the disagreements are more fun. I think I've finally caved on lesson study (Carl had Dylan Wiliam on his side, not fair), but we'll keep arguing about everything else under the teaching sun. This book has been a quantum leap in my own development and knowledge. Interviewing what is effectively the Harlem Globetrotters of education would benefit anyone, but especially those like myself who harbour that nagging feeling of being a rookie who got this far by dint of lucky breaks and a bit of hard work. Whatever you think of it, let us know. Talking, arguing, laughing, crying, and arguing again about teaching is basically our main hobby. Feel free to join in.

@robin_macp

DEDICATION

This book is dedicated to Dr Joanna Seldon, an inspirational teacher and author, and our valued colleague and friend.

INTRODUCTION

CARL HENDRICK & ROBIN MACPHERSON

TEACHERS HAVE BEEN GIVEN ANSWERS TO QUESTIONS THEY DIDN'T ASK.

EFFECTIVE RESEARCH IS A FORM OF LIBERATION WHICH GIVES TEACHERS A RICHER VOCABULARY WITH WHICH TO NAVIGATE THE COMPLEX LANGUAGE OF THE CLASSROOM.

WHAT WE WANT IS FOR THE QUESTIONS TO LEAD TO OPEN DISCUSSION AND INVESTIGATION, AND WE DEFINITELY WANT TO AVOID THIS JUST BEING ANOTHER ECHO CHAMBER.

GOOD PROFESSIONAL LEARNING – LIKE RESEARCH – SHOULD NOT ONLY IMPROVE PUPIL OUTCOMES BUT ALSO REDUCE TEACHER WORKLOAD

THIS BOOK IS OUR WAY OF PUTTING A LITTLE SOMETHING BACK IN. WE HOPE YOU FIND IT STIMULATING, PRACTICAL, AND ENERGISING.

Karen is late for period 1. In addition to her weekly workload of teaching, marking and planning she has spent the last week reading research on what she believes will motivate her students to reach their potential and has planned a set of activities to shift her class from having a 'fixed' mindset to adopting the more desirable 'growth' mindset. The lesson includes watching a video about the plasticity of the brain, group discussions on where the students had failed in their lives and what lessons could be learned. Karen has been dedicating ten minutes a week to similar tasks over the year and the students have been engaged and receptive, and yet she has noticed a fundamental problem: none of this appears to have made any noticeable difference in their attitude to learning or grades.

What Karen is experiencing is a common problem facing many classroom teachers today brought about by an often gaping chasm between research and practice. We have learned more about how students learn in the past 30 years than in the previous 300 yet we still struggle how to translate that research into practical use in the classroom. We know for example that the limitations of working memory can negatively impact student learning on a range of levels from behaviour to basic misconceptions, but what practical use is that when you're facing a tricky group of teenagers last period on a Friday?

In their book *Inside/Outside: Teacher Research and Knowledge*, Marilyn Cochran Smith and Susan L. Lytle outline a fundamental problem with our profession, namely that there has been an *outside-in* model of knowledge creation about what effective teaching is and a top-down model of school improvement. Teachers, they claim, have effectively been passive participants in the process of what constitutes good practice, and in research terms have traditionally been mere 'objects of study':

> The primary knowledge source for the improvement of practice is research on classroom phenomenon that can be observed. This research has a perspective that is *'outside-in'*; in other words, it has been conducted almost exclusively by university based researchers who are *outside* of the day-to-day practice of schooling.[1]

---

1. Cochran Smith, M. and Lytle, Susan, L. (1992) *Inside/Outside: Teacher Research and Knowledge*, Teachers College Press, p.6

In a very real sense, teachers have been given answers to questions they didn't ask and solutions to problems that never existed. For example, planning lesson content to match the individual 'learning style' of students is an undertaking that has now been proved to have been a waste of time trying to solve and a sad indictment of how much time and energy has been expended on approaches with little to no evidence to support them. Much research in education is often published in obscure journals, inaccessible to classroom teachers using obtuse and unnecessarily complex language. As Orwell reminds us, 'there are some ideas so wrong that only a very intelligent person could believe in them.' For education research to have an impact where it matters most, it should be accessible, relevant and above all, practicable.

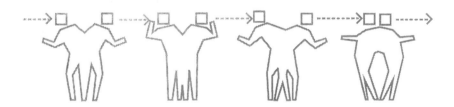

Even where there has been good evidence, a key problem has been implementation of that evidence. This usually manifests itself in a kind of Chinese whispers effect where researchers produce high quality research but by the time it filters down to the classroom, it's a pale imitation of its original form, devoid of any practical use. As we shall see in chapter 1, a good example of this is the way in which Dylan Wiliam's work on formative assessment was often implemented in a way that had very little impact on student achievement and a huge impact on teacher workload.

Another issue is the fact that research can only tell you what has worked in the past, not necessarily what will work in the future. Bernard Loomis notes that, 'the trouble with research is it tells you what people were thinking about yesterday, not tomorrow. It's like driving a car using a rearview mirror.' Just because a particular intervention proved to be effective with a group of undergraduate psychology students in California, it doesn't mean the same approach will work with a group of eight-year-olds on a cold November morning in Liverpool. However, what we are finding out is that children are often more similar than they are different in how they learn, retain and use knowledge and what we are now beginning to gather is a series of 'best bets' about effective practice in the classroom. These 'best bets' should be part of the arsenal of every teacher in how they plan effective teaching so that they can adapt and refine their practice according to the needs of their students. Many labour under the misconception that education research is merely the latest set of stone tablets telling teachers how to teach but when used judiciously, effective research is a form of liberation which gives teachers a richer vocabulary with which to navigate the complex language of the classroom.

It is a travesty that despite millions being spent every year on expensive professional development, many classroom teachers still have very little agency over what happens in their own classrooms, often at the whim of whatever fad or new initiative is currently in vogue. This is compounded by the fact that a lot of education research has come from the fields of sociology and anthropology with very little practical use for the classroom teachers. However, things are changing, and we are starting to see somewhat of a groundswell of support for the use of good quality evidence in the classroom at both local and national levels where many of the hard-won insights have very real implications for teachers like Karen who want to improve their practice but simply don't know how.

THE PURPOSE OF THIS BOOK

We started with the idea of writing a book ourselves about bridging the gap, but hesitated. If the purpose was to get classroom teachers to engage with research in a meaningful way, why not get them to ask questions directly? Rather than us writing several chapters on what we think, why not link up teachers like Karen with people who really know the research in a given area? This is where being part of a teaching school partnership came in useful. We work with three strategic partners: the IoE University of Reading; the IoE London; and the Wokingham Federation of Schools. There are currently 19 schools in the alliance and their diversity is a reasonable reflection of the sector at large, covering primary and secondary, faith-based, international, maintained and private, and special needs schools. We sent out an appeal to these schools to send us questions on the areas covered in the broad chapter headings. These came in by individual email, Twitter, and then in bulk from meetings that were held by professional learning leads.

We then had to evaluate and aggregate these questions. We had various questions all touching on a similar core theme, such as growth mindset or use of mobile phones in classes. Other questions were more niche but opened up important issues. Most appear exactly as they were asked, but where we have tweaked them it was because we thought the question would benefit from being more open, or less leading. You will be able to tell that questions come from NQTs as well as experienced teachers, and from those who have some understanding of research and those who have none. Some of the questions you will like, others you will not. We thought it was important to keep the authentic teacher voice, rather than substantially changing the line of enquiry or favouring those who already know a bit about the evidence base. What we want is for the questions to lead to open discussion and investigation, and we definitely want to avoid this just being another echo chamber.

We then put the questions to two experts in each field. The only steer we gave them before the interview was that the audience was classroom teachers (like Karen) so if they responded with practical examples it would be highly beneficial. Each person was interviewed separately and this was deliberate. Where they agree on a given issue, you can be fairly sure that the arguments and advice are sound. Where they disagree you will see that the evidence either isn't clear-cut, or the issue is yet to be explored fully. You will also notice that some questions have only been answered by one person, as the other interviewee preferred not to give an answer on a topic in which they did not consider themselves to be a leading authority. Suffice to say our respect for these people knows no bounds – they are honest and humble enough to wish to avoid posing as experts in a domain where they are not. Misleading teachers is the last thing that any of us wants to do, especially as a central theme of this book is to set teachers in the right direction in their pursuit of strategies that actually work.

We have written a brief intro to each area in order to set out the core issues and frame the debate. We have consciously avoided a strictly academic approach to our writing and to our referencing. This is because we want research to be presented in a way that makes sense for frontline classroom teachers; it is definitely not a case of dumbing down. The chapters and the questions within them are not intended to be comprehensive, but merely a starting point for debate and further enquiry. If teachers sit in their staff room at break-time and have a discussion about the answers to a question that they find intriguing then we will have fulfilled a key part of our mission statement.

The chapter on independent learning is a little different. This is a strong area of focus at the moment and the term is highly problematic. We therefore posed the same question to all 18 interviewees and the answers are fascinating. Rather than being a nebulous concept, there are themes and principles that emerge which can be of real use to teachers. Yet there are also diverging opinions that demonstrate the need for careful reflection before schools embark on this as an overarching strategy. We hope it is not too contentious to say that we all want our pupils to leave school with the capability to be self-sustaining, lifelong learners. How to achieve this in a curriculum that builds to a crescendo of life-changing external examinations is difficult. We hope that what you read in chapter 10 gives some food for thought, not least for policy-makers.

The final word goes to professional learning. We believe that there are some core principles to great teacher development. Firstly, teachers should have some say in what they learn rather than being forced to adopt specific targets extracted from a whole-school development plan and nothing more. Autonomy is vital if we want truly reflective practitioners with a high level of energy and morale. Secondly, good professional learning – like research – should not only improve pupil outcomes but also reduce teacher workload. We should be able to streamline what we do so that we can actually work more effectively and not expend effort on baseless initiatives. What is therefore vital is that professional learning informs and improves your practice rather than wasting your time. Thirdly, developing any serious skillset takes time and can't just be achieved on a one-day course. To this end, most professional learning is either low-cost or free, and works best when it is spread over time and leads to tangible benefit for your pupils. This is why we love reading as a form of professional learning, be it blogs or books like this. If teachers are going to help steer the nature and purpose of research, reading is the way forward. Wouldn't it be great if, for an inset day, your head took you to a good library?

With this book you don't need to read every line, or even follow it sequentially. Dip in and out as you see fit, cover the areas you are really interested in knowing more about, and then follow it up with the suggestions for wider reading. Teaching is the best profession in the world and has given us a huge amount of satisfaction. This book is, we hope, a useful contribution to the work of our fellow travellers. We hope you find it stimulating, practical, and energising.

CARL INTRODUCES

1

CHAPTER

ASSESSMENT, MARKING & FEEDBACK

DYLAN WILIAM & DAISY CHRISTODOULOU

> AT ITS CORE, FORMATIVE ASSESSMENT STRESSED THE NEED FOR ASSESSMENT TO BE SOMETHING THAT TEACHERS AND STUDENTS RESPOND TO IN ORDER TO REFLECT AND ADAPT THEIR PRACTICE BUT IN ALL TOO MANY CASES, THE 'ASSESSMENT' IN AFL BECAME MORE ABOUT COLLECTING DATA THAN IMPROVING LEARNING OUTCOMES.

> A CENTRAL PROBLEM IN THE AREA OF ASSESSMENT IN THE CLASSROOM HAS BEEN IN THE WAY THAT TEACHERS OFTEN CONFUSE MARKING AND FEEDBACK.

> A SET OF MARKED BOOKS IS TRADITIONALLY SEEN AS AN EFFECTIVE PROXY FOR GOOD TEACHING BUT THERE IS A LOT OF EVIDENCE TO SAY THAT THIS MIGHT NOT BE THE CASE.

> PERHAPS PART OF THE PROBLEM HERE IS THAT WE HAVE VERY LOW EXPECTATIONS OF WHAT STUDENTS ARE WILLING TO DO IN RESPONSE TO A PIECE OF WORK AND DO NOT AFFORD THEM THE OPPORTUNITY TO ENGAGE IN THE KIND OF TASKS THAT MIGHT REALLY IMPROVE THEIR LEARNING.

*'Judgement does not come suddenly; the proceedings
gradually merge into the judgement'*

Franz Kafka, The Trial

When Dylan Wiliam and Paul Black wrote their seminal work on assessment, *Inside the Black Box* in 1998, they could have had no idea that their work would later be mangled into a set of approaches that featured compulsory copying-down of learning objectives, an obsessive collection of data in the form of summative grades and students simply knowing what level they were working at without knowing what that actually meant. **At its core, formative assessment stressed the need for assessment to be something that teachers and students respond to in order to reflect and adapt their practice but in all too many cases, the 'assessment' in AFL became more about collecting data than improving learning outcomes**. Indeed, Wiliam would later say that he should have used the term 'responsive teaching' rather than formative assessment.

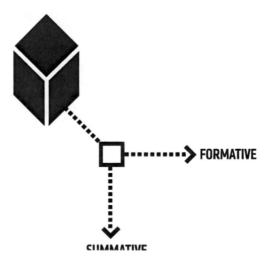

FORMATIVE

SUMMATIVE

A key problem with what assessment had become was the way in which it represented a final judgement as opposed to an opportunity to respond and improve. The fetish for collecting data in the form of individual grades (including sub-levels) was contrary to what Wiliam and Black originally envisioned. Later, Wiliam would reflect on this misappropriation and note that his original work had recommended that:

feedback during learning be in the form of comments rather than grades, and many teachers took this to heart. Unfortunately, in many cases, the feedback was not particularly helpful. Typically, the feedback would focus on what was deficient about the work submitted which the students were not able to resubmit, rather than on what to do to improve their future learning. In such situations, feedback is rather like the scene in the rearview mirror rather than through the windshield. Or as Douglas Reeves once memorably observed, it's like the difference between having a medical and a post-mortem.[2]

Like many initiatives in education, a key issue is in scaling up anything that looks promising and in this regard, policy-makers have often conflated the potential benefits of formative assessment with the more easily attainable summative assessment as Daisy Christodoulou points out:

> When government get their hands on anything involving the word 'assessment', they want it to be about high stakes monitoring and tracking, not low stakes diagnostics. That is, the involvement of government in AfL meant that assessment in AfL went from being formative to being summative: no longer assessment *for* learning but assessment *of* learning.[3]

A central problem in the area of assessment in the classroom has been in the way that teachers often confuse marking and feedback. As Wiliam points out in our discussion, there is an extraordinary amount of energy expended by teachers on marking and often very little to show for it in the way of student benefit. A set of marked books is traditionally seen as an effective proxy for good teaching but there is a lot of evidence to say that this might not be the case. Certainly students need to know where they make misconceptions or spelling errors and this also provides a useful diagnostic for teachers to inform what they will teach next, but the written comments at the end of a piece of work are often both the most time-consuming and also the most ineffective. For example, taking the following typical comments on a GCSE English essay:

· Try to phrase your analysis of language using more sophisticated vocabulary and phrasing.

· Try to expand on your points with more complex analysis of Macbeth's character.

2. Wiliam, D. (2011) *Embedded Formative Assessment,* Solution Tree Press, p.120
3. Christodoulou, D. (2017) *Making Good Progress?*, OUP, p.21

This is a good example of Reeve's 'post-mortem'-style marking. What is more useful to the student here: receiving feedback like that or actually *seeing* sophisticated vocabulary, phrasing and analysis in action? It's very difficult to be excellent if you don't know what excellent looks like. Instead of spending large amounts of time writing comments like these (over and over again) it may well be a better use of time to get students to evaluate the best three pieces of work produced by their peers and to critically evaluate the specifics of that successful writing, comparing it with their own and refining their own practice accordingly. As Dylan Wiliam reminds us, feedback should be more work for the recipient than the donor.

Often, teachers give both a grade and comments like those above to students, hoping that they somehow improve by the time their next piece of writing comes around a week later and then berate the student when, lo and behold, they make the same mistakes again. Perhaps part of the problem here is that we have very low expectations of what students are willing to do *in response* to a piece of work and do not afford them the opportunity to engage in the kind of tasks that might really improve their learning.

One of the more surprising things in many studies of feedback is not only that a lot of it has no impact, but that sometimes it can actually do damage. This can occur when feedback is given with too much frequency creating students who become too dependent on their teacher:

> Feedback that is given too frequently can lead learners to overly depend on it as an aid during practice, a reliance that is no longer afforded during later assessments of long term learning when feedback is removed.[4]

Lastly, an additional point to consider is that for many students, feedback is unwanted. If you have already decided that you are simply not good at maths, then why would you want to hear any more on the matter? Here is where the contextual factors around feedback are so important; **students will only act on feedback if they believe they can get better and so motivating students to believe in improvement itself becomes a key part of the challenge.** As we will see later on in chapter 5, motivation is an extremely complex dynamic where if students get a sniff that you are trying to 'motivate' them, they will often switch off. It may motivate a student more to walk them through how to complete an equation step by step and for them to bask in the glory of that achievement, however small, than to try to *motivate* them by talking about effort or belief. In this way, preparing the fertile seedbed of feedback, and more importantly

---

4. Soderstrom, N. and Bjork, R. (2015) *Learning Versus Performance*, p.23

a *response* to feedback, is about a lot more than marking books and assigning grades.

The questions we received from teachers largely reflected many of the issues outlined above in terms of how to give effective feedback in the classroom but also featured questions about larger issues such as the use of value-added data and the ways in which Assessment for Learning has been misunderstood and misused in schools. Answering these questions is the world's foremost expert in assessment, Dylan Wiliam, Emeritus Professor of Educational Assessment at University College London and the grand-architect of Assessment for Learning, along with Daisy Christodoulou, director of education at No More Marking and author of *Seven Myths about Education* and *Making Good Progress? The future of Assessment for Learning.*

> **DW**
>
> DON'T EVER GIVE FEEDBACK TO STUDENTS UNLESS YOU MAKE THE TIME THE NEXT TIME THEY ARE IN THE CLASSROOM WITH YOU FOR THEM TO RESPOND TO THAT FEEDBACK.

> **DW**
>
> IF THE FEEDBACK ISN'T HELPING THE STUDENT TO DO A BETTER TASK AND A BETTER JOB THE NEXT TIME THEY ARE DOING A SIMILAR TASK, THEN IT IS PROBABLY GOING TO BE INEFFECTIVE.

> **DC**
>
> THE DIFFICULT THING WITH SUMMATIVE EXAMS AND USING THEM DIAGNOSTICALLY IS THAT SUMMATIVE EXAMS ARE NOT DESIGNED TO BE DIAGNOSTIC.

> **DC**
>
> I THINK THE FIRST THING TO RECOGNISE IS WE'VE GOT INTO A BIT OF A SITUATION WHERE WE THINK THAT FEEDBACK AND MARKING ARE THE SAME THING AND ACTUALLY THEY'RE NOT.

CHAPTER 1   DYLAN WILIAM & DAISY CHRISTODOULOU

> **DW**
>
> IF THE STUDENTS DON'T HAVE A DESIRE TO IMPROVE, FEEDBACK IS UNWANTED.

> **DW**
>
> IF YOU PRICE TEACHER'S TIME APPROPRIATELY, IN ENGLAND WE SPEND ABOUT TWO AND A HALF BILLION POUNDS A YEAR ON FEEDBACK AND IT HAS ALMOST NO EFFECT ON STUDENT ACHIEVEMENT.

> **DW**
>
> THE BEST PERSON TO MARK A TEST IS THE PERSON WHO JUST TOOK IT.

ASSESSMENT
MARKING
FEEDBACK

> **DC**
>
> IN TERMS OF A FINAL ASSESSMENT, IF YOU WANT TO GIVE A GRADE ON IT, IT HAS TO BE ASSESSING QUITE A BIG DOMAIN, AND THE RISK I SEE HAPPEN A LOT IS THAT PEOPLE AWARD GRADES OFF THE BACK OF ASSESSMENTS THAT ARE QUITE NARROW IN THEIR DOMAIN.

What are the most effective ways of getting students to engage with and learn from feedback?

Dylan: I would say that the most important thing is to make the way students respond to feedback a direct task rather than just presenting feedback. So the way I describe it is to make feedback into detective work. For example, rather than saying to students, 'If you swap these two paragraphs around the story would be better,' you could say, 'I think it would be better if two of these paragraphs were reversed. Find out which two you think I'm talking about.'

So I think the important point is firstly, you have to give students a completable task in order to take the feedback on board and the second thing is you have to make them do it in front of you. I would say as a general principle, don't ever give feedback to students unless you make the time (the next time they are in the classroom with you) for them to respond to that feedback. After all, if it's important enough for you to give one-to-one advice to students, it's important enough to take lesson time to respond.

Daisy: I think that for students to engage with feedback and learn from it, it needs to be understandable. They have to understand what the feedback is and that might sound really obvious, but I think a lot of feedback is really hard for people to understand. My favourite example is one from Dylan Wiliam: where he once had a pupil who got feedback on their science project that said, 'You need to be more systematic,' and Dylan asked the pupil 'What does that mean to you?' and the pupil said, 'If I had known how to be more systematic, I would have been so in the first place.'

As Dylan went on to say, that's the equivalent of telling an unsuccessful comedian that in order to be better he needs to tell funnier jokes. So it's true, but is it helpful? There's not actually much you can learn from that. One thing is you need to frame the feedback in such a way that it is something that people can learn from, and in order to do that it has to be actionable. There has to be something they can go away and do in response to it. I think giving questions as feedback and particularly giving multiple choice questions as feedback can be really good because that's something that people can just do straight away.

It needs to be precise, so I think it needs to hone in on a specific thing that the people have misunderstood or got wrong and focus in on that. So

28

students need to understand it, they have to be able to take an action in response to it, and it has to be precise.

Q **'Feedback should be more work for the recipient than the donor.' How do you implement that?**

Dylan: An example in maths would be, rather than ticking 15 answers as correct and putting a cross beside five others, you could say to the student, 'Five of these are wrong. You find them; you fix them.' It is about getting into the habit of thinking about 'What concrete task do I want the students to engage in?' I think the important take-away here is that too many teachers focus on the purpose of feedback as changing or improving the work, whereas the major purpose of feedback should be to improve the student. If the feedback isn't helping the student to do a better task and a better job the *next time* they are doing a similar task, then it is probably going to be ineffective. So rather than asking students to do corrections, for example, which is in effect asking them to improve the work, I think we need to move the focus on improving the student's performance at some point in the future. That's why I think it is so important that feedback is more work for the recipient than the donor.

Daisy: Lots of students make similar mistakes to other people in the class and to people who have done the task before, so in a lot of cases you can anticipate the kinds of things they're going to say and therefore anticipate the kinds of feedback you should be giving. You can deal with lots of things at once, so I think the way for a teacher to cut down on their workload is to start to anticipate what's going to be a typical response and how they're going to respond to that.

For example, I was in a school the other day and there was a student who said, 'When you climb a mountain, the teacher told me that it gets colder on the top of the mountain, but actually it should be warmer. I think it should be warmer because you're getting closer to the sun.' That's a classic misconception. That child had come up with that themselves, but that is a really common misunderstanding, so it says to me that you can be identifying some of these really common misconceptions and thinking to yourself, 'What's the best way of responding to those?' That's one way a teacher can cut down on the workload, but I think in terms of them sort of upping the work or the challenge for their recipients, I think then it's something that goes back to what I said before about the actions. Students have got to be able to take some action off the back of the feedback they've got. Again, the idea of a question or a multiple choice question, or doing a bit of the work, or rewriting something, it's something that the student has to act on and have to think about. In that sense, probably the worst kind of feedback, I think, is when you get a written comment because written comments are way more work for the donors than for the recipients, because they take forever to write out written comments in each book, and yet students often just look at them and then look away and don't do anything in response.

It is said that feedback is more effective when students 'own' it. What does this mean exactly and how is it achieved?

Dylan: I think at the outset, it's important to say that we know very little about effective feedback. There are lots of people who say feedback is the most effective intervention there is, and people often quote an effect size of 0.8 but I don't think those things are realistic and they also ignore the studies that show considerable *negative* effects of feedback as well. And of course these effects may not be random. Even if feedback does, on average, improve achievement, without a better understanding of feedback, we may end up systematically giving students more of the kinds of feedback that has a negative effect on learning. More feedback could actually make learning worse.

Ideally, *owning* feedback would come from the students *seeking* feedback. If the students don't have a desire to improve, feedback is unwanted. If you think you can't get any better at something then all you want to know is whether you're good at it, and so feedback that shows you're not as good as you thought you were is unwelcome. People often call this a growth mindset but it is actually incorrect to describe it as that because the work of Carol Dweck (who coined the term) is specifically related to intelligence, rather than ability or skills. The starting point for effective feedback is students wanting to get better at something and seeing the feedback as being helpful in directing their improvement. Students really *own* the feedback when they *want* the improvement.

The problem in all this is that many teachers are giving their students feedback on things that the students don't really want to get better at, or think they *can't* get better at and that's why the feedback is unwelcome. What we do about this depends on how far back in that process we want to go, but recent research by David Yeager and his colleagues in the US suggests that one particularly important element is making sure that students understand why the feedback is being given. For example, a teacher might say, 'I am giving you this feedback because I think you can get better at this; I think you can do this.' David Yeager calls it 'wise feedback'. Yeager and his colleagues have shown that when teachers explain to students that critical feedback means both that 'I have high standards' and 'I think you can achieve these high standards', students had higher achievement at the end of the course and were more likely to complete high school. Just one sentence explaining to students *why* feedback was being given made a huge difference to their achievement. That's the really important point – seeing feedback as being part of a system of continual improvement and then building on that by showing students how acting on the feedback causes improvement. So when students realise that when they are given feedback and they act on it and get better, *then* students come to believe that more feedback can lead to even more improvement.

Daisy: Again, I think people just have to understand what it means and what it's telling you to do. You had this thing back with the APP, the pupil criteria, the assessment for the pupil group where they came up with pupil-friendly statements, but even the pupil-friendly statements were not actually that easy to understand. Even if you're saying to pupils in order to get a level four you need to be able to 'read between the lines', what does it mean to read between the lines? I don't think a student can own something unless it's clear to them what it means. I think to give feedback that's clear, they need some understanding of the domain in order to be able to understand the feedback.

It has to be very specific, very precise, and making sure that it's expressed in such a way and that it's dealing with something that the people already have some ownership of. That's why I'd say that questions are a good response, or something that is following up very immediately on something that people have just done. It's something they can act on instantly.

Q **Marking is probably the most time-expensive task any teacher can do. What strategies have you got to speed up the process and make the feedback more useful?**

Dylan: Yeah you are absolutely right. I once estimated that, if you price teachers' time appropriately, in England we spend about two and a half billion pounds a year on feedback and it has almost no effect on student achievement. In terms of what we do about this, I would say first of all, headteachers should lay down clear expectation to parents and say things like, 'We are not going to give detailed feedback on more than 25% of what your child does. The reason for that is not because we're lazy. It's because there are better uses we could make of that time. We could mark everything your child does, but that would lead to lower quality teaching and then your child will learn less.' Heads have to establish those cultural norms. If a teacher is marking everything your child does, it's bad teaching. It is using time in a way that does not have the greatest benefit for students.

I recommend what I call 'four quarters marking'. I think that teachers should mark in detail 25% of what students do, should skim another 25%, students should then self-assess about 25% with teachers monitoring the quality of that and finally, peer assessment should be the other 25%. It's a sort of balanced diet of different kinds of marking and assessment.

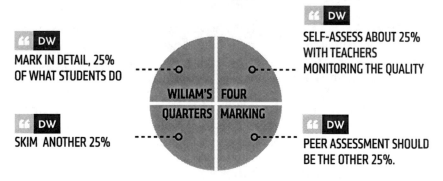

DW MARK IN DETAIL, 25% OF WHAT STUDENTS DO

DW SELF-ASSESS ABOUT 25% WITH TEACHERS MONITORING THE QUALITY

WILIAM'S FOUR QUARTERS MARKING

DW SKIM ANOTHER 25%

DW PEER ASSESSMENT SHOULD BE THE OTHER 25%.

One particular problem with feedback, especially in maths and science, is that teachers often find it difficult to give good feedback to students for the very simple reason that the tasks they gave the students to do did not effectively provide the teacher with any insights into the students' learning. If all you discover in giving students a mathematics exercise is that they couldn't do it, then it's no wonder that it's difficult to figure out what to say to the student. The reason you aren't able to give feedback is because you didn't design the task in a way that illuminated aspects of that student's thinking.

What this means is that the starting point for effective feedback is asking the right questions in the first place. English teachers never have any difficulty in feeding back to students about how their work could be improved, because the tasks they set are generally so rich, they almost always reveal something about the students' capabilities. I think we have to get into the habit of setting maths and science tasks in the same way – so that the task elicits evidence of the students' strengths and weaknesses, which then begins a dialogue with the student. Then, of course, it is essential to ensure that the students act on feedback in some way. I would say, in general terms – and school leaders don't say this often enough in my opinion – I think teachers should be spending twice as much time planning teaching as they do marking. However much time you have available, spend twice as much time planning teaching as you do marking. Then, make marking consequential, and focused on improving the student, not improving the work.

Daisy: I think the first thing to recognise is we've got into a bit of a situation where we think that feedback and marking are the same thing and actually they're not. There's lots of different ways to give feedback that don't involve marking, and a lot of marking isn't good feedback, and you're absolutely right, it is probably the most time expensive task. Even just to write, 'Well done, you have done well,' on 30 sets of books takes an awful lot of time.

I think there's a couple of ways you can cut down on it. One way is actually reducing the written comments, and I don't think you lose much by reducing written comments because I think too often they are just in that field of 'You need to be more systematic' type comments. Often, they're not actually very helpful, so I think cutting down on the written comment is a start. There are a few strategies I'm seeing a lot of schools using at the moment and if I pick three that I see that are really useful, I think one would be whole-class feedback, so instead of the teacher marking the books and writing a comment at the bottom of each one, scribbling comments all over the essay, the teacher reads the set of books and as they're reading they take notes on how the whole class have responded. Then in the next lesson they respond to the most frequent things that came up and maybe then also pick out one pupil's work, to really praise and kind of individualise that, show the whole class, and pick out another pupil who they're going to work with individually if that pupil is struggling. I think whole-class feedback where you're reading the books without writing on them but responding to common misconceptions is really effective.

I like also the idea of using VLOOKUPs on Excel and mail merge. They can be a little bit time consuming to set up, but once you have you're able to identify particularly the codes that the people are struggling with, and immediately. This is a feature on Excel where you can essentially come up with some notes and personalised feedback that doesn't involve you writing out the same thing over and over again.

The other thing that I think can work is responses that are questions, or multiple choice questions. Again, maybe a little bit similar to the VLOOKUP idea, but the idea that you've maybe got a bank of say five or ten questions, and depending on how people have answered in their question, you assign them one of those five questions based on their responses. One of those multiple choice questions might be a more advanced extension one if they've got everything right, and one might be targeting a common misconception. That's something that you can set up in advance and reuse and reuse and reuse and it doesn't involve you writing lengthy comments at the bottom of people's work.

Q **I've heard a lot about the power of the testing effect. How can I best harness it?**

Dylan: The testing effect is powerful and it seems to be fairly robust. The main benefit of testing is that you get practice at retrieving things from memory, as Robert Bjork has shown. When you retrieve things from memory successfully, that improves how well you know something. Relearning something or restudying is beneficial, but recalling it successfully yourself – *ie* retrieving it – is more effective than restudying it. Practice testing, regular practice testing, is beneficial to learning. The problem, of course, is that people think our students are tested enough as it is. To get around this, what I suggest is we should do different kinds of testing. The idea is that students should do regular tests, once a week maybe, certainly once every two weeks, where students are tested on what they've been learning. Then, the students are given the answers and mark their own work and don't even tell the teacher unless they want to. The best person to mark a test is the person who just took it.

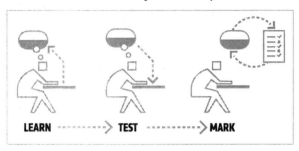

LEARN ----------> **TEST** ----------> **MARK**

There's two benefits here. One is the retrieval practice that you get when you actually sit down and do the test and the other is a psychological phenomenon called the hypercorrection effect. When you find out that something you thought was correct is in fact incorrect, the more confident you are that you are correct, the bigger the improvement in the change to your thinking. As I said, students don't get any extra benefit from testing when a teacher records a score in a mark book. The benefits of testing come from retrieval practice and hypercorrection and that's why the best person to mark a test is the person who just took it. So more testing and less marking.

Daisy: I think you need to identify the key things you want people to remember. What are those key things, and then test people on it repeatedly and space out that testing. An example I always give is a unit on *A Midsummer Night's Dream*. There is a part of the play that is really interesting and which is not straightforward, and we do a lot of testing on are questions like who loves who, and who is whose father, and who is whose lover, and who hates who *etc*. We do a lot of testing of that in our English Mastery unit here at Ark so it's the idea that in order to get them to remember those key things about the plot you keep testing them on it. When you repeat the testing, the effects of recalling something from memory is to say to pupils 'Who is Hermia in love with at the start of *Midsummer Night's Dream*?' the effect of struggling to remember the name Lysander actually helps to solidify that fact in long-term memory. I think identifying what are the key things you want them to remember and then spacing out that fact across time is really powerful.

I think also there's a real thing here where pupils can benefit from being told about the testing effect, particularly pupils who are coming up for revision, because I think there's a lot of research that the type of revision most people do is they reread the text and highlight it, and often this is not effective for revision. So if you tell pupils about the testing effect and tell them they need to self-quiz and test themselves, that is really helpful as well.

Q What are the benefits of using value-added data and where does it fall short when analysing student progress?

Dylan: The trouble with value-added data is most people don't understand how unreliable it is, and I'm using the term unreliable in the technical psychometric sense here. Any score, any test result, has a degree of unreliability. When you are calculating a value-added score, you're subtracting one unreliable number from another unreliable number and so the difference in scores is *extremely* unreliable – almost random at the level of the individual student. So what people don't like to hear but is actually psychometrically, demonstrably true, is that value-added measures on individual students are just about useless. They have almost no reliability. They're just basically noise. Progress measures for individual students are just not worth having, they're just a waste of time.

They can be useful at the classroom or school level. If you find that one class of 30 students has, over the course of a term, increased their scores by 10 marks, and in another class of 30 their scores have improved by 20 marks on the same test, then this difference is likely to be meaningful. The errors tend to cancel out because for each student who got a gain score larger than they should have got, there is likely to be another who got a smaller gain score than they should have. It seems to me that value-added is really not much more useful than the kinds of reports we had with RAISEonline. You look at groups of students and see if there is evidence of improvement. In fact, I would dispense with value-added at the student level entirely, for two reasons: One is because, as I said, it's unreliable. The second is because I think that value-added measures or gain scores can send the wrong message. A large gain in achievement over a particular period of time would indicate that a student is making good progress, but if they are so far behind that they're not going to be successful at the end of the learning sequence, then I think that's a problem. For this reason, I think we should focus on status, not progress. If this means that we need to put in three or four times as much work into one student to get them up to a level of achievement that most students have already achieved, then so be it. I say to teachers, 'If you're getting a bell curve of results, you're not doing your job because the bell curve is what nature gives us. Our job, as teachers, is to destroy the bell curve. Make sure that those who are struggling to get up to a level that they would be able to participate effectively in society get enough support to reach that level.'

That said, I think there is a role for value-added for evaluating schools and teachers – my first ever published academic paper was about value-added! Using value-added for schools ensures that we account for demographic differences in school populations, and within the school, they can be useful for looking at the progress of groups of students, but I think at the level of individual students, value-added measures are misleading and unhelpful.

Daisy: I think that the benefits of using value-added data are that you get an idea of where pupils are arriving. You've cleaned out the differences between attainment and progress, so you get an idea of where people are coming in and what therefore is good for them, and that cuts both ways because you might have a pupil who is attaining at a really high level, and you think, 'Oh fantastic, they're doing brilliantly and I don't have to worry about them,' but if you look at where their start point was, you realise actually they might be not attaining well and that's not as good as where they should be considering where they came in at.

Similarly, you can look at it in another way. A pupil may not be attaining something well, but if you look at where they came in at the start point, you see they've actually made enormous progress. So I think looking at value-added data is really powerful because in a sense it tends to remove some of the effects of prior attainment and actually prior attainment is I think the biggest influence on a pupil's attainment, and so value-added data helps you to see if you really are adding value or not.

The weakness of it is that where do you take the data from or what's your start point, and we know that all tests and subjects have got a measure of error. The risk is that you'll have a kid who gets the wrong kind of baseline measurement and that can throw out your judgement of whether you're adding value or not. I think the way you can square that circle is that value-added is particularly useful at a cohort level. For examples, if you look at a cohort of 100 kids and you see that, on average, they came in at grade four. If, on average, they leave at a grade of 4.5, you've added half a grade of value across that cohort. Now within that, some pupils have slipped back while some have made really exceptional progress, but some of those anomalies around measuring error, if you're looking at a cohort of 100 say, those measuring errors should be cancelled out because for every kid who under-performs there is one who cancels that out by over-performing.

So I think that value-added is a really powerful tool. I think it's probably most helpful to look at it at the cohort level and not at the individual level, and I think Progress 8 does that. I think the overall progress measures that you get when you look at a school Progress 8 I think is quite helpful and does tell you a lot of useful information.

Q **In what ways has AFL been used incorrectly in schools and how should I be using it properly in the classroom?**

Dylan: I think the confusion really began when David Miliband – the Schools Minister at the time – advocated the use of AFL as a way of monitoring student achievement. Certainly in secondary schools, AFL was reduced to a process of compiling complex spreadsheets that could be used to track student progress. Of course, in a way, there's nothing wrong with that. Any well-run organisation should be able to monitor its progress towards its goals. If you don't know whether students are learning anything, that's a problem. But the difficulty is that that kind of monitoring has a relatively small impact on student achievement. The research that Paul Black and I reviewed suggests that the biggest improvements in student learning happen when teachers use assessment minute-by-minute and day-by-day as part of regular teaching, not as part of a process monitoring.

So just to reinforce this point for me, Assessment for Learning does not belong in the Ofsted box called Assessment, Recording and Reporting. It belongs in the box called Good Teaching. It's about making sure that teachers have good evidence for the decisions they need to make. Teachers picking on students at random is still rare and classroom conversations are still dominated by the confident, articulate students. There are two issues here. One is that many students are not engaged (and therefore they're learning less). The other, and in some ways more serious issue, is that teachers are making decisions about what to do next with a class based on evidence only from the confident students. I believe that a teacher cannot possibly adequately address the learning needs of a diverse group of 30 students based on information only from the confident handful who are answering teacher's questions when they raise their hands. It's about getting better quality evidence for teachers' decisions, it's about feedback that students can use to improve their own learning, it's about harnessing the power of peer assessment and ultimately, it's about making sure that students become effective, self-regulating learners. As soon as teachers can get students managing their own learning, then the student can continue to improve even when the teacher isn't there.

In this regard, I think there's a lot we can learn from music teachers. Music teachers know that in the 20 or 30 minutes that the teacher gets with a student every week, progress is going to be very small. In that 30 minutes, not much improvement is going to happen. If students do get better at playing a musical instrument, it is because they have been practising productively at home. That is why music teachers spend a lot of time making sure that students know what they need to be doing when they're practising alone. Maths or science teachers tend to think that almost all the progress in learning happens in the classroom when they're teaching with homework relegated to a kind of optional extra. I think we need to take a leaf out of the music teachers' book and make sure that our students are able to go home and do productive development of their own learning when they're on their own, because they're self-regulating learners. Each of the strategies of formative assessment has a strong independent research base. Together, they're a very powerful framework for helping teachers reflect on practice.

Ultimately, it's a very simple idea. It's that teachers reflect on two things and their inter-relationship: What did I do as a teacher? What did my students learn? As long as teachers are reflecting on those two things, what did I do, what did my students learn, then they will always be able to further their practice.

 Daisy: I think there are two ways. Firstly, it became about the form and not the substance. It became about 'Am I using lollipop sticks? Am I using mini white boards? Am I using these surface features?' and it became less about specific things like pupils saying, 'It gets warmer when you climb to the top of the mountains because you're close to the sun.' What do I, the teacher, say when a pupil says that? For me, it became too much about that form and not enough about the substance of these real misconceptions, these persistent misconceptions that you need to try and address. That's not to say that I'm anti lollipop sticks or mini white boards, I think they're both useful. I just think they've got to be based on the underlying content of things that people struggle with. They've got to be based on how you respond to that.

The other way Assessment for Learning went wrong is, I think, too much of it became seen as also being about written feedback and less about responsive teaching and I think using this form of teaching is really important because when people talk about assessment for learning, the minute they hear the word 'assessment' they think, 'I need to write something.' They think formal assessment, whereas what we know from all of the research is actually it's not necessarily the feedback, but it's these ephemeral, real time moments that are happening live in the classroom that matter so much in terms of anticipating, avoiding, correcting misconceptions, keeping pupils on the right track, making sure they're always understanding what's happening. Even if you gave written feedback after every lesson, which is just not possible, but if you did give feedback after every lesson it would still not be as good as responsive teaching, which is responding in the class to the issues that are arising in the moment.

Q **How should past papers and exemplars be used most effectively in the run-up to exams?**

Dylan: Well it should be obvious by now that I think that practice testing is useful. Working on past papers is a valuable revision technique, particularly if, as with some examination boards, the papers are relatively predictable from year to year. The problem with this is that the teacher is then under pressure to mark the tests immediately to give the students feedback. One way round this is for the teacher to collect in the papers at the end of the mock exam, and then, next day, give students back their papers, and they work in teams of four to produce the best composite response to the exam paper they can. Then, the teacher can lead a whole class discussion comparing the answers from different groups to question one, question two, question three and so on. This technique gives students retrieval practice when they actually do the test, takes advantage of the hypercorrection effect when students find out their answers were wrong, and also provides an opportunity for peer-tutoring (which, the research shows, benefits both those who receive, and those who give, help). It's also less work for the teacher.

Daisy: I think that question has the answer within it. Past papers are great in the run up to exams, and by the run up to exams I'd say the few weeks before. Where I get worried is when you see past papers being used a year, two years, and sometimes three or four years before pupils are even going to take that exam. Past papers for most formal education should be about building the knowledge and experience you need to perform well in that subject. Then when you get close to exams, and by close I mean within a few weeks or maybe a couple of months max, then you do need to work on the specifics of exam technique and the specifics of that exam and then there is a case for teachers giving feedback on their whole performance on those past papers, but I think using them too far in advance is really counterproductive. Instead the role of the teacher in curriculum designing and the textbook should be to break down what people need to do in the exam and to teach those component parts instead, rather than always focusing on their past papers and on the questions.

Q How can I know if summative exams are diagnosing individual flaws/ lack of knowledge about individual topics?

Dylan: The basic answer is you can't. People think that assessments take up too much time, therefore people like to believe that large scale summative assessments can be useful diagnostically as well as providing some kind of summative role. Unfortunately, the evidence is that in most areas where we assess students, the inter-correlation between the different aspects of the subject is so high that diagnostic scores are basically meaningless.

Let me give you an example that illustrates this. In the days when we still had formal tests in English, mathematics and science at Key Stage 3, if a mathematics department wanted to predict a student's GCSE grade, they would probably look at the score the student got on the Key Stage 3 maths test. However, it turned out that the average of the three scores a student got in English, maths and science was a better predictor of their maths GCSE grade than the maths Key Stage 3 score alone. This seems odd, perverse even, but because the correlations between the English score, the maths score and the science score were pretty high, using the average of all three scores effectively gives you test that was three times longer, and, therefore, much more reliable. It's been shown time and time again. Nobody believes this but it's absolutely demonstrably true. If you want to predict somebody's performance on some *aspect* of performance – for example if you want to predict somebody's ability in biology in a science GCSE, the best predictor is their score on a general science test, not just their scores on biology questions. That's why diagnostic assessment just doesn't work. The idea that tests would be useful diagnostically is the Holy Grail of psychometrics, but unfortunately, it just doesn't work.

Daisy: The difficult thing with summative exams and using them diagnostically is that summative exams are not designed to be diagnostic.

I think a really important principle of assessment is to always be clear about purpose, and the purpose of a summative exam is not to be diagnostic. The purpose of a summative exam is to give you a national grade on a large amount of knowledge, to give you a way of comparing people to their peers nationally on a very broad domain of knowledge, like the whole of maths or the whole of English. That's great and that's valuable and we need that, but it is very hard to do that and to be diagnostic because in order to be diagnostic you need to be much more precise and much more specific and to focus in much more on the individual topic, or even the specifics in an individual topic.

To give you an example, suppose the pupil is struggling to decode text. You are not actually going to find that out reliably and effectively from a GCSE English language question because the GCSE English language question is not designed to find if a pupil can decode reliably or not. It's designed to do a much bigger thing. Similarly with the SATS paper at age 11, the reading paper is not designed to do that. A pupil might do badly on it, but you don't know why they're doing badly. Is it because they're not decoding, is it because they didn't know the words in that particular task? So one of the things we've done at ARK with our Year 7 pupils is at the start of the year we give them a reading test and the pupils who get a good mark on that, we follow up with a decoding test. With follow up it's a much more diagnostic test that tells you something much more precise and specific about how people are doing. So I think summative exams are great for their purpose, but they're not always great at being diagnostic.

Q I have to plan a six-week scheme of work and am thinking about how to build in the assessment. How would you go about it?

Dylan: First of all, if you're planning a six-week scheme of work, there's a couple of things you should do in terms of general design. The first one is *distributed practice*. Rather than doing one week on one element and another week on a second element and so on, it would probably more effective, in terms of long-term learning, to break it up. Two days on the first element, then two days on the second element, two days on the third element, and so on. Then, after two weeks, go back to the first element, and do two more days on that, then two more days on the second, *etc*. The important feature is that the practice gets broken up – the content of the course gets broken up. The second thing is that the scheme should involve a series of cumulative tests. At the end of week one, test them on what they were learning in week one. At the end of week two, test them on what they've learnt over the first two weeks in total (but giving slightly more weight to the second week's content depending on how cumulative the subject is). The key idea is that students should be required to accumulate knowledge and get regular retrieval practice on everything in the whole unit and then at the end of the six weeks, there should be an assessment covering everything in the unit. And again, I would recommend having the students assess their own work because you don't really need the grades. The learning you'll get from the students doing the retrieval practice and the hypercorrection of that will be more beneficial than you actually having some scores to put in a mark book.

Daisy: The first thing I would do is ask what's my ultimate end goal? What's the main reason that I want pupils to study this topic? Again, if I pick my example of *A Midsummer Night's Dream*, we could ask, 'Why do I want my pupils to study this?' Is it just so they can write an essay at the end of the unit, or is it because hopefully there's something that I want them to remember about this play or understand about this play in the following years at GCSE or even in later life? So first of all, I've identified my ultimate end goal of why am I doing this, and then I'd think about the final assessment. Again, with my *Midsummer Night's Dream* example. My end goal might be I want pupils to understand more about Shakespeare. I want them to know some specific quotations that they can remember, that they can use in their GCSE. I want them to totally love Shakespeare and that when they encounter Shakespeare later in life they're able to understand it more as a result of what they did here.

You then come down a level and say what's the final assessment? It could be a final assessment with an essay on one of the characters or one of the themes in *A Midsummer Night's Dream*, and then you come down a level again and answer what are the sort of building blocks that you need to do well on that assessment and towards my end goal? Maybe there's some quotations you need to learn, maybe you need to understand the relationship of the characters to each other at different points in the play, and with those small building blocks, if you like, are the key things you've tested throughout the unit of work and then I'd have one big assessment at the end of the unit that involves maybe a longer piece of work.

In terms of a final assessment, if you want to give a grade on it, it has to be assessing quite a big domain, and the risk I see happen a lot is that people award grades off the back of assessments that are quite narrow in their domain. The problem there is it's easy for pupils to get misleading grades, so if they get a high grade on something it might be because they've just spent six weeks studying it, but that's not actually a representation I feel of how they really are doing on the larger domain, which is ultimately what grades of summative assessments tend to do.

2

BEHAVIOUR

CHAPTER   TOM BENNETT & JILL BERRY

> MANY TEACHERS FEEL THAT THEY ARE NOT SUPPORTED WHEN DEALING WITH UNRULY PUPILS BECAUSE SANCTIONS AND SUPPORT FROM LINE MANAGERS ARE FLIMSY AT BEST.

> WHAT WE KNOW ABOUT BEHAVIOUR SHOWS THAT THE MOST SUCCESSFUL MEASURES WITH THE MOST TANGIBLE IMPACT COME FROM SCHOOL LEADERSHIP TEAMS.

> GETTING BEHAVIOUR RIGHT IN SCHOOLS IS A CORE INGREDIENT IN THE HEALTH OF THE PROFESSION. YET THERE EXISTS A WIDE RANGE OF APPROACHES TO THE PROBLEM.

> THE EVIDENCE COLLATED SUPPORTS THE CLAIM THAT THERE IS A NATIONAL PROBLEM WITH BEHAVIOUR, THOUGH THE WORD 'CRISIS' IS CONTENTIOUS.

> ONE-QUARTER OF TEACHERS ARE NOT HAPPY WITH BEHAVIOUR STANDARDS AND DON'T FEEL SUPPORTED, WHICH TRANSLATES INTO A QUESTIONABLE EDUCATION FOR THE CORRESPONDING QUARTER OF SOME EIGHT-AND-A-HALF MILLION YOUNG PEOPLE IN THE SCHOOL-AGE POPULATION.

'Behaviour is a mirror in which everyone displays his own image'
Johann Wolfgang von Goethe

Many research blogs have pointed out that a well-ordered classroom is a poor proxy for learning. However, if learning is to take place at all, then there needs to be an environment in which it can thrive. Behaviour is (to state the obvious) pivotal if pupils are to have a chance of success in their education. You will not find a school that can combine academic success and mayhem in classrooms and corridors. You will, sadly, find a typical pattern whereby schools with weak policies on behaviour combine this with poor academic performance.

Despite this being desperately obvious, many teachers feel that they are not supported when dealing with unruly pupils because sanctions and support from line managers are flimsy at best. Journalists who want to fill column inches with the (revelatory) claim that behaviour in schools in the UK is at crisis point have little trouble finding anecdotal evidence, and then they simply have to tack on some figures about exclusion rates. Yet do these claims hold up to critical scrutiny? And which approaches to behaviour management reap the greatest dividends?

What we know about behaviour shows that the most successful measures with the most tangible impact come from school leadership teams. If a teacher who is overloaded and up all night preparing lessons comes into a classroom that borders on anarchy because there is a lack of firm leadership at the top, then you have a toxic mix. Getting behaviour right in schools is a core ingredient in the health of the profession.

Yet there exists a wide range of approaches to the problem. On the one hand you have schools that preach traditional methods, zero tolerance and cultivate a reputation for being strict. On the other hand there are methods like restorative justice which argue that detentions don't work and that the rules should be developed and maintained by pupils. The Restorative Justice Council makes bold claims about the efficacy of a taking this innovative approach to behaviour issues:

> Restorative approaches enable those who have been harmed to convey the impact of the harm to those responsible, and for those responsible to acknowledge this impact and take steps to put it right. Restorative approaches refer to a range of methods and strategies which can be used both to prevent relationship-damaging incidents from happening and to resolve them if

they do happen. Becoming a restorative school has many benefits, including increased attendance, reduced exclusions and improved achievement. It can also alleviate problems such as bullying, classroom disruption, truancy and poor attendance, antisocial behaviour, and disputes between pupils, their families, and members of staff.[5]

Both strategies have produced serious heat in debates, as seen by the panel discussion at the 2017 Telegraph Festival of Education.[6] In 2015 Tom Bennett was appointed by then Secretary of State Nicky Morgan to head up a government task force on behaviour, in response to widespread claims that there was a behaviour crisis in schools. Tom is a long-standing blogger and researcher in this area. He has been very consistent in writing about the basic principles of behaviour management:

> I have visited a lot of schools in my time, and I'm afraid to say that my overwhelming impression is that the ones that have the best results also have the best behaviour, and it's almost always because they take it seriously: they talk explicitly about standards and boundaries and expectations; they revisit these regularly; they have staff dedicated to its execution, rather than simply expecting staff to absorb it into their existing timetables.[7]

Tom's report was published in 2017 and the findings make for fascinating reading. The evidence collated supports the claim that there is national problem with behaviour, though the word 'crisis' is contentious. Evidence from the Teacher Voice Omnibus carried out by the National Foundation for Educational Research showed fairly consistent responses from 2013 to 2015 about perceptions of behaviour standards in schools, and interestingly there is a marked improvement since 2008.[8] Approximately three-quarters of teachers think that their school has standards which are good or better, and feel equipped to tackle issues. Crucially, the report also shows that, 'there are many schools that demonstrate it is possible to improve in even the most beleaguered of circumstances.'[9] Whilst all of this seems very positive, the report also points out that one-quarter of teachers are not happy with behaviour standards and don't feel supported, which translates into a questionable education for the

5. www.restorativejustice.org.uk/restorative-practice-schools accessed 19/7/2017

6. www.youtube.com/watch?v=Kjh7x1NrUYw accessed 17/7/2018

7. www.tes.com/news/blog/two-biggest-problems-education-no-one-takes-seriously-1-behaviour accessed 16/7/2017

8. Bennett, T. (2017) 'Creating a Culture: How school leaders can optimise, behaviour, Independent review of behaviour in schools'. Department for Education, pp.15-16

9. Ibid, p.14

corresponding quarter of some eight-and-a-half million young people in the school-age population.

The questions we received about behaviour made for fascinating reading and discussion. Whilst many related to specific policies and strategies, a theme throughout was about cultivating a good relationship with pupils. There are undoubtedly students who have complex behavioural issues which require a wider support network than just the classroom teacher. Extreme behaviour issues are also clearly rooted in poverty and deprivation. However, for many pupils – and indeed classes – a strong relationship developed over time and a high level of intellectual challenge will do a lot to shape a positive learning environment and reduce low-level disruption. One of the most experienced heads and teacher trainers is Dr Jill Berry, author of *Making the Leap: Moving from Deputy to Head*. Jill has over 30 years' experience in teaching and leadership and has been working full time in teacher training and consultancy since 2010. Who better, then, than Jill and Tom to answer the questions from practitioners?

BEHAVIOUR

TB

PUNISHMENTS WORK WHEN THEY SUCCESSFULLY REINFORCE THE USEFUL SOCIAL NORMS YOU EXPECT TO SEE MANIFEST IN THE CLASSROOM.

TB

SO, IN A CLASSROOM WHERE THE OVERRIDING ISSUE IS POOR BEHAVIOUR, THE SOLUTION IS CLEAR; TACKLE THE BEHAVIOUR. VILIFY MISCONDUCT; LIONISE EXEMPLARY THOUGHT AND DEED.

TB

ENGAGEMENT IS AN OUTCOME, NOT A PROCESS, AND MANY SINS ARE COMMITTED IN ITS NAME.

TB

A CLASS CAN BE REBOOTED AT ANY TIME IF THE TEACHER IS SINCERE AND READY FOR THE LONG HAUL.

TB

TEACHERS NEED TO KNOW THAT STUDENTS WILL OBEY REASONABLE INSTRUCTIONS BECAUSE THEY SHOULD, BUT BECAUSE THEY WANT TO.

TB

RESEARCH HAS POINTED TO SIGNIFICANT LEARNING DEFICITS FROM CLASSROOMS WHERE DIGITAL DEVICES ARE IN PLAY.

JB

IT'S MORE ABOUT SENDING A MESSAGE TO THAT INDIVIDUAL, AND TO ALL THOSE AROUND THEM WHO WITNESSED THE BEHAVIOUR AND ITS CONSEQUENCES, ABOUT WHAT IS AND ISN'T ACCEPTABLE WITHIN THAT CONTEXT.

JB

LOW-LEVEL DISRUPTION IS DIFFICULT BECAUSE IT IS LOW LEVEL, AND YOU DON'T WANT TO OVER-REACT, BUT IT IS DISRUPTIVE AND SO YOU DO NEED TO TACKLE IT.

JB

I WOULD ALSO MAKE CLEAR THAT WE ARE ON THE SAME SIDE. WE WANT THE SAME THINGS. THEY WANT TO ACHIEVE, IN THE MAIN (I HAVE MET VERY FEW STUDENTS WHO DIDN'T, AND EVEN FEWER PARENTS) AND I CAN HELP THEM WITH THAT.

When do punishments work?

Tom: Punishments as part of education make many people recoil. But we have to consider what punishments represent, why they are used, and what form they take. Punishments can aim to be deterrents, revenge, retribution, rehabilitation … the most important sense in which they are relevant to school contexts is as a cue as to what is and what is not permitted or encouraged. Every classroom is a micro-culture, and every culture has social norms and expectations. It's how cultures survive. I find it amazing how easily people can come around to the idea if one describes punishments as sanctions, so laden with baggage is the term.

So punishments work when they successfully reinforce the useful social norms you expect to see manifest in the classroom. Every teacher needs to introduce and maintain the culture they want to see in the classroom, and that means they need to set cues about acceptable behaviour and attitudes. Sanctions are an essential part of that, by supporting clear boundaries and limits to acceptability. No society can endure without them; no community has been recorded in the history of human community that doesn't have rules, and sanctions to underpin those rules.

So: sanctions work when they support the behaviour you want to see in the classroom; when they are proportionate, predictable and just. As the old saying goes: the certainty of the sanction is far more important than the severity of the sanction. It is the hum of the fence that reminds us it is electric; it doesn't need to kill anyone to do what it must.

Jill: When they send a clear message to all involved (and on the periphery) about where the parameters of acceptable behaviour lie. Where they help young people understand about good and poor choices and decisions and where, ideally, these young people are motivated to choose more wisely in the future.

We hope for a positive change in future behaviour, but given the complexity of human nature I recognise it isn't that simple. If we only ever had to learn a lesson once, if we only ever broke a rule or a law, or made a mistake, once, learning from the repercussions and consequences of our actions, the world would operate very differently. Reality is more nuanced! So it isn't about punishing an individual as a deterrent so that they never again do what brought about the punishment. It's more about sending a message to that individual, and to all those around them who witnessed the behaviour and its consequences, about what is and isn't acceptable within that context. Good schools, good teachers and responsible parents help children to construct a framework within which they make their own decisions, choices and sometimes mistakes. Rewards and sanctions are part of that process, I would suggest. It's a key part of our education.

How do you promote creativity in a classroom where the overriding issue is managing poor behaviour?

Tom: This question is best tackled in reverse: whatever creativity is (and the subject is as philosophical as it is empirical) it is best served, encouraged, instilled by a classroom environment that is calm and positive. The only creativity that a chaotic classroom encourages is the tendency of the teacher to develop new and more novel ways to handle misbehaviour. You cannot reliably promote creativity in a poorly behaved classroom. This is because creativity is, at heart, supported and scaffolded by secure domain knowledge in one's subject. There is very little we can do to make children creative by itself; instead we are best occupied in our attempts to teach them content that they can be creative with. This, and every other school ambition, is best served by good behaviour. It is the necessary condition for every other school good. So, in a classroom where the overriding issue is poor behaviour, the solution is clear: tackle the behaviour. Vilify misconduct; lionise exemplary thought and deed. Then, and only then, can we say that creativity has its best atmosphere in which to breathe. There is no sense in believing that creativity somehow thrives in adversity. For every outlier for whom this is true, there are 24 other pupils who suffer instead.

Jill: I think if the overriding issue is managing poor behaviour, then you have to manage poor behaviour before you can achieve much at all. I really don't think you can promote creativity DESPITE poor behaviour. If children are behaving badly, in my experience they're not receptive to learning, and they're distracting and disrupting the learning of others. You have to focus on this before you can promote creativity. You have to establish some sense of calm, first, and I know that can be challenging. HOW you do it will depend on a range of factors – the age of the children, your relationship with them, the context in which you are teaching, the environment and whatever external factors are affecting the pupil behaviour. There are no easy answers and quick fixes. But I would say establishing positive behaviour and constructive routines in the classroom is non-negotiable. Learning can't happen if you don't have that in place.

What is the most effective way of engaging the disengaged?

Tom: The first thing to say is that engagement is a goal which is very easily misunderstood. Because every teacher wants their students to be attentive and interested in the class material, we value engagement to a fetishistic extent. But engagement is an outcome, not a process, and many sins are committed in its name. Another thing to consider is that disengagement occurs for many reasons, not all of them within the immediate ability of the teacher to remedy. If they are disengaged because they are bored by a poorly taught lesson, if the material is too far beneath or above their comprehension, then the teacher should look at their content and delivery. But far more frequently teachers have to wrestle with the obvious truism that not everything we teach is intrinsically fascinating, not everything we say will grip and animate our pupils.

The best way to make sure as many pupils are as focused as possible is to make it clear that the expectation is for high level and deliberate attention and effort to be given in the subject at hand. And when this attention drops below an acceptable level, an intervention from the teacher MUST occur. If not, the long, slow slide to carelessness begins.

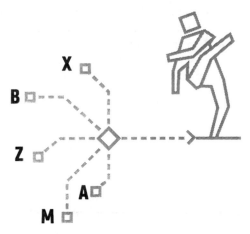

Jill: I think you need to examine root causes and be sensitive to context. Why are they disengaged and which part of this may be in your control? As teachers, do we have agency and how can we use it to best effect? We can't solve every child's problems – we can't 'fix' them all – much as we may love to do that. But we can work to establish the most positive relationship with each individual, show we care about them and their progress, separate the behaviour from the individual as far as humanly possible so that disapproval of behaviour, including lack of engagement, isn't seen as an attack on them personally. Rather it's about helping them to see what is and isn't acceptable in terms of behaviour/engagement, and why. I like the Doug Lemov argument about never accepting 'Dunno' and a shrug. Get across that it's fine to get it wrong and learn from that, but it isn't acceptable not to think, not to try, not to care. Get to the point where the individual vocalises the correct answer (perhaps provided by another student) and receives positive affirmation for that. We need to encourage students to take responsibility for their learning and to see what success feels like, building on the positives wherever we possibly can.

Again, it depends a great deal on the age of the children, what may motivate them, and what they see as desirable and undesirable experiences. It depends on your developing relationship with them. I'm a secondary specialist and I remember saying to older teenagers in my early years of teaching, 'If you choose not to work, and you don't achieve what you could, as a result, there is an argument that says it's your choice – it's your life, your responsibility. But if your words or actions stop other people learning, or take up so much of my time that I don't have the chance to support other people's learning, that's totally unacceptable. Because that's their life, and their choice, not yours.' In my experience, the vast majority of learners got that and it helped them to modify their behaviour. (They care about what their peers think much more than they care about what the teacher thinks, I reckon! And young people often have a great sense of fairness.)

I would also make clear that we are on the same side. We want the same things. They want to achieve, in the main (I have met very few students who didn't, and even fewer parents), and I can help them with that. If they fight me and make it more difficult for me to do that, they're shooting themselves in the foot. They will pass on through the school and I will teach hundreds more students but, for them, the English GCSE results they ended up with would stay with them for the rest of their lives. Sometimes this helped focus the mind and increase engagement.

 What's the best way of dealing with low-level disruption?

 Tom: By getting in front of it. Low level disruption is by far the most common misbehaviour in mainstream schools. It can never be eradicated completely, but it can be minimised; not by responding to it (although it is necessary to) but more importantly by laying clear behaviour expectations to the class from the start, and insisting as much as is reasonable that these levels are met. Designing and communicating clear, concrete routines to the class long in advance of any misbehaviour will minimise misbehaviour, because students will be aware of the classroom cultural norms. Driven home often enough, it can create tram lines for behaviour to default to. Instead of leaving behavioural choices to chance, the best strategy is for teachers to draw up exactly what is expected of their students from the beginning of the relationship.

In terms of dealing with misbehaviour after it occurs, the responses can be as varied as the offence. But generally, there needs to be a reaction as close to the behaviour as possible, in order to reinforce the connection between the misbehaviour and the negative reaction. Sanctions are often all that is required. For more difficult circumstances, contacting home or enlisting support may be more appropriate.

 Jill: Low-level disruption is difficult because it IS low level, and you don't want to over-react, but it IS disruptive so you do need to tackle it. You just need to address it in the least intrusive way you can. I think it's about establishing the most positive, constructive routines and clear expectations from the very beginning of your time with a new class, helping them to understand the rationale behind these routines and expectations, even perhaps devising those ground-rules in negotiation with the students so that they have some investment/buy-in when it comes to making them work: what routines and behaviours in this classroom will ensure everyone has the best possible chance of learning effectively and achieving success? Then, when everyone is absolutely clear about the expectations, be consistent in your application and reinforcement of them. Don't ignore low-level poor behaviour, which can actually be the most disruptive thing of all, because it can escalate, especially if it's motivated by attention-seeking (from their peers as well as from you).

Correct the poor behaviour in the least invasive way you can, though, so that the process of dealing with the behaviour doesn't itself overly disrupt others' learning. Again, Lemov is good on this, as is Bill Rogers. Consider: where you stand (sometimes just moving towards the source of the behaviour is enough); where and how you look; body language; quick use of a student's name (with perhaps a positive instruction, and a thank you, rather than a comment specifically on the undesirable behaviour). *Teach Like a Champion 2* is full of practical strategies for managing low-level disruption but, as always, you need to adapt to your context and to take into account your relationship with the learners. (I've worked with HMCTT trainees for the last three years and have suggested the book as essential reading.)

Q I often find that boys are lazier than girls. Are there behaviour strategies that are gender specific?

Tom: In my experience, very few. Human behaviour appears to be far more variable between classes and age groups than between genders.

Gender specific behaviour in the classroom appears to be as much a social convention as anything else. Which means that there are very few strategies that have greater efficacy with one gender against the other. Rather, more general principles of behaviour management – consistency, high expectations *etc* – seem to be the best way for all people, not just boys or girls. Which isn't to say that boys and girls can't display different behaviour patterns, especially in larger groups, but cod psychology approaches based on misapprehension of what constitutes a male or a female attitude seem doomed to failure. There appears to be no more evidence that boys are lazier than girls than any other scenario. Also, it doesn't matter what gender you present as a teacher; clichés about boys preferring a mother figure, or vice versa, are confounded by exceptions that suggest the reverse.

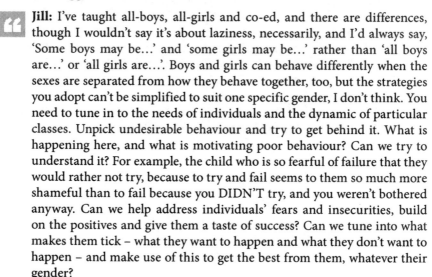

Jill: I've taught all-boys, all-girls and co-ed, and there are differences, though I wouldn't say it's about laziness, necessarily, and I'd always say, 'Some boys may be...' and 'some girls may be...' rather than 'all boys are...' or 'all girls are...'. Boys and girls can behave differently when the sexes are separated from how they behave together, too, but the strategies you adopt can't be simplified to suit one specific gender, I don't think. You need to tune in to the needs of individuals and the dynamic of particular classes. Unpick undesirable behaviour and try to get behind it. What is happening here, and what is motivating poor behaviour? Can we try to understand it? For example, the child who is so fearful of failure that they would rather not try, because to try and fail seems to them so much more shameful than to fail because you DIDN'T try, and you weren't bothered anyway. Can we help address individuals' fears and insecurities, build on the positives and give them a taste of success? Can we tune into what makes them tick – what they want to happen and what they don't want to happen – and make use of this to get the best from them, whatever their gender?

How can a teacher be helped to repair a working relationship with a class when this has broken down?

Tom: This is hard, especially if the relationship has broken hard, such as if the teacher has really lost them due to extreme mishandling, *eg* calling them disgusting, or something equally personal. That said, human relationships are remarkably flexible, and students can relearn their habitual responses quite quickly. Observe how differently a student can act from one teacher to another, in a heartbeat.

The best way to go about it is to be upfront, assertive and positive: 'Things need to get better so we can all learn, and I believe they can.' A class can be rebooted at anytime if the teacher is sincere and ready for the long haul. Reiterate the classroom expectation, assuming they have slid. And then – the hardest part of what is essentially a simple equation – hold fast this time. Set as many detentions as needed but also encourage and reinforce acceptable or encouraged behaviours. The key thing is to convey fairness and high standards, rather than partiality or uncertainty. The longer the classroom teacher can persist on this course, the greater the chance that a relationship will emerge where the students see the teacher as an authority figure than an interloper into their culture.

Jill: I think sometimes it's a question of admitting to the fact that this has happened, that it isn't acceptable, and that you're all going to start again. I've known teachers who have done this and who have been able to claw their way back to a more productive and mutually respectful working relationship: 'We started off on the wrong foot and we're going to start again this term/half term.' Even, 'I got this wrong but I care about your learning, I care about you, and I'm going to try again.' I know that may be hard!

Seek advice from others – you're not on your own. Can you observe another teacher with the same group and analyse the strategies they are using which you could perhaps adapt? Could that teacher observe you and give you some specific feedback about your classroom management? Just maybe suggest ONE thing you could focus on in the next few lessons and, if that has a positive impact, then try a second different thing. You're not asking anyone to solve your issues for you, but you're asking for guidance and advice about what you can do next – perhaps from someone who has more experience and confidence than you currently have, and perhaps a peer rather than a manager/leader. Talk through with them what you've tried, what has happened, what you COULD try, what might happen, where you might go from there. Talk through, and even practise with someone else, possible scenarios.

Make the most of the support network you have. And build on the positives – there may be times when things go better, so what can you learn from that and how can you apply that elsewhere to try to achieve more success?

When I was a head, there was a year when we had a tough Year 9 cohort – there were some fantastic students within that year BUT there were also a fair few who were harder to manage and they were strong characters whose behaviour was having a negative impact on the dynamic between some teachers and their Year 9 classes. We were dealing with some of these individuals, but felt we needed to do more. Over a two-week period, senior leaders, pastoral middle leaders and I called into a large number of Year 9 lessons – on our own, and only for 15 minutes or so each time, to observe and learn. All those who taught that year group knew they might receive a visitor at some stage of the lesson. Then all those of us who had been observing got together to discuss what we had seen WORKING, and we did a presentation to the whole staff on what we had witnessed having a positive effect with this particular year group. I hadn't heard of Appreciative Enquiry at that time, but I realise, in retrospect, that this is what we were doing. It did help.

 Should you really not smile before half term?

 Tom: This is folk wisdom with a grain of truth that is frequently misunderstood. Taken literally it is perhaps obviously mistaken. To not smile in circumstances that would normally demand it would be to appear synthetic and odd. That said, the relationship between student and teacher is best seen as a professional one. It can be warm and positive, but at all times it needs to be authoritative, or it is merely baby-sitting. Teachers need to know that students will obey reasonable instructions not because they should, but because they want to. On that basis, it is wise if teachers begin their relationships with pupils as sternly as they feel comfortable with. It is far easier to start a little strictly, and then ease into a more comfortable register with pupils, than the reverse. Classes frequently see over-familiarity as an invitation to be overly familiar. Once this tone is activated, it is hard to defuse or reverse. Because of this, the best course for teachers is to attempt to be more than usually formal.

Jill: You definitely should! I would say smile MORE, smile often, and show you are pleased to be there (even if you really feel you would rather be anywhere else). Be at the classroom door and smile at each individual as they arrive. Show your warmth, your humanity, your compassion, your interest in them. It certainly doesn't mean you're weak. You can be (you must be) firm/strong AND kind. Be clear, consistent, but be warm.

 What's the best way of liaising with parents of a poorly behaved child?

Tom: As if they were part of a possible solution rather than a problem. The vast majority of parents care for and know the student far better than we ever will, and yet a common mistake is to talk to parents as if they were a problem, or somehow to be blamed because of a current infraction. I rarely advise scripts, but when it comes to parental encounters, the best way to approach them, is to accept that they want they best for the child, just like you and say something like:

'Hello is that Parent X? I'm [teacher] from [school] and I teach [pupil] [subject]. He can be excellent, but today he let himself down a bit and I want to talk to you about what we do next.' That's the approach: positive but assertive, Accepting that the parent will want to help, and putting them at their ease. Some parents of badly behaved children resent multiple intrusions in any given day, so do check with the Head of Year/Learning to see if the parents have been phoned on multiple occasions recently.

Jill: You have to build the relationship and help them to see you are on the same side – the child's side. Fighting each other is definitely not in the best interests of the child at the centre of your relationship. If you are critical of their child's behaviour, you are not attacking the child personally and you are not attacking their parenting. You recognise parenting is the hardest job in the world (harder than teaching!) and you want to support them, just as you need them to support you and the school. Whatever has happened in the past, you want to work together to find the best way forward. Sometimes the most important thing to do is to ensure they have a clear and accurate picture of what has happened (rather than the potentially distorted version filtered through their child's perspective!).

I know this can sound a bit pat and the reality is much harder, but keeping this in mind can help you to stay calm, be professional, even if you feel you are under attack. I fully understand that sometimes parents are waging their own battles with adolescent offspring, so if they have the chance to fight their child's corner against the school they grab it because they think it will help them to forge a more positive relationship with their son or daughter. Sometimes they are really motivated by love of their child. You have to explain you care about their child too (though not in the same intensely emotional way – you have a wider perspective that comes from the fact that you care for ALL the children in the school). Helping the child understand what is and is not acceptable behaviour, and taking responsibility for the consequences, is what you and the parents need to do together to help young people construct the guiding framework I talked about earlier.

It's so much easier if you've already earned their respect. I used to feel that you earned 'credits' through a positive relationship with parents which you sometimes then needed to trade in if times got tough! So establish a constructive relationship early on, if at all possible. Certainly as a new form tutor I would want to contact the parents of my tutees to introduce myself and say I looked forward to getting to know them and their son/ daughter better and to supporting the student to achieve their best – perhaps just a quick email so they also have contact details. This may be something some schools suggest all teachers do for their new classes – it depends on the school policy. If your first contact with a parent is positive, that's so much better than if the first time they hear from you it's because there has been a problem with their child's behaviour. Get to know the child, get to know the parents, and show you have high aspirations but that your role is to support behaviour and learning, and to find solutions, not to hector/blame if the child hits a rocky patch.

Q **What do you do when you're not supported by the school leadership, for example when the behaviour policy has inconsistencies?**

Tom: This is one of the hardest problems for a teacher, as it involves them reacting against their school system rather than working smoothly with it. It is also one of the most common problems I used to tackle on social media. To be frank, some school systems are inadequate. Many are not, but some are. And new teachers need to be aware of this in order not to a) pick up bad habits or b) blame themselves. The key thing is to seek out someone in the chain of command who will support you. Secondly, manage upwards: know the school behaviour system backwards, then if support from the school isn't forthcoming, they can be 'reminded' of procedures that have been publicly agreed. Set time-limited headlines from them, keep a note of all conversations, and meet with them regularly to discuss the progress they are making on your support. It usually turns it around quickly, and to be fair many staff do just need a reminder to help.

Jill: As I said above, you can always use peers if you don't have faith in your immediate line manager/senior staff, though I would think it's unlikely that you feel unsupported by ALL those in leadership roles in your school. Find who you can connect with, talk to, and ask for advice and guidance as you work to establish high standards and solve your own issues.

We all have to do the best we can within the constraints we inevitably have. I really do believe that if we can get relationships right in our own classrooms, we can achieve a huge amount, whatever is happening elsewhere. How are things going to work in your lessons, and what routines and protocols can you apply which you think will support learning? Where can you access support and guidance from others and where can you OFFER support and guidance to others? Where is your agency and how can you make best use of it? What is beyond your control and can you ensure you don't waste your time and energies beating your head against the wall? Pick your battles.

If you get relationships and communication right within your own classroom, and within the team of which you are a member, you can achieve a huge amount, whatever whole-school systems/policies/ structures you're working within. But if you don't rate or respect the wider school systems/policies/structures, think what you're learning from this negative example and resolve to be better when YOU are a Middle Leader/ Senior Leader/head!

Should mobile phones be banned in classrooms?

Tom: There's no simple yes/no to this, because all classroom cultures vary – some can easily sustain a norm where phones are out and in use. To be honest I think far more children would benefit from environments where phones were rarely, if ever, seen. There are so few essential services a phone can provide to the learning experience that cannot easily be reproduced by low-tech solution that it seems fair to ask if they are needed at all when we consider what a distraction they are to pupils. Research has pointed to significant learning deficits from classrooms where digital devices are in play. I usually advise that phones stay in their bags, on pain of confiscation. There are very few circumstances when I would agree with children carrying phones, especially smart phones.

Jill: I know this is a tricky one, but I would say no, not these days. I think it's about educating children to make the most positive and constructive use of all technology, not trying to police, restrict and control their use of it. I would rather have the phone on the desk and in use when it has educational purpose and value, rather than banning and confiscating.

Things have moved on since I left headship in 2010. We did say then that mobile phones should not be seen in school (though we knew students had them and used them on their journey to and from school). Each child had a lockable locker and we said phones should be locked away during the school day. In actual fact, I suspect just about every child had them on their person/in their bag, and used them surreptitiously, but if we saw them they were confiscated and the child had to collect them from me (or my deputy if I was out of school) at the end of the day. Names were taken, and a second offence within the same term meant the phone was kept by the school office until the parent came to collect it.

I think our reliance on mobiles has become much greater in the last seven years, and the capacity of handheld devices to be harnessed and used in the classroom, rather than just being a distraction, has increased, so I would take a different tack now and try to use phones constructively rather than banning them. But it is a tough one. Because the pupils in my school couldn't openly use their phones, including at breaks and lunchtime, they did interact with one another rather than huddle round devices or all be on their phones instead of talking to their friends. I think this is a difficult issue to address!

3

CHAPTER

READING AND LITERACY

DIANNE MURPHY & ALEX QUIGLEY

> IT HAS BEEN CLAIMED THAT READING FOR PLEASURE IS THE SINGLE MOST IMPORTANT INDICATOR OF THE FUTURE SUCCESS OF A CHILD (OECD, 2002), AND THAT LITERACY HAS A "SIGNIFICANT RELATIONSHIP WITH A PERSON'S HAPPINESS AND SUCCESS." (NLT, 2008)

> IF YOU JUDGE WHAT 'WORKS' THROUGH READING SCORES, THEN THE WEIGHT OF EVIDENCE WOULD SEEM TO BE ON THE SIDE OF PHONICS INSTRUCTION BUT IF YOUR FOCUS IS ON OTHER MEASURES THAT ARE MORE HARD TO QUANTIFY THEN CLEARLY READING MEANS A LOT MORE THAN PASSING A TEST.

> READING IS VERY MUCH AN UNNATURAL ACT AND REQUIRES CLOSE INSTRUCTION AT LEAST FOR NOVICE READERS.

> LIMITED VOCABULARY IS NOT JUST A PROBLEM CONFINED TO ENGLISH OR LANGUAGE SUBJECTS, INDEED MANY TEACHERS OF SCIENCE FIND THAT WITHOUT A ROBUST DOMAIN-SPECIFIC VOCABULARY, MANY STUDENTS ARE SIMPLY UNABLE TO ANSWER FUNDAMENTAL QUESTIONS IN THEIR SUBJECT.

> THE GROWING BODY OF EVIDENCE AROUND PHONICS INSTRUCTION STILL DOESN'T SOLVE THE ISSUE OF PUPILS WHO CAN READ BUT SIMPLY REFUSE TO DO SO.

'A word after a word after a word is power'
Margaret Atwood

We know that reading has a profound impact on young people's lives. It has been claimed that reading for pleasure is the single most important indicator of the future success of a child[10], and that literacy has a 'significant relationship with a person's happiness and success'.[11] Given this, it would seem incredible that decades of research into reading and literacy has not come to a consensus and that we are still debating the most effective way of furnishing young people with the kind of key skills that can have such an important impact on their lives. Again there is the need not just for good evidence but also for ways of implementing that effectively in the classroom.

Such has been the debate around the best way to teach children how to read that the phrase 'reading wars' was used to characterise the level of animus between two very different camps in the 1990s. On the one side you have phonics instruction which explicitly teaches the relationships between units of sound (phonemes) and their corresponding letter or group of letters (graphemes), and on the other hand you have the whole-word, or sometimes called whole-language approach, which claims that learning to read in a more natural way through whole words is a better approach and engenders a more immersive engagement with reading through authentic tasks. Whole-word advocates claim that phonics instruction focuses on dull drills and repetition that can stifle a child's engagement whereas phonics advocates claim that the basics need to be mastered first in order to read effectively.

Although this debate is often characterised as a late 20th century one, it goes back as far as the mid-19th century. In America, Horace Mann, the first US education secretary of Massachusetts, campaigned fiercely for a whole-word approach which was then picked up by Dewey in the 1920s and Goodman and Smith in the 1970s. Central to this debate is the degree of agency a child has in the reading process. (William Gray once referred to phonics as 'heartless drudgery.') Phonics advocates claim their approach may be more challenging in the short term but leads to greater long-term benefits, while whole-word advocates claim their approach leads to a lifelong love of reading unencumbered

---

10. OECD (2002) 'Reading for change: Performance and engagement across countries. Results from PISA 2000', New York: Organisation for Economic Cooperation and Development.
11. National Literacy Trust (2008) 'Literacy Changes Lives An advocacy resource', www. literacytrust.org.uk/assets/0000/0401/Literacy_changes_lives_2008.pdf

by the slog of rote and drill. Today there is generally a balance of the two approaches but many teachers still ask, which one is more effective?

The answer to this is complicated. Certainly if you judge what 'works' through reading scores, then the weight of evidence would seem to be on the side of phonics instruction, but if your focus is on other measures that are more hard to quantify then clearly reading means a lot more than passing a test. However there does seem to be one issue with the claim that learning to read is a natural skill. For Dan Willingham, in order for something to be natural it needs to fulfil three criteria: firstly, it needs to be done without great difficulty and can usually be achieved through observation; secondly, as part of our human inheritance it should be observable in all cultures across the world; and lastly, it should be evolutionarily old and not something that has appeared in the last few thousand years. Reading would not appear to fulfil these criteria, however, as Willingham explains:

> These three features – easily learned by everyone, observed in all cultures, and evolutionarily old – are true for some human skills: walking, talking, reaching and appreciating social interactions, for example. But almost none of them is true for reading. Most people don't learn to read through observation alone, and there are peoples in the world without a written language. Finally, writing is not evolutionarily old. It's a cultural invention that is no more than fifty-five hundred years old.[12]

Seen in this light, reading is very much an unnatural act and requires close instruction at least for novice readers. However, how do you address the issue of the reluctant reader? The growing body of evidence around phonics instruction still doesn't solve the issue of pupils who *can* read but simply refuse to do so. Clearly there are a lot more distractions available to an impressionable young mind now than there were before the advent of the internet for example, and there do not appear to be any easy answers to the age-old question of encouraging kids to step away from the lure of the screen and open a book.

Many of the questions we received from teachers were focused on vocabulary and the question of how to broaden the range and depth of words available to students. This problem is a perennial one and one not just confined to English or language subjects. Indeed, many teachers of science find that without a robust domain-specific vocabulary, many students are simply unable to answer fundamental questions in their subject. Not all words are equal, however. Beck, McKeown and Omanson offer a three-tier model: tier one words are simple

12. Willingham, D. (2015) *Raising Kids Who Read*, Jossey-Bass, p.79-80

and usually require no instruction such as *dog* or *run*; tier two words consist of words that are 'high utility for mature language users'[13] such as *contradict* or *precede*; and tier three words are domain specific or technical words that are quite low in frequency such as *pantheon* or *epidermis*. Tier two words would appear to be of vital importance to children who have mastered the basics and, as pointed out in our discussion below, helping students have a rich vocabulary is the responsibility of every teacher. But how much explicit vocabulary instruction occurs, particularly at secondary level?

To help us answer these questions and navigate our way through the 'reading wars', we asked Alex Quigley, an English teacher and Director of Huntington Research School, York and the author of *The Confident Teacher* and *Teach Now! English*; and Dianne Murphy, founder of 'Thinking Reading', an intensive, one-to-one intervention synthesising well-evidenced teaching methods which won the Teach First Innovation Award in 2016.

---

13. Beck, I., McKeown, M., Kucan, L. (2002) *Bringing Words to Life*, Guilford Press, p.9

> **DM**
>
> OVERALL THERE IS EVIDENCE OF A SLIGHT DECLINE ACROSS OECD COUNTRIES IN READING FOR PLEASURE.

> **DM**
>
> STUDENTS NEED TO LEARN WORDS THAT ARE NOT YET PART OF THEIR EVERYDAY VOCABULARY BUT WHICH CAN BE READILY INCORPORATED INTO SPOKEN LANGUAGE AND STUDENTS' WRITING.

> **DM**
>
> FIRST OF ALL, YOU NEED TO KNOW HOW WELL THEY CAN READ. THIS IS NOT ALWAYS OBVIOUS.

> **DM**
>
> DOES SCREEN TIME AND NEW READING GADGETS CHANGE THE WAY WE READ, OR EVEN TRANSFORM THE BRAIN? WELL, PUT SIMPLY: NO.

> **AQ**
>
> COMPARISONS WITH READING IN THE PAST ARE VERY TRICKY. WHETHER TECHNOLOGY HAS MADE A DIFFERENCE FOR GOOD OR ILL IS UNCLEAR.

> **AQ**
>
> PUT SIMPLY, ENSURING OUR STUDENTS READ A GREAT DEAL IS A VITAL ASPECT OF DEVELOPING THEIR VOCABULARY.

> **AQ**
>
> WE CAN HELP FOSTER 'WORD CONSCIOUSNESS' IN OUR STUDENTS: THAT IS TO SAY, A CURIOSITY FOR WORDS, BY HIGHLIGHTING STORIES ABOUT WORD ORIGINS, AND MORE.

> **AQ**
>
> AS GEORGE SAMPSON SAID, BACK IN 1921: "EVERY TEACHER IS A TEACHER OF ENGLISH BECAUSE EVERY TEACHER IS A TEACHER IN ENGLISH".

READING AND LITERACY

CHAPTER 3   DIANNE MURPHY & ALEX QUIGLEY

What does the evidence suggest about how much pupils are reading compared to the past, and about the ways in which they are reading?

Alex: Ask many people, including teachers, what they think of reading habits of the children of today and the likely response is a negative one, with sad anecdotes of classic novels being supplanted by SnapChat and Sony PlayStations.

Some concerns about young people's reading habits are well founded. The National Literacy Trust, in their annual study of reading habits of children, found a significant fall in the reading enjoyment of boys, falling from 72%, aged 8 to 11, to 36% at ages 14 to 16.[14] In 2011, the international PIRLS (Progress in International Reading Literacy Study)[15] offered hope in that the highest attaining students in England were amongst the best readers in the world, but then, crucially, our lowest attaining students sat at the bottom of the international ladder.

Comparisons with reading in the past are very tricky. Whether technology has made a difference for good or ill is unclear. The potential benefits of using technology for increasing the rate of reading remain small[16], so we are best off focusing on improving standards of basic literacy, in the hope that reading competence leads to confidence, with more of England's children reaching the lofty heights scaled by our very best readers.

Dianne:

Reading for pleasure

Overall there is evidence of a slight decline across OECD countries in reading for pleasure. The majority of children read independently but about 23% say they do so rarely or not at all: 'In terms of frequency Clark (2011) found that most young people read outside of class every day (29%) or two to three times a week (26%). Sixteen percent of pupils said they rarely read outside the classroom and 7% did not read outside of class.' (DfE, 2012)

14. National Literacy Trust (2016), 'Celebrating Reading for Enjoyment: Findings from our annual literacy survey 2016', www.literacytrust.org.uk/assets/0004/1119/Celebrating_Enjoyment_of_Reading_2016-_Final.pdf

15. Twist, L., Sizmur, J., Bartlett, S. and Lynn, L. (2012) 'PIRLS 2011: Reading achievement in England', Slough: National Foundation for Educational Research, www.nfer.ac.uk/pirls.

16. Cheung A., and Slavin, R. E. (2011) 'The Effectiveness of Education Technology for Enhancing Reading Achievement: A Meta-Analysis', Baltimore, MD: Johns Hopkins University, Center for Research and Reform in Education.

However, such surveys do not necessarily describe how much children are reading overall, which can vary considerably depending on the curriculum their school follows.

Screen time versus book time

The fifth national survey by the National Literacy Trust in 2015 found that while overall time devoted to reading had not shifted significantly over the previous five years, the average time dedicated to reading materials online (including texts, emails and blogs) was twice as high as reading books. However, other print media was also read in the form of magazines, comics, manuals, plays, and poetry.

The most concerning trend is that children from disadvantaged backgrounds tend to read less, to read less well, and to see themselves as non-readers. We still have a gap of around 20% of children arriving at secondary school unable to read fluently for their age (Read On. Get On. 2015; DfE, 2015). For children who find reading effortful and slow, reading is aversive.

As a primary teacher, how can I broaden my students' vocabulary?

Alex: We know that the breadth and depth of our students' word-hoards is strongly bound with their ability to read and succeed in school. At primary school, most children increase their word-hoard by something like 3000-4000 words a year. We know that good readers can read around 1,000,000 words a year, in stark contrast to weak readers, who can read as little as 50,000 words in a year.

Put simply, ensuring our students read a great deal is a vital aspect of developing their vocabulary. Good readers have the benefit of a bigger personal word-hoard, often bolstered through lots of talk and interactions at home, as well as in the classroom. Well-structured talk and debate, using academic vocabulary can help develop ours students' vocabulary, but we need to twin this with lots and lots of reading, as much of our students' vocabulary is developed implicitly in the act of reading.

Also, focusing on explicit word learning strategies can prove very beneficial. First, simply introducing children to a new word effectively matters a good deal, breaking down the process into accessible steps, for example:

1) Pronounce the word;

2) Write it clearly;

3) Give a student-friendly explanation (dictionaries are often a challenge to negotiate) with examples;

4) Practise using the word in sentences;

5) Identify any word families or word parts, such as common prefixes or word roots;

6) Repeat exposure to this new word (as much as ten times in a given week or teaching cycle).

We can help foster *'word consciousness'* in our students – that is to say, a curiosity for words – by highlighting stories about word origins, and more. For example, how might the word *'attraction'* link to a *'tractor'*? Well, search out the Latin root *'tract'* and find out.

 Dianne: (The main source in this section is Beck, McKeown and Kucan, 2013)

Selection of words

Students need to learn words that are not yet part of their everyday vocabulary but which can be readily incorporated into spoken language and students' writing. Beck calls these 'Tier Two' words, 'likely to appear frequently in a wide range of texts and in the written and oral language of mature language users'. These can be selected from stories that children are exposed to but also related to relevant topics. For example, the words *merchant, required, tend, maintain, perform, fortunate* and *benevolent* were selected from a story likely to be of interest to third and fourth graders (Years 4-5). Such words allow students greater precision and clarity in language use.

Definitions or explanations?

Remember that dictionary definitions are usually not very helpful compared to explanations that show how a word may be employed in practice. Two or three explanations of how the word *'artistry'* is used are much better for teaching than the often rather abstract definitions provided by a dictionaries.

A range of contexts

Teach to ensure that students have encountered and thought about a word in a range of contexts. For example, where students offer responses very similar in context to the one that they have encountered in print, guide through questioning to consider wider contexts. So, a description of an *intrepid* explorer could lead to a discussion using *intrepid* to describe a football team, a fire officer, or a child giving a speech to a roomful of adults.

Be systematic and intentional

Plan to revisit the words introduced over time, weaving them into discussions and written work. Beck *et al* suggest that students need to encounter words at least ten times before they are likely to be reproducing them in their own speech and writing.

Q **As a secondary school teacher I've noticed that very few of my students read for pleasure. How can we encourage them to do so?**

Alex: The *'reading for pleasure'* conundrum is as old as records about reading. Teenagers have been turning off to reading for decades. So many options abound for them with the social media net seemingly enveloping them endlessly. Of course, many children are reading ceaselessly for homework and so reading for pleasure becomes something of a busman's holiday.

So what are we to do? Well, we should focus on making our students effective readers and in doing so make them much more *likely* to read for pleasure. When you can't read very well, and you have a limited vocabulary, then reading simply isn't very pleasurable.

We can do our very best to steer our students to the best of contemporary fiction, as well as to timeless classics. As we lead them to water, we may coax them to drink in Orwell, Austen, Dickens or Dostoevsky, or equally get them page-turning Stephen King, Suzanne Collins, Meg Rosoff, or the ubiquitous J K Rowling.

Reading pretty much anything will do, as long as we help them find *their* pleasure in so doing. We can steer and nudge, perhaps recognising that they have too little time to read as they stuff their homework in their bags. A little word of encouragement can still go a long way. A hint, or a tip off may work as well as some coordinated reading programme, whereas students who are forced to open a book under duress, or '*drop everything and read*', will demonstrate no little reluctance.

Dianne: First of all, you need to know how well they can read. This is not always obvious. Some students with decoding difficulties are verbally fluent and very good at masking their problems. Others can decode accurately but have difficulties with comprehension. Reading accurately is not enough – students must also be able to read fluently to support working memory leading to deeper understanding.

Any student who finds reading laborious or embarrassing will avoid the task, and teacher encouragement alone is unlikely change that. Therefore your school needs to have systematic testing in place to ensure that all students with various types of reading difficulty are identified and given appropriate help. Until such help is given, reading for pleasure is an unrealistic – and unfair – expectation for these students.

On the other hand, there are many who can read, but tend not to. As a result they are not making the progress in vocabulary, general knowledge and thinking about texts that they could (Cunningham & Stanovich, 2001).

Gambrell (1996) listed four key points that were important to creating a motivating climate for reading: availability of appropriate texts; opportunities for choice; familiarity with books; and social interaction.

Text choice

Students will be more likely to read about subjects they like – not just because they are interested, but because their background knowledge makes it easier for them to understand and think about the subject matter. It's essential that there are good quality texts available for a wide range of interests.

Text difficulty

Have a range of difficulty levels available and encourage students to read gradually more demanding texts so that they are not presented with steps that are too big. However, it is through encountering more challenging texts that students develop their grasp of vocabulary, syntax, style and text types.

Guidance towards new topics

It is essential to broaden students' experience of texts, so the teacher and librarian have an important role to play in extending the types of texts that students encounter. The quality of personal interaction here is important to students' perceptions of themselves as readers.

Reading promotion

Reading promotion schemes can be of benefit to some children: recent EEF research showed some benefits for more able readers but none for those who are not yet independent. Such schemes usually provide extrinsic rewards as additional motivation: quiz points, reading mileage, tracking information for competitions and recognition. However, any use of extrinsic motivation should include a plan to move towards increasingly intrinsic motivation, including spacing out rewards and fading them out entirely. The schemes generally in use in schools do not take this into account, which is why they tend to have short-term effects on pupil motivation.

For more information on these topics, see: Gambrell, 1996; Cunningham & Stanovich, 2001; DfE, 2012.

Q **As a history teacher, should I be correcting pupils' spelling, punctuation and grammar when I mark their work?**

Alex: A history teacher should be correcting spelling and grammar errors. As George Sampson said, back in 1921: 'Every teacher is a teacher *of* English because every teacher is a teacher *in* English. We cannot give a lesson in any subject without helping or neglecting the English of our pupils.'[17] Little has changed. The standards of accuracy we demand in history become the writing norms that our students internalise.

And yet, we should recognise that no one teacher or subject has the singular responsibility of teaching spelling or teaching grammar. The academic code of school is explicit in every subject. Of course, we need to support every teacher, from physics to Physical Education, to better understand *how* to teach spelling and grammar, whilst communicating with skill and accuracy.

The teaching of spelling is, in the main, something that is seldom addressed in every secondary school subject, primarily because there is too little knowledge how we do so. Spelling tests and word lists are a start, but they are unlikely to help children learn to spell consistently and well.

We need to supplement these traditional spelling methods with a more systematic approach. From deliberately teaching prefixes (like 'un-' and 're-'), to foregrounding word parts (the study of morphology), we give our

---

17. Sampson, G. (1921) *English for the English: A Chapter on National Education*, London: Cambridge University Press.

students an awareness that words are made of composite parts and form pretty reliable patterns. By doing this explicitly with numerous subject-specific words, we begin to develop habitual high standards and our students can internalise such strategies.

Dianne: Yes. The evidence about the usefulness of marking is inconclusive, partly because there are different notions of what marking is for. However, correcting errors is core business for teachers. The problem in implementing this is that a teacher can spend vast amounts of time correcting spelling, punctuation and grammar errors for very little return.

A straightforward workload tip here is to use simple codes to identify that a particular type of error has occurred – *eg* spelling, capital letters, paragraph break required, *etc* – and then set aside time for pupils to identify and correct the errors. You can save further time for yourself by using peer checking to see if their partner agrees that they have found and corrected all the errors.

The alternative, as those who have tried to ignore student errors will know, is that the mistakes become habits and are then very difficult to remove. On the other hand, if you identify and praise those students with few or no errors, or students whose error rate has dropped markedly, you will be reinforcing the behaviours you wish to see increased. In short, reward accuracy and make sure there is a cost for students in time and effort for mistakes.

How do you motivate white working-class boys, especially with reading and writing?

Alex: Well, as we have established, first we need to make sure they can read *well*. When they can read well, speaking with some confidence about what they have read, they'll be ready to write with confidence and competence too.

Evidence by Professor Daniel Muijs and Daniel Reynolds[18] shows that students don't become more motivated and confident by being lavished with praise or told *'you can do it'* cheerleader-style. They need to experience achievement, such as writing a great story, or reading a challenging poem, and finding real insight therein. The more experiences of learning and success like this that we foster, the more motivated our students can become.

We know that some students we label (sometimes lazily so) as white working class may lack reading role models. Their home may not foster literacy, reading and writing, like their word-rich peers, but, of course, we cannot wait for poverty to end. By having the highest expectations of our students' writing, helping them craft and draft, with relentless cycles of expert teacher modelling, we can instil increased motivation. By having sky-high expectations of every student we can challenge social stereotypes, even smashing down barriers of inter-generational illiteracy.

We make a start by reading one great text, or writing one great piece of writing. We set manageable goals, just out of the reach that they thought possible. In seizing this singular success, we whet their appetite for more.

 Dianne: See the points earlier regarding motivation to read. White working class boys are the least likely social group to read recreationally – and they are also the most likely to have difficulties with reading (Read On. Get On. 2015). These two problems are closely related. Address reading needs first, then worry about motivation.

In terms of motivation to read, work with the school librarian to match texts to interests, and then gradually extend students' worldview through more diverse and challenging texts. Throwing something completely unfamiliar at them is unlikely to have the same impact as gradually shaping their outlook. This may take a lot of thought and planning – but has the potential to change outcomes in the long term.

Remember that achievement is more likely to lead to motivation than *vice versa*. It is a reasonable inference that students who are demotivated by an activity probably find that activity difficult. This requires systematic

18. Saunders, K. (2012) 'Effective teaching: Evidence and practice – By Daniel Muijs & David Reynolds', *British Journal of Educational Technology*, 43: E37–E38. doi:10.1111/j.1467-8535.2011.01274_5.x.

teaching of key competencies, for example combining and altering sentences, becoming more fluent at spelling and punctuation, and so on. On a broader scale, students need instruction in strategies for planning, revising and editing (Hattie, 2009). For motivation, consider emphasising purpose, and writing for a real audience. Social interaction can be a powerful motivator, especially if it is contingent on completing a piece of work (*eg* for peer review). Publishing student work in print or digital anthologies can be motivating. Remember to use praise judiciously. Praise can be de-motivating if given in ways which are perceived as embarrassing or inauthentic.

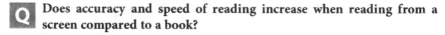

Q **Does accuracy and speed of reading increase when reading from a screen compared to a book?**

Alex: Much has been made of the transformative effects of technology. Do screen time and new reading gadgets change the way we read, or even transform the brain? Well, put simply: no. Humans have only been reading, as we know it, for a few thousand years. In relative terms, reading without technology makes up only a hair's breadth of human history.

There is little reliable evidence that would indicate the speed of reading increases when reading from a screen compared to a book. Most people read around 280 words per minute. If a Harry Potter novel is *circa* 77,000 words, that means we could read the entire book in around four hours.[19]

If you want to try and speed read, then good luck to you, but in skimming across words and sentences you lose accuracy. If you are reading on a screen, well, you have the added temptation of getting lost down the bottom of the Google garden, but other than that, there is largely no distinguishable difference.

Myths abound, but the truth is more quotidian. Reading is effortful and requires concentration. If we write good written notes and talk about what we have read, we may have a chance of remembering it more accurately. 'Memory is the residue of thought', as Dan Willingham states, so if we think hard about what we read, we can likely learn and remember what we have read. Whether it is a screen or a real book doesn't matter too much.

Dianne: There have been a number of studies in recent years on this theme, partly because of the rising popularity of digital textbooks. The evidence is mixed, but key points so far are:

---

19. Seidenberg, M. (2017) *Language at the Speed of Sight*, New York: Basic Books.

- Paper is a preferred medium over screen reading by most users. This may partly be due to greater familiarity with the medium – in which case, we might see a change in preference over time (Kretzschmar *et al*, 2013).

- Readers read faster and more accurately on paper, but this is not because technological features like light emissions, but probably because of the additional sensory clues that paper gives us as we handle it, jot notes on it, turn pages *etc* (Myrberg & Wiberg, 2015).

- Reading times on screen tend to be higher, though this is perhaps because of an associated tendency for multi-tasking when using a computer. Multi-tasking does not produce simultaneous cognitive processes – these are slowed down by the task of switching between processes. In other words, multi-tasking is a myth (Levitin, 2016).

- Interestingly, a study in Norway found that students scored significantly higher in reading comprehension on paper compared to reading the same texts on screens (Mangen, Walgermo & Brønnick, 2013).

As any teacher who has tried to get a classroom full of teenagers to research a topic on the internet knows, some students are too addicted to their online profiles and networks to be able to resist connecting to their email and social media accounts. Use with care.

 As a science teacher, what is my responsibility for whole-school literacy?

 Alex: As a science teacher, you are primarily responsible for your students knowing and understanding science. Of course, every science concept we teach and learn is clothed in language. Ergo, language and communication is your responsibility. Whole-school literacy is language and communication.

Glad we have got that settled.

Obviously, the question about whole-school literacy is bound up in the messy reality that we all mean different things by whole-school literacy. Too often, it is reduced to a bedraggled literacy coordinator, worn down by the unrealistic expectations of the role, promoting reading or writing in one-off events that are bound to fail in the bigger scheme of things. When we recognise that whole-school literacy is not a tick-list of dress down days where we wear fancy dress, drop books, pick up pens, carry placards, and the rest, and that it is instead the essential fabric of each and every subject discipline, then we will get somewhere.

We should talk more of '*disciplinary literacy*'. How does a scientist read, write and talk? What is the unique lexicon of biology or bhemistry? What reading strategies are required to unravel the complex threads of a scientific text?

When we move from vague cheerleading to meaningful, structured academic communication, we move onto the hallowed ground of great teaching. It is the stuff of science lessons as much as any English Literature lesson.

 Dianne: If language is the medium by which you instruct and assess students, then it follows that precise, accurate and efficient use of language will have a significant effect on your students' learning. To put it the other way around, if our use of language in the classroom is inefficient, unclear or inaccurate, we are holding students back. This is so in any subject domain, including science. Science teachers have every incentive to guide their students towards more accurate and precise written and oral expression, sound verbal reasoning, and accurate use of technical vocabulary. Such skills are essential for developing subject knowledge – and in turn are built by subject knowledge (Hirsch, 2003).

The 'elephant in the room', of course, is that many teachers are not confident in their own language skills and therefore avoid talking about language, including correcting students' mistakes and eliciting more sophisticated use of language. The first step in addressing this is developing a strand of CPD around language and literacy. Such CPD can be based on low-threat, fun and interesting tasks – like a pub quiz on grammar and punctuation, for example.

At a whole-school level, there should be a clear policy that supports consistent standards across all subjects.

 Why is there still no agreement over phonics versus meaning-based reading interventions?

Alex: Do I dare enter the phonics fray? The '*reading wars*' have raged for decades and show little sign of abating.

Why there is no common agreement is complex and likely beyond my capabilities in such a short response, but as training on reading can prove so variable for teachers, our shared knowledge and understanding can prove equally mixed and subject to the personal preferences of how teachers *want* to teach in the classroom.

The evidence is pretty comprehensive that that basis of effective reading relates to the teaching and learning of the *'Big Five'* (taken from the seminal American National Reading Panel of experts[20] back in 2000):

1. *Phonemic Awareness* (knowledge that spoken words are made up of individual sounds – phonemes)

2. *Phonics* (the explicit linking of sounds – phonemes – and the corresponding letters – graphemes)

3. *Fluency* (reading with the appropriate speed, accuracy and expression)

4. *Vocabulary instruction* (vocabulary is largely learned incidentally, but explicit instruction can help)

5. *Reading comprehension* (understanding what you read – built upon the other four components)

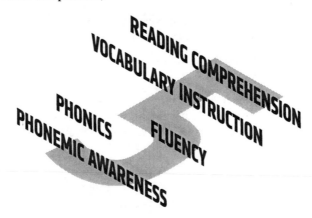

Clearly, phonics is a core aspect of teaching early reading (although not the *only* one). It does not preclude reading for meaning at all, quite the opposite. Good early phonics teaching can lead to fluency, and then onto accurate, successful reading for meaning.

The battle rages on – perhaps because different philosophies of reading are so muddled and clash. With some more training and professional

---

20. National Reading Panel (U.S.), & National Institute of Child Health and Human Development (U.S.) (2000) 'Report of the National Reading Panel: Teaching children to read : an evidence-based assessment of the scientific research literature on reading and its implications for reading instruction: reports of the subgroups', Washington, D.C.: National Institute of Child Health and Human Development, National Institutes of Health.

dialogue regarding developing reading, one fine day, we might all just learn to get along!

Dianne: There is in fact considerable agreement in the scientific community. The evidence for the efficacy of phonics as the basis for successful reading continues to converge. Likewise, there is little or no evidence in support of meaning-based approaches (Hattie, 2009; Hempenstall, 2013). A recent UK study found a very large advantage for code-based over meaning-based approaches to teaching artificial languages (Taylor, Davis & Rastle, 2017).

The differences of opinion in education on this matter are therefore to do with other motivations, ranging from ignorance of the science, to intransigence to change, and to good old-fashioned ideology. Stanovich (2000) puts it like this: 'I believe in letting scientific evidence answer questions about the nature of the reading process. Nothing has retarded the cumulative growth of knowledge in the psychology of reading more than failure to deal with problems in a scientific manner.'

I notice the same spelling errors crop up again and again, how do I break the cycle?

Alex: Improving the spelling of our students requires a deep understanding of words: their meanings, histories, families and their composite parts. In short, breaking the cycle of spelling errors will require much more than a few correction exercises and a spelling test.

It is important to have some basic understanding of *why* students are making spelling errors. It can of course simply be down to laziness and weak writing habits, or the problems can prove more deeply rooted.

We can draw deliberate attention to words and their spellings – helping students recognise word families and common word parts (such as prefixes and suffixes), pre-teaching some words and their spelling patterns. We can highlight common spelling issues, like homophones (write/right; bored/board), silent letters (ghost/ghastly), complex vowel clusters (conscious/conscience) and double letters (suddenly/surrounded).

A little etymology – the history of the word – can unlock its meaning and spelling. For example, '*cred*' comes, unsurprisingly, from Latin, meaning 'to believe'. That knowledge can help a child understand, remember and spell words like 'credibility', 'incredulous' and 'incredible' correctly.

Often, a child can spell effectively in a spelling test, but when undertaking the complex act of writing, with lots of different moving parts to consider, students make mistakes. This can be helped by reading a great deal, internalising patterns of words, but some deliberate focus on teaching spelling practice is essential. As experts in our subject domain, we should pay close care and attention to complex words, particularly with tricky spelling. Foregrounding and pre-teaching such words and their spellings raises our students' consciousness of spelling patterns and can help raise the standard of their spelling.

Dianne: Spelling is a written representation of spoken language. English allows for a sound to be represented by a number of different letter combinations – sometimes one letter but also two: sh (shot) and th (thing and that); three: igh (light) and oul (could); or even four: aigh (straight).

As a result, students need to be able to segment a word into its constituent sounds and write a 'spelling' for each sound. To check the accuracy of the spelling they then blend the sounds together based on what they have written.

A powerful way of ensuring that students learn from their errors is the 'match to model' procedure described by Okyere and Heron (1991). A page is divided into three columns. The target words are written in the first column by the teacher, and then folded under. The student's attempts are written in the second column. After testing, students uncover the first column, and use a simple four-item code to identify what types of errors they made. They then rewrite the word in the third column correctly, using the original model. Interleave practice so students have the opportunity to revisit the words they found tricky.

Remember that you can have students develop individual spelling lists and work with a partner to test and record. Visual feedback from charting their cumulative progress is also motivating.

Joshi and Moats (2008) identify three main areas for teachers to highlight in explanations, in order to help students develop their spelling skills: word origin and history (etymology); syllable patterns and units of meaning (morphology); letter patterns (phonics). Teaching students explicitly about language patterns that are largely implicit to us can be challenging. For example, words ending in '-able' or 'ous' are pretty much always adjectives; many so-called 'irregular' words in English are Anglo-Saxon in origin, so the spellings *do* follow patterns, but from a more archaic form of the language; no words in English start with 'ns', but a few Greek-origin words do begin with 'mn'. Systematic knowledge of the language is required to teach it systematically.

Q **How do you prepare students for the step up to sixth form where a much deeper level of reading is required involving lengthier texts?**

Alex: First, I think it is essential to dispel the notion that deeper reading, or complexity, equates directly with lengthier texts. Any student, or adult, reader of *The Waste Land*, by T S Eliot, can testify to that! I suspect the question is probing how more complex texts being read at A level require more independent reading skill and knowledge, whether the subject is English Literature, science, or history *etc.*

I would say that the solutions are not too far away from the issue of teaching complex texts to younger students. We need to pre-test the essential background knowledge of a given A level text, which invariably proves gaps in our students' background knowledge. For example, in a great deal of classic literature, like the aforementioned Eliot, a sound knowledge of the language and rituals of Christianity is vital to unlock an understanding of the text. This needs to be coupled with pre-teaching essential vocabulary knowledge.

It is of course essential that we put in place really good diagnostic assessment to know exactly what our A level students know and do *not* know. Recently, I spoke to an A level politics teacher who was aghast when students couldn't explain basic political vocabulary like democracy *etc.*

As every A level teacher knows, there is no substitute for knowledge. We need to foster, encourage and structure wider reading wherever we can. We need to make our A level classrooms rich with academic debate, talk and lots of reading of complex texts. Reading around the subject should be more than encouraged; it should be mandated. Even if this mandate is not much more than the vital enthusiasm of a teacher conveying a deep-seated passion for their subject, it is likely to help our students better make the learning leap to A level.

Dianne: It's necessary to start as early as possible. Students need to be reading challenging texts and developing more sophisticated vocabulary in Key Stage 3. Recent research by Dr Jessie Ricketts shows that students with poor vocabulary on arrival at secondary school remain well behind and do not catch up (Ricketts, 2017).

Even when students have a reasonable vocabulary for Key Stage 4, the leap to A level is much more difficult – the sheer volume of reading required, and the cumulative nature of the knowledge and connections between texts required, is too intense for some, especially in the exam context.

However, if we begin as early as possible and systematically work on building students' reading skills, vocabulary and subject knowledge, the leap does not have to be so large. Key Stage 3 and 4 curricula should both include a wide range of texts and require extensive reading, in order to build the cultural knowledge which is so important for comprehending text at A level. Required reading for students must therefore go well beyond the texts required for GCSE and introduce them to classics as well as important recent texts. This is particularly so for disadvantaged students who are much more reliant on education services to help them bridge this gap. Reading lists and recognition for progressing through them are straightforward structures for teachers to implement – though, in the context of GCSE exams, it can be difficult to maintain momentum. It is important to start the process as early as possible.

4

SPECIAL EDUCATIONAL NEEDS

CHAPTER

MAGGIE SNOWLING & JARLATH O'BRIEN

> THE FIRST ATTEMPT TO RECOGNISE AND CLASSIFY CHILDREN WHO REQUIRED PARTICULAR PROVISION WAS ONLY MADE IN THE EARLY 1970S.

> IN 2005, WARNOCK WROTE A PAMPHLET WHICH CHALLENGED THE BASIS OF ALL SEND PROVISION IN THE UK AND ARGUED THAT A MAJOR OVERHAUL WAS NEEDED.

> TEACHERS NEED TO BE AWARE THAT THIS IS AN EVER-SHIFTING LANDSCAPE WHERE PRACTICE MUST ALWAYS BE CUTTING EDGE.

> IT IS NOT ONLY THE SENCO'S JOB TO BE AWARE OF THE LATEST IN EFFECTIVE RESEARCH, IT IS THE RESPONSIBILITY OF ALL TEACHERS.

> IF YOU DO KEEP UP TO SPEED WITH THE LATEST IN RESEARCH - OR, PREFERABLY, HAVE A RESEARCH LEAD WHO WORKS EFFECTIVELY WITH THE SENCO - THEN YOU CAN DEAL CONFIDENTLY WITH SITUATIONS THAT ARE ARGUABLY THE MOST SENSITIVE FOR THE MAJORITY OF TEACHERS. THIS WILL ENSURE THAT CHILDREN WHO REALLY NEED SUPPORT - THE KIND WHICH IS LIFE CHANGING IN NATURE - WILL GET IT.

An apocryphal story is often told about a Confederate veteran of the American Civil War, who spent countless hours regaling his grandson with tale after tale of his experience in battle at places like Antietam and Gettysburg. The young lad meekly enquired, 'Who won?' to which his grandfather said, 'It's too early to tell.'

The same might be said of the battle to provide adequate support for children with special educational needs and disabilities. It is, after all, relatively recently that such a group of young people has even been acknowledged. If you are reading this as an educator working outside of the UK, then perhaps spend some time reviewing the history of SEND in your country. Here, the first attempt to recognise and classify children who required particular provision was only made in the early 1970s (so after the Swinging '60s – a subtle clue that difference existed in British society). A commission was set up to investigate, chaired by Mary Warnock. Her 1978 report provided the basis for the 1981 Education Act, which accepted some – but not all – of what had been recommended in this area. In 2005, Warnock wrote a pamphlet which challenged the basis of all SEND provision in the UK and argued that a major overhaul was needed. Her one solid conclusion is revealing:

> No serious suggestions for reform can be made without proper research and a proper reliance on evidence. This is why I regard it as essential that there should be a government-funded independent Committee of Inquiry into the current state of special education, empowered to make recommendations based on the evidence of experts, especially teachers. This is my only firm conclusion.[21]

Nearly a decade passed before serious response was implemented, when the SEND Code of Practice was issued. A pivotal part of the government's strategy was a team of SEND Pathfinders who were tasked with making the system less bureaucratic, increasing choice for families and quality of provision for learners aged 0-25. This was also supposed to be based on a robust evidence base. Did it work? It's too early to tell...

This is an area plagued by major ideological divides, made all the harder to navigate by all sides making impassioned and logical points. Should all children be educated under one roof to avoid segregation and labelling? Or should children be placed in an environment where their emotional and educational needs are met? Wading into this is about as problematic and dangerous as a pub debate on Israel/Palestine. So what are your responsibilities as a classroom

---

21. Norwich, B., Terzi, L. and Warnock, M. (2011) *Special educational needs*, London, p.44

teacher? Indeed, what are the responsibilities of a parent? We know several heroic people who are both. What does the research say?

This is a huge area and the approaches taken in different schools – and countries – shows how fraught with difficulty it is. The example of Finland is fascinating, where every school is legally obliged to have a child welfare team in place. The issues are clearly set out in Lucy Crehan's excellent *Cleverlands,* where she argues:

> The purpose of child welfare work in Finnish schools is to 'create a healthy and safe environment for learning and growing, protect mental health, prevent social exclusion and promote the wellbeing of the whole community'. I think it is an advantage that children's mental health and wellbeing is just as important as (as well as closely related to) their educational achievements.[22]

Yet she also acknowledges that the system, however well intentioned, has had mixed reception with Finnish teachers as the first level of support must come in the classroom and evidencing need has added to teacher workload. Whilst this may be true, these are the pupils that are worth the extra time and effort.

So we come back to the questions of teacher responsibility and the role of research. Teachers need to be aware that this is an ever-shifting landscape where practice must always be cutting edge. Relying on the SENCO is not enough; familiarity with the likely needs that pupils have is a precursor, and knowledge of the school's system and the links with the wider support network is vital if needs are to be met. Even if a system is good (and in this area, that's a massive presumption internationally), it will fail if its users don't know how to navigate it. Even then, any system can be improved and streamlined. This is where the research element comes in. It is not only the SENCO's job to be aware of the latest in effective research, it is the responsibility of all teachers. After all, who wants to be out of touch at a parent conference where you are the least-informed person in the conversation? If you do keep up to speed with the latest in research – or, preferably, have a research lead who works effectively with the SENCO – then you can deal confidently with situations that are arguably the most sensitive for the majority of teachers. This will ensure that children who really need support – the kind which is life changing in nature – will get it, and that difficult decision of whether a child stays in a mainstream school or goes to a special needs school will be made with the best evidence available.

This is an emotive area for obvious reasons. The questions that follow, and the

---

22. Crehan, L. (2016) *Cleverlands*, Unbound, p.29

answers that are given, are intriguing and worth reading carefully. Given the range of possible questions, we could think of none better than Professor Maggie Snowling and Jarlath O'Brien as responders. Maggie is an expert in reading difficulties and has transformed our understanding of the field, particularly in understanding the genetic component in learning difficulties. She was awarded a CBE (a British distinction given by the Queen, so not your typical teacher 'pat-on-the-back') and her answers show a degree of understanding that can only come from many years of practice and research. She is also President of St John's College, Oxford, which quite incredibly and generously allowed us past the Porters' Lodge. Jarlath was appointed head of Carwarden House Community School in 2011, a special needs school for young people with an Education, Health and Care Plan (EHCP), and is author of *Don't Send Him In Tomorrow* (top tip – order a copy now). The conviction and expertise in their answers will, we hope, inspire you to spend more time on how to improve your classroom knowledge, and your school's provision, in this area. It's the one and only chapter where we will depart from our mantra on reducing teacher workload and tell you to up the effort. It always reaps rewards for those who need it most. Get stuck in.

MS FOR ANY CHILD WITH SPECIAL EDUCATIONAL NEEDS IT'S VERY IMPORTANT TO RECOGNISE THOSE NEEDS AND TO ENSURE THAT THEY KNOW YOU RECOGNIZE THEM.

MS I AM CAUTIOUS ABOUT SAYING 'WHAT STRATEGIES WORK', IT'S REALLY ABOUT BEING A SKILFUL PROFESSIONAL WHO WILL LOOK AT THE BEHAVIOURS, RECOGNISE THAT THESE ARE ON THE SURFACE AND TRY TO UNDERSTAND WHAT THE CAUSES ARE.

JO IT IS IMPORTANT TO REALISE THAT ALL BEHAVIOUR IS PURPOSIVE – THAT IS TO SAY THAT WE ALL BEHAVE IN CERTAIN WAYS FOR A REASON.

JO I TAKE THE VIEW THAT BEHAVIOURAL DIFFICULTIES ARE SKILLS GAPS TO BE FILLED MUCH LIKE WE DO WITH READING AND SPELLING.

MS FROM A TECHNICAL PERSPECTIVE, I CALL THEM NEURO-DEVELOPMENTAL DISORDERS. SCHOOL SYSTEMS CALL THEM SPECIAL EDUCATIONAL NEEDS. THEY'RE HIGHLY, HIGHLY HERITABLE.

MS YOU GIVE CHILDREN EXTRA TIME IN AN EXAM, BUT HOW ARE THEY GOING TO USE IT? THEY NEED TO BE INSTRUCTED IN HOW BEST TO USE EXTRA TIME.

MS TEACHERS CERTAINLY SHOULDN'T BE EXPECTED TO BE DIAGNOSING OR TREATING A MENTAL HEALTH ISSUE IN THE CLASSROOM.

MAGGIE SNOWLING   CHAPTER 4   JARLATH O'BRIEN

SPECIAL
EDUCATIONAL
NEEDS

Q **What strategies work with students who have social, emotional and behavioural difficulties?**

Jarlath: Firstly it is important to realise that all behaviour is purposive – that is to say that we all behave in certain ways for a reason. It does not mean that the behaviour is acceptable or appropriate, but it is a response to a person's interaction with others and with their environment. I like to think of this as 'all behaviour is the right behaviour'. In this way I view negative behaviour as the communication of an unmet need (a great example of this is the research showing that between 35-50% of children with speech, language and communication needs also have behavioural difficulties). This does not absolve the child of the responsibility of owning their behaviour, but it really helps me to understand what may be happening to this child for them to behave this way. The unmet need may be something that you can do little or nothing about at that immediate moment, but if you don't seek to understand then you will be perennially frustrated at what you see in front of you. I use a personal example to illustrate this. I find singing and dancing very stressful things to do. I am not good at either of those things, they make me feel very self-conscious and I feel as if everyone is looking at me and laughing. I will blush deeply and I will feel very stressed. Fortunately I am in a position in life where I can avoid both of these things and people generally can't make me do them, although I had to have lessons for the first dance at our wedding! If your lesson involves singing and/or dancing, which you might think will be fun and enjoyable for everyone, then I'll do pretty much everything within my power to get out of taking part. You can threaten me with any punishment you like – all are preferable as long as I'll avoid singing or dancing. For me it's singing and dancing, for some children that might be reading aloud, or swimming, or maths. All behaviour is the right behaviour, remember, so for me the right behaviour involves doing what I can to protect myself from embarrassment. I still know that it is wrong – don't take this to mean that we are not in control. That emotion overrides any behaviour policy sanctions you can throw at me. However, if you understand this about me and start from where I am, be gentle with me and help me retain my fragile confidence then I am far more likely to do what you would like me to do.

Secondly, I take the view that behavioural difficulties are skills gaps to be filled, much like we do with reading and spelling. Ross Greene says, 'Children do well if they can'; and the late Joe Bower extended that to: 'Doing well is always more desirable than not doing well, so when a child is not doing well, it is likely that their environment is demanding skills they are lacking.' I think this way about behaviour. Take my singing and dancing example above. If I was a top-notch singer and dancer there would be no problem. But I don't have the skills and need you to start from where I am at. I would also add to Joe Bower's comment that your definition of doing well might differ from the child's. Doing well for me might be escaping that lesson and will remain so until my skills are such that I am confident enough to take part. I have worked with many children who have this view about reading – teenagers with learning difficulties who, in their own words, 'can't read' – but, as I remind them constantly, can't read as well as they would like. We must be sensitive to this.

Thirdly, I came to learn through long experience that punishments and sanctions were largely ineffective for most of these children most of the time: the logic being that these are deterrents yet didn't work, and punishments were a fact of life for many of them that they just factored into their day. Again, don't jump to the conclusion that I support the idea that children should be allowed to get away with things. They are still responsible for their behaviour. Instead I came to learn that restorative approaches worked best. Making it clear to children the consequences of their actions on others and themselves and their responsibilities for fixing situations and relationships that they had damaged is far more powerful and effective. I have always thought it silly that we expect children to change their behaviour by simply depriving them of time in school in the form of a detention or away from school in the form of exclusion. This places the problem as being innate to the child and they simply need to go away and think about what they did. If you are going to use things like detentions then make sure that the time is used productively in a restorative way to prevent reoccurrence. If the same children are receiving detentions and fixed-term exclusions time and time again then it is legitimate to ask if those are effective behaviour-improvement strategies.

Lastly, many children I've worked with in special school who have been excluded from mainstream schools have come to the conclusion that schools are unsafe places to be for them – they're given work they don't feel they can do, punished for not doing it, yet advance no further forward. This may be an unfair conclusion from the teacher's perspective, but we ignore it at our peril. They need to know that you are there to support them and that you understand them – I call this 'We're here to catch you, not catch you out'. They need to be convinced that their struggles will be met with unstinting support, not withering criticism. They're used to people giving up on them, so they're waiting for you to do the same. Far better to quit on their own terms, goes their logic, so you may sometimes see children sabotage situations. They need to know that you're not going to give up on them.

Maggie: My answer to this question is probably going to be similar to the answer to some of the other questions about special education needs, because I want to start off by saying that we can think about strategies, but fundamentally we have to think about individuals and we need to adapt the strategies and the plan to individual. The other two things I would say is that for any child with special educational needs it's very important to recognise those needs and to ensure that *they* know you recognise THEM. You can help them to understand THEIR STRENGTHS AND WEAKNESSES and by listening to them, you can also understand what the needs are. For all special needs, a very important thing is to affirm the good things that the child does and to affirm their strengths. Don't be patronising and just say everything is good, because they know if they've done something and it's not good, but selectively praise the parts of their behaviour which are positive. That raises the whole issue of monitoring, progress and evaluating what you are doing.

With regard to children with social, emotional and behavioural difficulties, THIS IS really an umbrella term. You need to have enough space to assess the situation, what's causing the social, emotional and/ or behavioural difficulties, and to be thinking about causes. Causes are just hypotheses. If you have a hypothesis about what causes a difficulty you then need to intervene, but you ALSO need to monitor whether that intervention is effective. If not, that hypothesis can probably be discounted and there might be another reason. One of the significant causes of these sorts of difficulties are problems with spoken language and communication – often hidden disabilities in the classroom. A child who doesn't understand can easily get frustrated and can behave badly. A child who perhaps is struggling at school can fail to communicate their difficulties with attainment and can internalise the problem, so these can become emotional difficulties. Social difficulties can often be problems to do with communications with peers.

Now that's not to say that social, emotional and behavioural difficulties can't have origins in the family, and they can. I think it's very important to involve the family in discussion ABOUT the difficulties, but explore hypotheses one by one before you actually turn to the strategies that are available. These would cover a very wide range of strategies depending on the nature of the problems, and depending on whether or not you have to bring in family support, whether or not you have to bring in some behavioural management techniques, or whether you think, ultimately, that this child is vulnerable and needs referral to a mental health practitioner. So I am cautious about saying 'what strategies work'; it's really about being a skilful professional who will look at the behaviours, recognise that these are on the surface and try to understand what the causes are. That's the first step in planning the programme.

Q **Can you give me three simple tips to use to support a child in my class with dyslexia?**

Maggie: Well this is a difficult question because it will depend upon the age of the child and also the stage of their reading development – that is, the level of literacy that they've reached. In general, you must be positive about strengths, and not let the child suffer in terms of ever-decreasing self-esteem, which is a real problem for children with dyslexia. Generally teachers need to think about differentiating the work the child has been required to do, perhaps putting in particular supports. For example, read the question in maths, don't expect the child to have to read the problem and also do the maths, because maybe they can do the maths perfectly but they can't read the questions. So think very carefully about the content of the work that you're asking a child to do, and also be careful when you mark the work. Don't mark every single error, that's terribly demoralizing. Pick one or two teaching points, share with the child what you're going to be focusing on this week, and focus your marking on whether or not the child has achieved that particular aid, that particular teaching point.

So to move from the generic to the more specific, with a very young child with dyslexia, or a child who has not learnt to read in the first year in school, you must ask about their oral language development. Spoken language is the foundation for literacy, if a child is having difficulty learning to read there is a very strong possibility that the problem actually is to do either with understanding or producing spoken language. A language problem can prevent the child acquiring the phonological awareness skills that are important for them in learning to read. So that's the first thing; maybe you need to put in some support with the development of speaking and listening skills.

Assuming these are okay and in the 'classic' child with dyslexia, spoken language is not usually an issue. You then need to be thinking about a tiered approach, so the child in the early years will be receiving systematic phonics teaching in some form. Put in an extra TA-supported small group where you can, focusing in on letter-sound knowledge and phonological awareness and also sensible writing exercises. If the child doesn't catch up through that, then you should be thinking about a more individualised approach. The evidence here is very clear that children with a dyslexic profile you need to be working on phonological awareness, letter-sound knowledge, linking the two things together through writing and also reading from books. Those books need to be selected to be at the right level so that they're not too hard for the child to access.

When you get a bit further up the age range (and by which I also mean off the basics of learning to read), you need a lot of work on spelling, helping children to organise their spelling lists according to shared spelling patterns, and helping them very early on with their creative writing. You can be talking to them about what they want to say and perhaps then just ask them to write some of it and not all of it. In other words, you're differentiating the work so that the child can achieve. With older children we are talking about arrangements like extra time, perhaps putting in spell checkers, or allowing work to be submitted using a digital voice recorder sometimes rather than having to write. Therefore the emphasis is on combining specific intervention work with a differentiated approach to class work.

Finally, although the evidence base for early phonological approaches is very strong, there is much less evidence further up the age range. Always combine what you do with a very positive approach to affirming things that they have done well, so I think that's very important for supporting self-esteem.

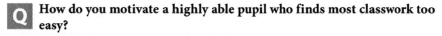

How do you motivate a highly able pupil who finds most classwork too easy?

Maggie: This is something on which the evidence is not very strong. I think good practice differs and it depends very much upon the child, the school context and the child's emotional maturity. Also the area in which they are gifted is important because I don't think any child is going to find every aspect of class work too easy. Generally the approaches involve trying to offer enrichment to the curriculum in their area of particular interest. Some stretching is needed, so if there is flexibility in the school, try shadowing or attending classes in the year above for particular curriculum areas. Sometimes there are ways teachers can use quizzes just to challenge children, give them something else to do rather than the regular classroom work.

The other thing that I think is helpful is encouraging those very bright kids to give support to their less able peers, because sharing knowledge is also a very good way of deepening one's own knowledge. It's a way of really affirming that this is a continuum; for that particular subject area they're at the higher end but there are kids at the lower end and they can benefit from the help that they give. That can also help social skills and integration, so those are the sorts of things that I'd recommend.

Q **What strategies can you use to support students who find it very hard to concentrate?**

Jarlath: There can be many underlying reasons for such difficulties. The research above on the overlap between speech, language and communication difficulties and behavioural difficulties is one obvious route to look for. It is clear that if a child has receptive language difficulties (*ie* listening difficulties) then they may find it challenging to absorb large amounts of verbal information from a teacher (and we do this a lot, don't we?). If you have rattled off a list of five things to do there may be some off-task behaviour in the near future when the first thing is completed, but the child has forgotten the other four. Schedules help here – either break the task down into manageable chunks to be completed one at a time, but let the child know what the whole task is to ensure they are clear on the context of what they're doing, or list the steps to full completion. The child can tick them off as they go. This is a very common strategy in special schools – the use of visual timetables, First-Next-Last strips, *etc* all help to promote independence and mean that you aren't questioned every 90 seconds on 'What do I do next, miss?'

I work with many children with sensory issues – they are over- or under-sensitive to light, temperature, noise, clothing such as ties, blazers, zips, buttons and labels. They may chew their clothes, squirm in their seat, hold their hands over their ears (think behaviour and unmet needs here). That sensory need is going to be met somehow and it can distract from their attention on the task at hand. There are many ways to help with sensory input such as weighted gloves, scarves or blankets or by being reasonable with adjustments to uniform that can make a big difference to a child's ability to concentrate for longer periods.

Maggie: Well this of course is also very, very difficult because it depends on why they're not concentrating. Sometimes children can't concentrate because their thoughts are grappling with emotional issues, some which they might bring from home. Other children may have some underlying attentional issue. Other children might be not concentrating because they have a learning difficulty, so typically dyslexic children don't concentrate very well because if they're not properly engaged due to their literacy problems, they can be distracted. One has to, again, think carefully about why the child isn't concentrating.

Techniques that help: sit the child near to the teacher; gently remind them to keep concentrating; give them frequent breaks and again, how many breaks depends on the individual child. You can actually use some kind of timer, so that the child knows for themselves that they have to work for five minutes before they can take a breather. Some children with attention problems actually suffer quite a lot from distraction. There is a little bit of evidence, and I don't know how up to date this is, that some kids actually benefit from having music in their ears, but I wouldn't want to push that too strongly. I think it depends a little bit upon the nature of the problem, but always think, 'Is it a real problem with attention control, or is it because the work is hard?' If the work's hard, then you should be asking, 'Can this work be differentiated so that it's more engaging?'

The other thing to remember is that lots of kids with attention problems do have really significant cognitive difficulties with the appreciation of time. Now you ask them, 'How long is 10 minutes?' And they'll tell you after two minutes or after an hour. That's a real problem for time management, that they need help with that because it's not just having the time management plan, they actually don't appreciate time.

All of these, from a technical perspective, I call them neuro-developmental disorders. School systems call them special educational needs. They're highly, highly heritable. There's a strong genetic component to this. The genes act through the environment. For example, if you have parents with dyslexia who don't read very much, the home environment doesn't add in the books, so you're getting a double whammy.

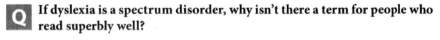 **If dyslexia is a spectrum disorder, why isn't there a term for people who read superbly well?**

Maggie: Well, there's the term 'hyperlexia', which is used for children who can decode very well and often in advance of their age and mental abilities. That's of course a problem, though a different sort of problem to dyslexia – in a less extreme form we refer to that as reading comprehension impairment. Reading comprehension impairments are about as frequent as dyslexia, but they can be hidden because teachers just focus in on whether the child can read aloud. Children who can read aloud very well are thought to be doing okay. It's really quite important that those children have their reading comprehension assessed properly, because sometimes they've got enormous problems there.

But just more generally, all cognitive skills are dimensional, so whether we're talking about language or reading or numeracy, we're talking about dimensions. Cut offs, labels, or categories like dyslexia or language disorder or autism spectrum or ADHD, are arbitrary. They depend upon external criteria that might be determined by a local authority or a government policy – they're not hard and fast. There's no clear cut distinction. That's why we use the term 'spectrum'. When we're talking about these spectra, from a perspective of special educational needs, we're not concerned about people who are above a threshold and are doing well, because they are within the typical range that can be accommodated in the classroom. However, at the lower end you have the majority of children with special educational needs. Then at the extreme higher end in terms of talent and giftedness and so on, we have equal numbers who we should be paying attention to, but more generally those children don't get labelled.

Q **Do you think technology assists or inhibits pupils with SEN issues, and if it does assist what can you recommend?**

Jarlath: It has undoubtedly been a significant support to young people with SEN. To see a child use an eye-gaze machine (a computer that allows a person to select words into sentences which then speaks for them solely by their eye movements or helps them make choices) is a revelation. This kind of technology literally changes the lives of these children.

Dictation software for young people with significant literacy difficulties has also been very important. The physical act of writing, itself very important and not something to be ceased obviously, can significantly slow down the pace of work for some children because of their fine-motor control issues, for example. Their brain may work far faster than they can get ideas down on to the page, so simple use of a computer or dictation software can really help.

The use of datalogging technology in subjects such as science can help support students with SEN too. Learning to read the scale on, say, a thermometer is valuable in and of itself, but if the point of an investigation is to learn about insulation and heat loss you may find the difficulty in reading the scale on the thermometer the biggest barrier to a successful lesson, yet it is unimportant to understanding the concepts you are teaching. If the point of the lesson is to learn to read the scale, then fine. If not, consider using such technology that lowers that barrier for that child or children so they can focus on what you really want them to learn.

Maggie: The research evidence here is qualitative, so we don't have any robust evidence of the type that might say, 'If you take children with dyscalculia and you randomly allocate them either to receive calculators or not, what is the outcome for their maths achievement?' The evidence which is available tends, as far as I know, to be with older children and it's more of the type, 'How have you used the software? Has it been helpful? What do you find good about it? What do you find difficult about it?' We are here in a very new and important area, but we are grappling to know really what works.

I've always been a strong advocate of children with specific learning difficulties being allowed to use calculators, because many may have mathematical abilities which are stymied because they can't do arithmetic, but I don't think a calculator should just remove the need for them to learn to calculate. It's about using a calculator well and still knowing how to do the calculation, so you've got the conceptual development, but using it as a sort of prop.

I'm also quite a strong supporter of early introduction to voice recognition software for children with dyslexia. These devices have really improved, and the earlier a child can get used to using them the better, because higher up in the school grades essay-writing really is quite important and also at university. If the child is fluent, then this is a good way of them producing writing. I think writing is still ultimately the most difficult area for children with a specific learning difficulty affecting literacy. Touch-typing is an old fashioned term, but obviously using keyboard skilfully is an important task. You shouldn't just assume you can put in a computer and the child will benefit. They have to be taught how to use the computer, how to use it well.

There is also quite good software for things like revision and so on. I'm really out of date with them, but I think what you need to do here is, when you're analysing what the child finds difficult, trial software solutions, but you should monitor and check that they are helpful. Also a word of caution: don't assume that the child doesn't need training to use the software of the piece of technology. It's a similar thing with extra time. You give children extra time in an exam, but how are they going to use it? They need to be instructed in how best to use extra time, because if you don't do that, all you find is you're increasing the length of exams that children with specific learning difficulties have to take over a given exam period, so they end up more exhausted than their peers. It's really important with any support, any arrangement, to try and do proper training and proper evaluation of how it's working.

Q **What are the best early interventions a teacher can make to mitigate learning difficulties?**

Jarlath: Bear in mind with interventions what it is that the child is missing when they're doing this work. Can your support for this child be done within the context of what the class is doing? I know many children who ricochet from intervention to intervention all week long and spend little time with their peers. It is difficult for them then to feel part of their class if they're always somewhere else with a TA. You may be inadvertently adding to their sense of isolation.

The children that come to my secondary special school, almost all from mainstream primary schools, have a very wide range of different needs and conditions. However, they almost always have the following difficulties in common:

- Problems with working memory.

- Problems transferring learning to long-term memory. It is frustratingly common for our children to appear to have learned something and for it to be gone the next day.

- Speech, language and communication difficulties.

  – Pre-teaching vocabulary for topics (like earthquakes and volcanoes or World War Two, for example) will help support these children if and when they come up against new words for the first time.

  – Teach them explicitly the language to explain how they're feeling. This helps with conflict resolution and will help them explain to you when they're struggling.

- Literacy difficulties. These come in many different forms, but continued work on this cannot be overstated.

Anything you can do to support these common difficulties will be welcome, but remember to keep an eye on what is intervention and what is just good teaching.

Maggie: I would just say language, language, language. Language is a foundation for so much of education and so much of learning. In all educational systems, the curriculum is transacted through language. Children have to be able to understand language to benefit from teaching, and they have to produce language to demonstrate that they're learning. Language is the foundation from which we get the development of phonological awareness, which is a key step to literacy. The more non-phonological aspects of language, like vocabulary and grammar, are absolutely crucial for reading comprehension.

If one of the important targets of primary education is to be able to read with understanding, language is really crucial. It's also important for numeracy; arithmetic is verbal, it requires language, mathematical problems are cast in language. Language is also important for self-regulation. Children who can't concentrate often haven't got that kind of inner speech telling themselves to sit still, don't jump up, we're supposed to be listening now, we're supposed to be looking now. I think language is very, very important and it should be worked on to help mitigate learning difficulties.

The other things are just to remember that children with learning difficulties will take more time to learn. Don't expect them to learn at the same pace as everyone else. I think where we can we need to involve parents, but we need to be mindful that there is a genetic component to most learning difficulties, and parents of children with learning difficulties are highly likely to have the same learning difficulties themselves. We cannot assume that a child with a reading problem will have parents at home who are highly literate and can do lots of reading practice with them. So think about who else can be brought on board – grandparents, older siblings, kids in the class who don't have reading problems. We need to support parents of children with learning difficulties.

There has been an increase in awareness of mental health issues. What are my responsibilities as a teacher when it comes to identifying and diagnosing a pupil's problem?

Jarlath: I feel uncomfortable identifying or diagnosing any health issues as we're teachers and not health professionals. If we have concerns there are colleagues within school, Heads of Year, SENCo, SLT, who we should discuss these with and they can help us seek the right support from other professionals.

There is, however, lots we can do to support children by making our classrooms the most welcoming places they can be. If we are teachers who provide an environment that feels like it is 'high challenge, low threat', as Mary Myatt would say (remember from above 'We're here to catch you, not catch you out'), then we're well on the way. It has always been important for me that learning is a rewarding experience for our students. If it is characterised by high stakes (think Year 6 SATs or GCSE) then pressure can build if we're not careful and issues arise. I cannot help but contrast my experiences of teaching in a comprehensive compared to teaching in special schools. In special schools we're largely free of the culture of performativity, the end-point narrative of Progress 8, SATs scores, floor standards and 5 A*-C including English and maths and I firmly believe that teachers are under far less pressure to 'perform' in ways that the performativity culture demands. This pressure in schools seeps into every corner and affects children. There is a purity of purpose that remains in special schools that I see tainted by exam pressures, looming inspections and results days in August in mainstream schools. Protecting children as much as possible from the professional pressures that teachers face is surely a major step in the right direction. As an example, I don't talk about Ofsted in my school at all. It is a fact of life for me, but I cannot have it playing on the minds of the staff. They need to go about their work doing things because they're the right things to do, not because they have been told by me that that is what Ofsted want (Ofsted have done much to remove these myths thankfully) or because it is to meet a need of mine (think behaviour and unmet needs again and think how that influences the behaviour of headteachers too!).

Maggie: I don't know the current guidance in schools, so I'm going to answer this from what I consider to be the current guidance in higher education (university teaching), which is what I know about. I suspect the principles are the same. The first thing is I think all teachers need an awareness of mental health issues. They need to have some form of training, and organisations like MIND provide this training so that you can identify mental health difficulties before they escalate.

When you have a suspicion about a mental health problem, I think you need to be discussing your concerns with someone in school who is more expert, and they may recommend a meeting with the parents. Almost certainly you would do that, to see whether the problem is also apparent at home (*ie* triangulate it) or if it is something about the school situation. Beyond that, really, I think the responsibility is to refer the child to the appropriate professionals. Teachers certainly shouldn't be expected to be diagnosing or treating a mental health issue in the classroom.

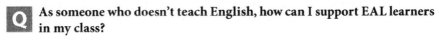

Q **As someone who doesn't teach English, how can I support EAL learners in my class?**

Maggie: This is a difficult question, because EAL covers something like 200 languages in the UK, so we don't know the background language often, and we may not have access to anyone who does. There are a number of strategies that I think are very helpful. One is to identify the key vocabulary in the subject area. This sort of strategy is also good for children with language disorder. In history, you might be going over something like the Roman Empire, and there'll be some key terms that will be introduced which are the backbone of the topic. I think it's very helpful if you can provide a glossary of those terms and what they mean and maybe even get Google translator to provide the version in the home language, so that before the lesson happens, the child is prepared with some kind of framework for understanding what the teaching is going to be about.

Again, family can be very helpful. Older siblings can be very helpful in this direction. Just plan a little bit about what the child's going to find difficult before you actually find the child in the class hasn't understood. In terms of the writing component, I think the usual sort of supports. Allow different recording techniques, don't mark down for poor use of English grammar or poor vocabulary.

In an ideal world allow the child to use their home language and to switch between the languages, but of course that's not really realistic in the context of what is still primarily a monolingual society that we have. This is a huge problem globally, multilingualism, and we just need to think about practical sorts of solutions. Think ahead and give the child a framework, or use visual images. If it's geography, you can have a map and pictures to get across the framework, so then they've got much more chance of keeping in touch with the lesson.

Q **I've got a pupil with ADHD in my Year 8 class. What advice can you give on how to get the best out of them?**

Jarlath: Understand what ADHD is in as much depth as you can first. It is unfortunate that ADHD is often considered to be naughty children with feckless parents. It isn't. Understand how ADHD manifests itself in that child and how you can best support them. Understand, if they are on medication, what that medicine is for and how it helps the child. It is not a cure for ADHD, so seek to understand what it actually does. Talk to the child about how it makes them feel; when do they feel successful, when do they feel that they struggle and need you support? What support do they say they need?

Maggie: This again is a question of understanding the nature of the ADHD and what works for them. It's very important to find out whether the child has had a proper medical opinion, because if this really is ADHD, many of these children would benefit from some form of medication and that's your responsibility. There is good evidence that medications can help. There is a reluctance often of parents and teachers to think about medical intervention, but there is strong evidence that this is probably as helpful as much of the behavioural evidence that one could give.

It's a question of setting a plan that takes account of the nature of the ADHD, and your Year 8 student should well be able to comply with this. Work out what periods of time they can work for. Work out whether there are supports like listening to music through headphones that help them concentrate better. Work out whether they need to take more regular exercise. Work out how diet might feed into this, or if there are certain things that they need to avoid. It's the usual sorts of things. In the classroom, have some management. Once you've planned, decide how long they're going to work without a break and then keep them to it so you're very consistent in your approach. With all behavioural problems, consistency is the real issue. Set the plan so they know what's required, what's expected, and be very consistent, but also very positive.

Many children with ADHD have communication problems. They blurt things out. They interrupt people. These sorts of pragmatic language difficulties may, in and of themselves, require some intervention that can be helpful, and speech and language therapists can be consulted about that sort of problem. Once again, it really is about the individual and planning what's best for them.

5 MOTIVATION

LUCY CREHAN & NICK ROSE

> MOTIVATION DOESN'T ALWAYS LEAD TO ACHIEVEMENT, BUT ACHIEVEMENT OFTEN LEADS TO MOTIVATION.

> IT COULD BE THE CASE THAT USING TIME AND RESOURCES TO IMPROVE STUDENT ACADEMIC ACHIEVEMENT DIRECTLY COULD BE A BETTER AGENT OF PSYCHOLOGICAL CHANGE THAN PSYCHOLOGICAL INTERVENTIONS THEMSELVES.

> ARE SCHOOLS CREATING A KIND OF COGNITIVE DISSONANCE BY HOLDING ASSEMBLIES TELLING STUDENTS THAT A FIXED MINDSET IS BAD BUT THEN GIVING THOSE SAME STUDENTS FIXED TARGET GRADES IN THE CLASSROOM?

> MOTIVATIONAL POSTERS AND TALKS ARE OFTEN A WASTE OF TIME AND MAY WELL GIVE STUDENTS A DELUDED NOTION OF WHAT SUCCESS ACTUALLY MEANS.

> IN THINKING ABOUT HOW TO MOTIVATE STUDENTS IT'S PROBABLY MORE HELPFUL TO THINK ABOUT THE KINDS OF THINGS THAT WILL GIVE STUDENTS A SENSE OF AUTONOMY AND MASTERY IN THE LONG TERM THAN A SENSE OF INSPIRATION IN THE SHORT TERM.

> *'While none of the work we do is very important, it is*
> *important that we do a great deal of it'*
>
> Joseph Heller, Catch-22

When looking at how research is implemented in the classroom one of the central problems is a fairly consistent confusion between methods and outcomes. This is especially prevalent in the difference between novices and experts where we often assume that to become an expert you should do what experts do; however, a large body of research shows that this approach is often problematic. If you want to become proficient in playing the guitar, probably the worst thing you can do as a beginner is to try and play the guitar like an expert. Instead, it is far more expedient to break the complex domain of an expert guitar player into its constituent parts of scales and chord formations and practise those before moving onto the more complex demands of playing a complete song. We would all want our eight-year-old son or daughter to be able to play football like Lionel Messi but if they try to dribble past five players before mastering the essential skills of close control, drags and step-overs they will become frustrated and disheartened. In any given class, the range of ability is often more similar than it is different with most students having the *potential* to achieve, yet often students who should get an A end up with a C and other students who were predicted a C can end up getting an A. This is often put down to great teaching and quite often this is the case; but more often than not, this is down to the student's own motivation, so how do you affect this?

Psychologists Edward Deci and Richard Ryan have offered the concept of self-determination theory (SDT) as a way of thinking about motivation which claims that the interaction between intrinsic and extrinsic motivation is the key determinant in any form of achievement. They describe intrinsic motivation as 'the inherent tendency to seek out novelty and challenges, to extend and exercise one's capacities, to explore, and to learn'[23] but that this is not sustainable without 'some form of supportive conditions, as it can be fairly readily disrupted by various nonsupportive conditions'.[24] Getting the balance right between these two aspects of motivation is key in creating the conditions of learning for any student and is still a source of great contention in the field.

Probably the most influential theory of motivation in education today is the

---

23. https://selfdeterminationtheory.org/SDT/documents/2000_RyanDeci_SDT.pdf p.70
24. https://selfdeterminationtheory.org/SDT/documents/2000_RyanDeci_SDT.pdf p.70

work of Carol Dweck and the notion of a growth mindset as being a key driver of student achievement. This theory claims that beliefs about intelligence as being 'fixed' or malleable have a huge impact on how well students do in many aspects of their lives and is backed up by decades of solid research. However, recent studies[25] in how to actually affect student beliefs about intelligence have failed to replicate and once again point to the difficulty of how to implement research in the classroom. It may well be the case that a growth mindset can have a dramatic impact on students, but how exactly do you change those who have a fixed belief about their abilities? Furthermore, are schools creating a kind of cognitive dissonance by holding assemblies telling students that a fixed mindset is bad but then giving those same students fixed target grades in the classroom?

One of the consistent things about research on motivation is just how counterintuitive it is. It seems fairly straightforward to claim that once you motivate students then the learning will follow but research shows that this is often not the case. Motivation doesn't always lead to achievement, but achievement often leads to motivation. A lot of what drives students is their innate beliefs and how they perceive themselves, and while there is a strong correlation between self-perception and achievement and we tend to think of it in that order, some research has shown that the actual effect of achievement on self-perception is stronger than the other way round (Guay, Marsh and Boivin, 2003). It may well be the case that using time and resources to improve student academic achievement directly could be a better agent of psychological change than psychological interventions themselves. Daniel Muijs and David Reynolds (2011) note that:

> At the end of the day, the research reviewed shows that the effect of achievement on self-concept is stronger that the effect of self-concept on achievement.

Despite this, a lot of interventions in education seem to have the causal arrow pointed the wrong way round. Motivational posters and talks are often a waste of time and may well give students a deluded notion of what success actually means. Teaching students how to write an effective introduction to an essay through close instruction, specific feedback, worked examples, careful scaffolding and then praising their effort in getting there is probably a far more effective way of improving confidence than giving an assembly about how unique they are.

The other problem is that even when students are engaged, it doesn't mean they are learning anything. This again is quite a counterintuitive claim; why is

---

25. www.sciencedirect.com/science/article/pii/S0191886917303835

engagement is such a poor proxy indicator for learning? Surely the busier they are, the more they are learning? This paradox is explored by Graham Nuthall who claims that:

> Our research shows that students can be busiest and most involved with material they already know. In most of the classrooms we have studied, each student already knows about 40-50% of what the teacher is teaching.[26]

Nuthall's work shows that students are far more likely to get stuck into tasks they're comfortable with and already know how to do as opposed to the more uncomfortable enterprise of grappling with uncertainty and indeterminate tasks. Robert Bjork describes some of the activities like these as 'desirable difficulties', which refers to the kinds of things that are difficult in the short term but which lead to greater gains in the long term. These point to a range of strategies that teachers can do such as spacing out learning, interleaving topics and enabling students to engage in retrieval practice through frequent quizzing (dealt with in chapter 6) and also things that students can do such as taking more ownership over the process of feedback (dealt with in chapter 1).

Motivation represents a highly complex domain with many variable factors and, like creativity, is a mercurial force that often eludes us when we need it the most. In thinking about how to motivate students it's probably more helpful to think about the kinds of things that will give students a sense of autonomy and mastery in the long term than a sense of inspiration in the short term. Motivational posters might look nice around a school but they are unlikely to help Lisa with quadratic equations. Motivation is also something that is probably domain specific as opposed to a general disposition that can be applied in all subjects – students might be highly motivated to learn about the French Revolution in history but have no motivation whatsoever to learn about Newtonian motion in physics. Allowing students to experience the hard-won gains of learning a tricky concept through scaffolded activities might just lead to more motivation than talking about motivation itself.

To answer these questions we asked Lucy Crehan, who spent time working in schools and living with teachers in six 'top-performing' education systems as the basis for her book, *Cleverlands: the secrets behind the success of the world's education superpowers*, one of *The Economist's* 'Books of the Year 2016'. On her return, Lucy wrote a book on teacher career structures for IIEP UNESCO, and spent a year working as part of a team advising foreign governments

---

26. Nuthall, G. (2007) *The Hidden Lives of Learners.* NZCER Press, p.24

on education reform at the Education Development Trust. We also spoke to Nick Rose, who worked as a post-graduate researcher in psychology – working with Susan Blackmore at the University of the West of England in Bristol. As a Leading Practitioner for Psychology and Research, Nick created evidenceintopractice.wordpress.com – for which he was shortlisted for a *TES* award in 2015. He joined TeachFirst as a researcher in March 2016 and is the co-author of *What Every Teacher Needs to Know About Psychology.*

MOTIVATION

LC EAST ASIAN STUDENTS, TEACHERS AND PARENTS ARE MORE LIKELY TO THINK THAT EFFORT PLAYS A BIGGER PART IN ACHIEVEMENT THAN INNATE ABILITY.

NR IN ALMOST ALL CASES, THE EVIDENCE ISN'T THERE TO SUGGEST A CAUSAL LINK BETWEEN TRYING TO CHANGE PEOPLE'S ATTITUDES AND THEN THAT LEADING TO AN IMPROVEMENT OF OUTCOMES.

NR MOST PEOPLE THINK OF GENETIC INFLUENCES IN VERY DETERMINISTIC WAYS; THE IDEA THAT YOU'RE BORN WITH GENES AND THAT PRE-DETERMINES SOME KIND OF OUTCOME. BUT THE SCIENTIFIC EVIDENCE DOESN'T SUPPORT THAT DETERMINISTIC VIEW.

LC THE EAST ASIAN APPROACH TO THIS APPEARS TO BE TO OVERRIDE THIS CONCERN FOR AUTONOMY IN THE FIRST INSTANCE, AND MAKE CHILDREN DO THE UNDESIRED TASK ANYWAY, WHETHER THAT BE DOING THEIR HOMEWORK, OR PRACTICING AN INSTRUMENT.

NR THERE'S ALSO SOME EVIDENCE THAT USING RETRIEVAL PRACTISE MAY ACTUALLY HELP TO REDUCE SOME OF THE SENSE OF ANXIETY THAT STUDENTS HAVE WHEN COMING UP TO EXAMS.

LC WHAT WE CAN, AND IN MY OPINION SHOULD, LEARN FROM THE EAST ASIANS IS THEIR HIGH EXPECTATIONS OF ALL STUDENTS, AND THE ATTITUDE THAT ANYONE CAN SUCCEED WITH THE RIGHT SUPPORT AND EFFORT.

Q Can extrinsic motivation encourage intrinsic motivation in the long term?

Lucy: According to self-determination theory and research on motivation in adults, intrinsic or autonomous motivation (a term that incorporates intrinsic motivation and the motivation to do something because you believe it's important, even if you don't enjoy it) is brought about by creating environments that fulfil three basic human needs: the need for relatedness, the need for competence, and the need for autonomy. How do you create an environment that meets the needs for all three?

The relationship with the teacher is very important in getting children motivated by a subject. In Canadian schools I visited, staff talked a lot about the importance of each child having at least one adult that they trust and respect, and this is one reason they have a lot of extracurricular opportunities and school counsellors. Competence is, of course, what we are trying to get students to achieve in the first place, and taking a mastery approach to learning can help in this respect, as addressed elsewhere in this book, and in my own.

Autonomy is the tricky one here, as if you give children autonomy over whether they partake in an activity they don't already enjoy, they will typically choose to not do it! An alternative is to introduce some choice into how they do it, but this must be carefully planned to ensure that all options will still lead to learning. The East Asian approach to this appears to be to override this concern for autonomy in the first instance, and make children do the undesired task anyway, whether that be doing their homework, or practising an instrument. 'Tiger mother' Amy Chua sums this up nicely in her book, *The Battle Hymn of the Tiger Mother*:

'What Chinese parents understand is that nothing is fun until you're good at it. To get good at anything you have to work, and children on their own never want to work, which is why it is crucial to override their preferences. This often requires fortitude on the part of the parents because the child will resist; things are always hardest at the beginning, which is where Western parents tend to give up. But if done properly, the Chinese strategy produces a virtuous circle. Tenacious practice, practice, practice is crucial for excellence; rote repetition is underrated in America. Once a child starts to excel at something – whether it's maths, piano, pitching or ballet – he or she gets praise, admiration and satisfaction. This builds confidence and makes the once not-fun activity fun. This in turn makes it easier for the parent to get the child to work even more.'

Despite this approach, research carried out in 2009 on a sample of Chinese and American children found that the Chinese children were actually no less intrinsically motivated than American children were, suggesting that perhaps a bit of extrinsic motivation is one way to get children into the reinforcing loop of intrinsic motivation and achievement, in the context of a supportive relationship with a teacher and well-designed learning activities.

Nick: There's been a great deal of debate about this. Some of the evidence suggests that when individuals are already very highly intrinsically motivated, so they're already really engaged and very interested in a particular subject, offering them rewards for it – extrinsic motivators – may not actually be very effective. In some cases it may even reduce their intrinsic motivation. If we're only doing things in the expectation of receiving a reward, when those rewards stop coming, then obviously the very logical thing we might do is withdraw our effort from those endeavours. On the other hand, we're not intrinsically motivated to do everything. I can think of occasions across my career where getting up in the morning has not been something I've been intrinsically motivated to do; however, the subtle extrinsic motivation in receiving a salary, having professional responsibility, being accountable, is enough to overcome my reticence to get up and get on with the day.

Learning a musical instrument is a classic example, particularly when you're first starting out. You're just playing scales and it can seem extraordinarily dull. One cannot always really see the purpose or the point of it and lots of people give up, sometimes quite quickly. That's because it's not terribly intrinsically motivating to learn the very basics of these things. And here, perhaps, extrinsic motivation can play a part. Whether that's very subtle in terms of encouragement, or just praise for committing the effort to these endeavours. Or whether it's having a sense of accountability. There's an extrinsic motivation for doing these things, because you're accountable to other people, even if that's just friends or family around you. Particularly for adolescents when they start moving from looking for approval from adults in their environment, particularly their parents, to being much more focused on their peer group, the use of extrinsic motivators to overcome that bump in the road, that effort gradient beyond which you actually start seeing the benefits of your labour, feeling a sense of success and becoming intrinsically motivated, is where a bit of extrinsic motivation can help.

Can you teach students to have a growth mindset?

Lucy: There is a lot of research on cultural differences in approaches to learning between 'the East' and 'the West'; typically, comparing Chinese or Japanese students with English, American or Canadian students. This research does not mention growth mindset *per se*, but investigates behaviours and attitudes that are closely associated with it. These studies consistently show that East Asian students, teachers and parents are more likely to think that effort plays a bigger part in achievement than innate ability. East Asian students are more likely to persist in attempting tasks they find challenging, or that they believe they are failing at. And East Asian parents are more likely to point out their children's weaknesses, and then support them to improve.

These Chinese and Japanese students are not consciously taught about growth mindset, but messages about the relative importance of effort over ability, and the possibility of success, no matter your starting point, are shared with children through the actions of their teachers and parents, as well as more explicit sayings and stories. One Chinese idiom is 'A clumsy bird that flies first will reach the forest soonest', sharing the idea that even the less able can beat their peers if they make the most effort. Young children are brought up with the story of famous scholar Kuang Heng, who wasn't able to continue studying into the night as his family could not afford lamp oil, and so studied by the light of his neighbour's house, which got in through a small chink in the wall. My own observations and stories from Japanese and Chinese people suggest that East Asian teachers are more likely to praise students for the effort they make, rather than their accomplishments. There is no need to teach children about growth mindset if their teachers and parents have this orientation themselves, and speak and behave in such a way as to bring about this belief in children.

Nick: Growth mindset is part of a field of psychology called Attribution Theory and the idea that on some occasions we see our capabilities as somewhat fixed, while other times we might see them more open-ended, is certainly an area of Attribution Theory that's got a fair amount of evidence around it. Many psychologists would refer to it as a difference between a learning and performance orientation. So when we feel like we're on the spot and we have to perform well, not look stupid, hopefully make a good impression, or whether we see it really as an ongoing process, a learning process, and if we make errors and things like that, we'll learn from them.

Now, the extent to which we can teach students to have these mindsets around their work is the open question. The recent failure to replicate some of the effects around praise certainly casts something of a shadow over it; however, there has been some successful interventions apparently using feedback in order to encourage students to have a growth mindset around things like mathematics but whether or not they can be genuinely scaled is an interesting question. Many of these interventions that have apparently worked have been extraordinarily subtle, very short-lived and the idea is really what you're trying to do is nudge the student into a more virtuous circle. So, the idea being that by encouraging them to adopt more of a learning orientation towards a particular task, it encourages them to apply more effort and to not be concerned about looking stupid or whatever else and from that, there then comes a sense of success, which then builds on itself.

So rather than try to teach a growth mindset, I think what proves better would be to try and create the conditions around which students are more likely to adopt a learning orientation and in terms of what that might be in the classroom using techniques like formative assessment in order to diagnose possible misconceptions or areas where students can improve and I might try and relate it to some of the EEF toolkit evidence on mastery learning. So, trying to achieve a very high success rate before moving on and I think it's a case of building that sense of self-efficacy, that sense of achieving success, which probably drives the conditions around which students are more likely to adopt the learning orientation, rather than a performance one.

It's important to realise that both of these mindsets are adapted in different circumstances. If you've got a job interview or you're about go into a high-stakes exam, it's quite natural and probably quite sensible to adopt that kind of performance orientation to that particular task. And also the fact that perhaps we draw effort from particular domains, particular subject areas, whether that's PE or maths, is again probably adaptive. If your constant experience is a sense of not achieving very much, despite your efforts, then obviously withdrawing that effort seems to make a great deal of sense. So, rather than trying to manipulate mindsets, I think it's about trying to think about the conditions within which people can achieve and experience a genuine sense of success and I suspect that would then drive the mindset differences that we're seeing.

Q **Does motivation increase achievement or does achievement increase motivation?**

Lucy: Whether motivation leads to achievement, or the other way around, depends on whether you're talking about intrinsic motivation or extrinsic motivation. Of course, common sense tells us that intrinsic motivation can lead to greater achievement in some areas – if you enjoy doing something, you do more of it, and if it's the kind of behaviour that you get better at with practice, then this will make you more accomplished. Reading is a classic example. Being accomplished at something can also make it more enjoyable, and so increase intrinsic motivation. So, it isn't that one causes the other, but that they are mutually reinforcing.

Nick: There's a major review by Stephen Gorard back in 2012 that attempted to examine a whole range of things about attitudes, things like self-confidence, self-efficacy, to educational outcomes and were all these mindsets actually making any direct influence on people's outcomes? What's really interesting about the article is that in almost all cases, the evidence isn't there to suggest a causal link between trying to change people's attitudes and that leading to an improvement of outcomes. You see the same thing across the whole variety of other kinds of domains in psychology for example, the value action gap. So for instance, organ donation is a classic example. You can ask people about their attitude about donating organs and most people will say that seems like a really great idea. You can give them information about how important it is and how necessary it is and how easy it can be. But despite having changed the attitudes, people aren't more likely to sign an organ donation scheme so, this is a problem we might face, the directional arrow between motivation and outcomes is not a simple one. So I think for a teacher in a classroom, again it goes back to trying to create these conditions where students can meaningfully perceive themselves to be seeing some progress and seeing some success in what they're doing and I suspect that probably drives the attitudes, at least as much, if not more than attitudes drive the outcomes.

Is motivation a heritable trait like intelligence or can it be manipulated?

Nick: This is an interesting area. Most people think of genetic influences in very deterministic ways; the idea that you're born with genes and that pre-determines some kind of outcome. But the scientific evidence doesn't support that deterministic view. Better to think of a range of potential influenced by our genes, but within this we have extraordinary behavioural flexibility. That's the thing about human beings, such interesting animals, is the fact that we're able to adapt our behaviour to such a wide variety of circumstances and use the environment in such incredible ways to overcome barriers, that we're not genetically well suited to do. The fact that we can fly around the world is not something we've evolved to be able to do!

However, within the complex relationship between motivation and genetics, there's something called gene-environment interactions, which means that we're more likely to be drawn towards things we might be genetically well suited to, where we have the capability of doing very well in particular tasks. There's a reason I'm not a basketball player. However from the point of view of a teacher in a classroom, we can't know the genetic potential of any of our students. And we certainly can't be certain about how interactions between the influence of the environment and our genes will impede or bring out potential. All we can really do is consider the classroom environment that we're creating for those students. We tend to be motivated by things we think we're good at and things that we think are valued by the people around us. And so it's probably better to think of our motivation as not necessarily something that's genetic in a deterministic sense, but rather to think about what we can do that will best allow students to fulfil whatever their genetic potential might be.

There's an issue about *how* we do that. I think some of the arguments around trying to manipulate students' effort through praise and similar techniques tends not to work predictably because young people are socially aware. They have the benefit of a long evolutionary heritage of people trying to manipulate people. Very young children may willingly engage with the game in which they're manipulated to behave well, for instance, but as we get older, certainly when going through adolescence, we typically sense quite quickly when adults are trying to manipulate us; whether that's through rewards or through praise, and where they detect this, they will often reject these things.

Do you think that starting schooling at a later age is better for long-term motivation?

Lucy: The UK is fairly atypical in starting compulsory schooling at five. Most countries begin formal education at age six, and many – including top-performers Finland and Shanghai – start school at seven. Starting school at a younger age isn't a problem if what children are expected to do is appropriate for them. While it isn't the case that children develop in the same way or at the same speeds, it is the case that children need to understand or learn some things before being expected to do other things – for example, they need to have a sense of number before they will gain any benefit from learning to add up, and they need to have a solid grasp of letter-sound correspondences before they are expected to spell words which break these rules. This understanding may happen at different times for different children, but approximately two-thirds of summer-born children don't meet minimum expected standards in reading, writing, speaking, maths and other developmental skills at the end of their first year of school (compared to a third of older children), suggesting that what is expected of many of them is too much, due to their age.

What does this have to do with motivation? Firstly, there is some research which finds that children who have formal, instructional approaches to education at an early age are less motivated, and have poorer wellbeing outcomes, than those who take part in more playful learning at the ages of five and six. This is a hotly contested topic, and not all agree with what the research ultimately tells us. I hope that what all can agree on though is that children need to have a good grasp of the foundations of learning – not just numeracy and literacy, but how to self-regulate and how to interact with others – before rushing ahead with the syllabus. If children experience early failure by being expected to do things which are beyond their current abilities, particularly in a culture which does speak about intelligence like it is something you either have or you don't, then we shouldn't be surprised if children become demotivated.

Nick: I'm not sure that there's any really good evidence on the relationship between the age at which we start school and motivation. I think one of the caveats here would be the idea of age appropriateness. Perhaps there's a bit of a hangover to Piaget's ideas about the stages of cognitive development. It's not uncommon for people to still have the idea that certain things, perhaps more formal learning or more abstract ideas, are simply not suitable for younger children. In fact, when more carefully conducted experiments have taken place, younger children turn out to do surprisingly more and more things. Very young children are capable of learning quite abstract ideas, are capable of engaging with some of things that would be considered 'formal operational' in Piaget's model. Typically, it's their prior knowledge that's probably a better starting point for thinking about what children can learn at different ages. I think that the jury's out as to what age children should start school; but we do know that really good early years provision can, if supported across the child's experience across their later school years, produce quite some potentially major gains. So I think the key thing is just not to get trapped into the idea that certain things are off the table because of the child's age and to consider whether the child has the foundations of prior learning to build more formal learning on top.

 How can we motivate sporty boys who see academic work as tedious?

 Nick: My problem with school was precisely the reverse. I was rubbish at sport. I'm a late summer baby, so I was likely the youngest kid in my school and therefore nearly a year's development behind my peers when it came to sport. And funnily enough, my motivation was much greater in things like science and maths and English than it was in PE. In fact I hated PE with a passion and I suspect the reason was that I never really experienced any success in PE – I was always the smallest, the skinniest, so when it came to climbing ropes I consistently humiliated myself by failing to get even halfway up.

I think we've got to see that the challenge of motivation extends across the curriculum. If students see themselves as very successful in sport, but unable to achieve any success within other subjects, then quite logically they'll withdraw effort from areas where they don't feel they're being very successful and they'll be quite keen to invest their effort into areas where they are doing well. So, your question reversed would be 'How would I have been more encouraged to be motivated in PE and get my nose out of the maths books?' The answer in both cases is to provide an environment where students can genuinely see themselves being successful within each subject area: whether that's a sporty boy achieving well in mathematics or a weedy nerd like myself not achieving in PE These things can be tackled in a similar way: it's about what kind of support you can give that allows both individuals to perceive themselves as being successful. I think where they can see themselves being successful, there's a logical process by which they will invest more effort within those kind of domains and I think it's likely that their motivation will increase as well.

 There seems to be an increased anxiety around exam pressure. How best can we help pupils cope?

 Nick: In the context of our classrooms, we can create an environment where hopefully students are adopting more of a learning orientation towards their work. So hopefully we're focusing on things they can improve and the strategies they can use, and it's not accompanied by a high stakes sense of anxiety. However, across all aspects of life, not just school, there will be occasions where we adopt more of a performance orientation – because we are being put through our paces; whether that's a big sporting fixture, a cup final or whether it's a job interview, or a high-stakes exam. These things generate anxiety because they're important to us and because we know that we need to put in our best effort in order to achieve what we want. So, what can we do about that? Well we can't spare students ever having the experience of having a high-stakes performance at some stage in their lives. Indeed, it would probably be wrong for us to remove all of those experiences from their childhood as we learn to cope with such adversities by experiencing them; and hopefully experiencing some success despite that adversity.

So what teachers should do to help is focus on what kind of preparation will genuinely help students when they get into that high-performance, high-stakes exam. There's an interesting review of the various study skills that students use when preparing for exams and unfortunately some of the most common things, like rereading notes, or highlighting or underlining materials in preparation for exams, turn out to be the ones that are probably the least useful in terms of helping students do well. The review by Dunlosky *et al* identified retrieval practice as a highly effective way of preparing for exams and improving outcomes. And there's another reason why that might help, there's also some evidence that using retrieval practise may actually help to reduce some of the sense of anxiety that students have when coming up to exams.

I think the reason for that is fairly logical. All teachers will remember that sense of impending deadlines with the exams looming. I think what frightened me most is that feeling of walking into the exam, seeing the question and just my mind going blank and the information not being there when I needed it. This is why retrieval practice might help to protect a little bit against some of that anxiety. If you know that can reliably recall material, regardless of the situation, and you have practice recalling the information that you need, that's quite deeply reassuring, I think. When it comes to getting ready to go into an exam, if you *know* that you know it, and you know that it will come to mind when you need it without any concern, then I think that can plausibly help reduce some of the very highest levels of anxiety around going into exams.

Before performers go on stage, they often describe butterflies in the stomach. It's worth noting that some anxiety isn't necessarily a bad thing; in fact a bit of anxiety is actually very good for our performance. If we're a bit too relaxed, if we're sleepy and non-committal about it, we don't tend to do our very best. So, what we need to do is identify what it is that will support students, so that despite some understandable and inevitable sense of anticipation for a high-stakes event, that they're prepared well enough and they can trust themselves to be able to recall what they need to know and what they'll be able to do what they need to do. There's the concept called self-efficacy, which is our confidence in our ability to perform well within a particular domain, even when the stakes are high. Whilst I think trying to tackle this at the level of 'building self-efficacy' is wrong for the reasons I've given before, I think that creating a set of strategies and techniques that the students can really use to build for themselves a sense of self-efficacy from the evidence of their own experience can help to moderate the anxiety they feel when it comes to exam pressure.

Q **The UK has been performing poorly in PISA. Are students in the West less motivated than students in the East?**

Lucy: The UK has been performing averagely in PISA, but it is certainly notable that most of the top spots in the PISA tables are taken by East Asian systems. This is due to a multitude of differences, including teacher training, teaching style, tutoring, and curriculum. But there is certainly some truth in the idea that there are also cultural differences that affect children's motivation, as I've alluded to earlier.

The expectations of children are different. In Shanghai, if you don't do your homework, or forget to bring it in, you have to stay after school to do it – sometimes several times over. I'm sure this is the case in some English schools too, but in my own experience, a key difference is the extent to which parents support this intervention. Education is highly valued in East Asian countries, and is seen as the only way to a better life. Entry to the best jobs is based on attendance at the best universities, and entry into these are governed by entrance exams. If you combine the high-stakes nature of these tests with the Confucian belief that anyone can succeed if you put in enough effort, you get a highly pressured culture in which children spend a lot of their time studying. I'm not sure that we would want this culture in the UK, even if it did bring us higher PISA scores.

What we can – and in my opinion should – learn from the East Asians is their high expectations of all students, and the attitude that anyone can succeed with the right support and effort. Having students persist at problems, and practise things they fail at because they believe that they can improve, is hugely powerful. In one particularly memorable 'almost-study' by Stevenson and Stigler in the 1990s, they had planned to give

American and Japanese students a maths problem that was impossible to solve, and to record how long the students tried for. They report that they weren't able to complete their study, because in the initial trials the Japanese teachers had found that their students wouldn't give up, and said that it wasn't fair to let them keep trying. In a more recent study by Heine *et al* Japanese and Canadian students were made to feel that they were either good or bad at a particular task, and then given the option of spending more time on it. Canadian students spent less time on it if they thought they'd done badly – the Japanese spent more. They were motivated by failure. It is impossible to say for sure whether these attitudes lead to better learning and higher scores in PISA, but it seems pretty likely to me.

Nick: There's some evidence about more explicit forms of instruction, suggesting the techniques are potentially more used in some East Asian countries that perform well. However, another thing is we know there is a great amount of tutoring, a very strong culture of tutoring, in many of the same countries. So beyond cultural differences it's a difficult question to unpick exactly what it is that causes the UK to underperform in PISA compared to East Asian countries. What's interesting is that East Asian second-generation immigrants living in Australia, there are research studies that suggest that they still perform extremely well in comparison – which does suggest that something potentially stemming from family culture has a strong influence on a child's commitment and the effort they put into their learning.

In terms of motivation, one of the issues is that when we've done something and repeatedly experienced failure at it, it's quite adaptive to withdraw some effort from it. There's a reason I'm not sporty, and the reverse process likely underpins why I worked hard in mathematics: I achieved some sort of measure of success with it, which encouraged the long-term motivation to pursue that as a subject. With football, at the end of the year, I still wasn't very good at it and that experience probably led me to withdraw effort from that particular subject.

So again, it's answering your question in a roundabout way I guess, we should really focus on what it is around the kind of experiences for students have that builds that sense of success that leads to greater long-term motivation towards that subject. We shouldn't get confused between that instant engagement or gratification and long-term motivation, a deep interest in a particular subject that the student wants to pursue for many years after leaving school.

How do you build resilience in pupils without knocking confidence?

Nick: Resilience is one of those tricky concepts. Someone I interviewed had a great quote on this: to paraphrase, 'My concern with it in education is it comes up in every conversation. I would love to ask 30 people to write down one paragraph on 'what is resilience?'; and I'll get 30 different answers.' I think part of the problem with a concept like resilience is that it can mean all things to all people. If we were trying to bring it down to something very simple, we might use the concept of self-efficacy, which I was talking about before. It's that sense of confidence within a particular domain, so that even if there are obstacles, you're still confident you're going to do well and overcome any problems that you encounter.

How do we build that up that sense? Well, to a certain extent it is about having the effective strategies, and experience of using them when challenged, that builds a sense that we're able to do those things again when we need to. Facing adversity without those strategies for dealing with it or never experiencing any kind of adversity probably both undermine our ability to build resilience against similar future challenges. If we want children to be successful, despite the obstacles and barriers that they will inevitably face in life, then actually the safe environment of school and the kinds of mild adversity that schools put in their way are probably ideal. Whether that's a big sporting event or a maths challenge or an end-of-year exam, all of these things are adversities to students; but having the experience of being successful despite those adversities is likely a key way we build a sense of self-efficacy for future occasions. So, what people describe as resilience, the ability to press on when faced with adversity or perhaps bounce back from disappointment, relies very much on our experience of being able to successfully deal with similarly difficult occasions before. So, how do we build resilience? I think within the safe and caring environment of a school, it is to provide students with low-stakes (to us, it will feel high-stakes to them) examples of adversity for them to test themselves against and the knowledge and strategies required to succeed at them.

How do you encourage independent learning in a society that promotes dependence and instant reward?

Nick: I would like to take issue with the latter half of that proposition. I don't know that we live in a society that promotes dependence and instant rewards. Our ability to be independent individuals is probably greater now than it has been in any other period in history, if you think of peasants working in 12th-century villages or factory workers during the industrial revolution. In terms of instant rewards, there's a difference perhaps between the momentary gratification provided by sex, drugs and rock 'n' roll – or the films and computer games I grew up with – and that longer term reward from having a kind of gratifying career or family life; and some of those things probably haven't changed.

In terms of encouraging independence, I think one of the things I'd refer back to is the Dunlosky study looking at the kinds of ways that students approach studying. When they're trying to be independent, that study identified that some of the really common things that students do, like rereading, highlighting, and underlining, are essentially pretty ineffective ways of building up the knowledge required for exams and skills they might need. So I think that if we want children to become independent in their learning we need to teach them the kinds of things that are more effective in that regard. My hope would be that their experience of being able to use these techniques, and seeing the effectiveness of it, would encourage them to do it in the future. So I think one way in answering that question, would be again, some of the research looking at, for instance, the benefits of spaced retrieval practice or the kinds of support required for techniques like summarising to be useful, in order for those to be effective as opposed to some of the things students think they do. A classic example of this would be flash cards: you get students conscientiously rushing off to make them, but perhaps the content is wrong or they just sit there staring at them; rather than getting guidance on what content needs to be on them, they simply turn them over and try to recall what was on the cards. So an example from psychology teaching would be Milgram's study of obedience, to try to recall from a limited cue (the sort of stem in an exam question perhaps) the details of the method, results and conclusion. I think when students use some of these techniques and see how effective they can be, it encourages them to be more independent.

6 MEMORY AND RECALL

CHAPTER   PAUL A KIRSCHNER & YANA WEINSTEIN

> WHAT WE WANT STUDENTS TO LEARN AND WHAT THEY ACTUALLY LEARN ARE OFTEN TWO DIFFERENT THINGS.

> AN IMPORTANT THING FOR TEACHERS TO KNOW IS THAT REDUCING THAT STRAIN OR 'COGNITIVE LOAD' TO AN OPTIMUM STATE INVOLVES PLANNING EFFECTIVE LEARNING OPPORTUNITIES WHICH HARNESS BOTH THE LARGE CAPACITY OF LONG-TERM MEMORY AND WHICH OFFSET THE SMALLER BANDWIDTH OF WORKING MEMORY.

> AS TEACHERS WE OFTEN FORGET THAT FOR MANY STUDENTS, LEARNING A NEW TOPIC IS A LOT LIKE LEARNING TO DRIVE AND TOO OFTEN WE CAN SEND THEM ONTO A BUSY INTERSECTION WITHOUT THE REQUISITE SKILLS OR KNOWLEDGE TO NAVIGATE THEIR WAY EFFECTIVELY.

> TEACHERS SHOULD PLAN LESSONS THAT MINIMISE THE STRAIN ON WORKING MEMORY AND ALLOW OPPORTUNITIES FOR STUDENTS TO BUILD UP THE KINDS OF MENTAL MODELS THAT WILL ALLOW THEM TO FLOURISH WHEN FACED WITH CHALLENGE.

> LONG-TERM MEMORY WOULD SEEM TO HAVE A HUGE CAPACITY TO STORE INFORMATION WHEREAS WORKING MEMORY HAS A FAIRLY LIMITED CAPACITY.

'Memory believes before knowing remembers'
William Faulkner, Light in August

'Understanding is remembering in disguise'
Dan Willingham

Why is it that we can remember random things from our childhood or the names of obscure Russian football players but yet we can't remember where we left our keys five minutes ago? We've all had that experience where we have meticulously planned a series of lessons, delivered them well and get the sense that students have learned the material, but then discover two weeks later that they have forgotten most of what we taught them. What we want students to learn and what they actually learn are often two different things.

In recent years, findings from cognitive psychology have revealed that the mechanics of memory have a huge impact on learning. We know that the academic success of students largely depends not just on their ability to store salient information, but more importantly on their ability to recall and use that information in a range of disparate contexts in order to create new connections and meaning. Broadly speaking, we can think of two elements of memory; working memory and long-term memory. Long-term memory would seem to have a huge capacity to store information whereas working memory has a fairly limited capacity. In the 1950s, it was thought that the average working memory can store between five and seven items of information but more recent research[27] places that number as nearer to four. Dan Willingham outlined what he described as 'just about the simplest model of the mind possible' overleaf:

---

27. Cowan, N. (2010) 'The Magical Mystery Four: How is Working Memory Capacity Limited, and Why?' www.ncbi.nlm.nih.gov/pmc/articles/PMC2864034

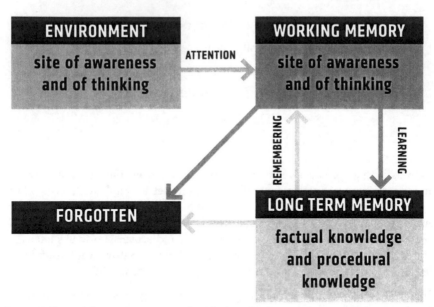

Essentially, working memory is the 'desktop' where information is processed either from the environment or from long-term memory and if too much strain is placed on working memory then students can get confused, frustrated and often give up. An important thing for teachers to know is that reducing that strain or 'cognitive load' to an optimum state involves planning effective learning opportunities which harness both the large capacity of long-term memory and which offset the smaller bandwidth of working memory. One of the ways to do that is by introducing information in particular ways. Dual-coding theory, for example, claims that processing information both visually and verbally has a more powerful effect in storing that information. Labelling diagrams of the limbic system appropriately helps biology students encode that new information more effectively than if they were simply told what it is.

John Sweller's Cognitive load theory (CLT) has generated a large amount of interest recently; in fact, Dylan Wiliam claims it's the '**single most important thing**' for teachers to know. Essentially it states that the amount of mental effort it takes to complete a task is finite and that teachers should plan lessons that do not overload students' working memories. A good way of doing this is to model problem-solving through worked examples before allowing students to attempt the same task.

Keeping cognitive load within an optimum state is key for effective learning

The limitations of working memory can be illustrated through the following example. If you were asked to look at the following sequence of letters for 30 seconds and tested on your ability to recall them in sequence, how well do you think you would do?

XKD JSD PRL MXG LWK

Most people would struggle to get past seven or eight but suppose you were asked to remember the same number of letters, grouped in a similar order but they looked like this:

BBC FBI ATM TLC CIA

You would do far better on the second sequence because instead of having to remember 15 items you would be able to group or 'chunk' those 15 items into five items which is well within most people's capabilities. You can do this because the three letters of 'BBC' are already encoded in your long-term memory and so count as one item, not three. Another good example is learning to drive a car in which your working memory is asked to remember a large amount of new information at once and so becomes easily overloaded. Through carefully guided instruction from an experienced expert, you gradually encode in your long-term memory the ability to change gears, control the clutch and to look before signalling. After a while these smaller skills become automatic and your working memory is then freed up to concentrate on more demanding tasks like how to navigate roundabouts or enter/exit motorways. As teachers, we often forget that for many students, learning a new topic is a lot like learning to drive and too often we can send them onto a busy intersection without the requisite skills or knowledge to navigate their way effectively.

Anders Ericsson uses the term 'mental representation' to refer to a 'mental structure that corresponds to an object, an idea, a collection of information, or anything else, concrete or abstract, that the brain is thinking about'.[28] These mental representations, or schema, are important for two reasons: firstly, they allow us to draw up a robust understanding of a particular problem or situation fairly rapidly; and secondly, they free up our working memory to be able to work on ways of solving that problem without falling at the first hurdle. If you had to go shopping in your local town centre, you would know where to go, how much money you'd need, how to read the labels of different items you require and so on. However, if you had to complete the same task in a village in Greece you would struggle on all of those fronts because you lack the requisite mental model needed to complete the task. You would have to look up online which stores sell what you need, or ask where to go, figure out if the labels mean what you think they mean, where to queue and how to pay – all of which would overload your working memory.

Unfortunately, the way to create these robust mental representations depends greatly on the level of complexity of the task and seems to require repeated exposure to the material. As we'll see in chapter 9, for many students a limited vocabulary means that when reading a complex passage, their working memory is very quickly at full capacity from simply having to remember or even guess what certain words mean, so being able to engage with the deeper thematic concerns of that passage will prove a lot more difficult than the student who can automatically read that same passage. Teachers should plan lessons that minimise the strain on working memory and allow opportunities for students to build up the kinds of mental models that will allow them to flourish when faced with challenge.

Yana Weinstein is an Assistant Professor at University of Massachusetts, Lowell. She received her PhD in Psychology from University College London and had four years of postdoctoral training at Washington University in St Louis and is co-founder of the Learning Scientists blog which focuses on learning science and its application to instruction. Paul A Kirschner is Professor at the Open University of the Netherlands, Visiting Professor of Education with a special emphasis on Learning and Interaction in Teacher Education at the University of Oulu, Finland, and Doctor Honoris Causa (honorary professor) of that same university. He is an internationally recognised expert in the fields of educational psychology and instructional design and is the author of several hugely influential publications including *Ten Steps to Complex Learning: A Systematic Approach to Four-Component Instructional Design*.

---

28. Ericsson, A. and Pool, R. (2016) *Peak*, Eamon Dolan/Houghton Mifflin Harcourt, p.58

PK

WHEN YOU LEARN, YOU DON'T PRACTISE ONE SKILL UNTIL IT'S LEARNED AND THEN GO ON TO THE OTHER, BUT RATHER MIX THE PRACTICE BY SWITCHING FROM ONE THING TO ANOTHER.

PK

I DON'T HAVE MULTI-CORE PROCESSOR. IT'S JUST THAT SIMPLE.

YW

THE WORKING MEMORY CAPACITY OF YOUR STUDENTS WILL VARY, SO SOMETHING THAT MIGHT OVERLOAD ONE STUDENT WON'T NECESSARILY OVERLOAD ANOTHER.

MEMORY AND RECALL

CHAPTER 6   PAUL KIRSCHNER & YANA WEINSTEIN

PK

HOW MANY TEACHERS FOR EXAMPLE START A BIOLOGY LESSON WITH THREE MINUTES OF "WHAT DO WE REMEMBER ABOUT THE HEART?" BEFORE THEY START.

PK

IF YOU JUST PRESENT SOMETHING WITH PICTURES, STUDENTS MIGHT REMEMBER THE PICTURE BUT POSSIBLY NOT THE PRINCIPLE BEHIND IT. SO IT'S THE COMBINATION OF TWO MEMORY TRACES: AN ICONIC TRACE AND A SEMANTIC TRACE.

YW

BY FAR THE MOST IMPORTANT STRATEGIES ARE SPACED PRACTISE (SPACING OUT STUDYING THE SAME INFORMATION OVER TIME, I.E., NOT CRAMMING); AND RETRIEVAL PRACTISE (PRACTISING BRINGING INFORMATION TO MIND, RATHER THAN RE-READING INFORMATION OVER AND OVER AGAIN, OR DOING A SHALLOW TASK SUCH AS COPYING OUT NOTES).

Q **How should I plan a lesson to ensure I don't overload my students' working memory?**

Paul: The simplest answer is to create learning tasks that are of the proper level of complexity depending upon the student's prior knowledge and skills and then make use of techniques that require as little extraneous mental effort or cognitive load as you possibly can. For example, there are techniques or principles which help manage cognitive ability in such a way that you minimise extraneous cognitive load such as worked examples where you show students how it's done before they try it. By choosing a task that's really complex (that is, many new information elements for the learner and lots of interactivity between the elements), you'll cause quite a lot of intrinsic load on the student. A very complex task in itself has a high level of cognitive load and the complexity of the task is highly related to the expertise level of the learner so basically, don't give things that are too complex for the learner and choose instructional techniques that eliminate as much extraneous cognitive load as possible.

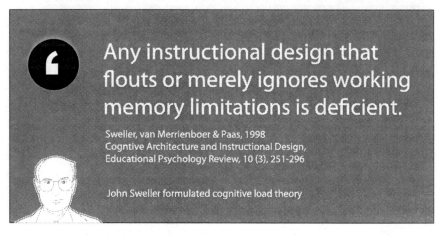

> Any instructional design that flouts or merely ignores working memory limitations is deficient.
>
> Sweller, van Merrienboer & Paas, 1998
> Cogntive Architecture and Instructional Design,
> Educational Psychology Review, 10 (3), 251-296
>
> John Sweller formulated cognitive load theory

So, if you're working on a book, don't put the diagram on one page and the explanation on the next page or the page after (it can best be nested in the diagram) or if you're presenting something for a class, don't introduce it and then explain it five minutes later. Both are examples of the split-attention effect with the former relating to spatial contiguity and the latter to temporal contiguity. Also, if you're giving a lesson, make use of things like goal-free tasks and worked out examples which induce little extraneous cognitive load.

And finally, take the level of the learner into account and don't choose a load-improving or load-inducing technique that doesn't match your learner. I'm not talking about learning styles, I'm talking about the expertise reversal effect: certain instructional techniques that you can and should use for experts will not work for novices, and certain things that work for novices won't work for experts or can even hinder their learning, so it's a combination. Choose the proper technique for the relevant expertise level of the learner.

 Yana: The working memory capacity of your students will vary, so something that might overload one student won't necessarily overload another. However, you can try to keep a few rules of thumb in mind that will help everyone:

- do not include unrelated information (*eg*, images that decorate without illustrating) on your teaching materials.

- similarly, it may not be a good idea to present redundant information, unless there is a particular need for it in your classroom (*eg*, students who are hard of hearing and thus need closed captioning on all videos shown in class).

- try to break instruction down into small, concrete steps, and build students up to tackling larger problems/tasks.

- provide lots of concrete examples, because working memory resources may be used up by students trying to figure out what you are referring to when you describe abstract concepts.

FEATURE	DESCRIPTION	WHAT IT MEANS
ACTIVE PROCESSOR	Working memory is the conscious part of the brain that thinks, solves problems, and learns.	Teachers must engage working memory for learning to occur.
CAPACITY LIMITS	Working memory can only hold a few items at one time. When working memory fills, its processing capacities slow down.	Teachers must avoid overloading working memory for learning to occur.
DUAL CHANNEL	Working memory has a separate area for storing visual and auditory information.	Teachers can extend working memory capacity by using the visual and auditory components.

Colvin Clark, R and Lyons, C (2004) Graphics for Learning, Pfeiffer

 How should I plan a scheme of work to make use of the spacing effect?

 Paul: There is no ideal length; how you use it depends on what you're doing, whom you're doing it for and what you're attempting to achieve. Set it up in such a way that you encourage studying in smaller amounts closer to the moment that they studied it and discourage the mass practice at the end. Use multiple testing moments of smaller pieces of learning as suggested by research on the testing-effect – also known as retrieval practice – instead of one large exam because if all you do is the one exam at the end of six weeks, then the only reason the students will practise is for the exam.

In Dutch, we use the term 'the calculating student' and I don't mean that in a pejorative way. What it means is that the student will just do that which he or she *needs* to do. So you have to create the necessity of spaced practice for them by setting up your instruction and redesigning your curriculum in a way that the practice is phased, and don't leave it up to the students to organise their practice.

 Yana: There are difficult ways that require a lot of planning, but there are also small adjustments that you can make to your teaching in order to incorporate spacing. The difficult ways involve creating a spiral curriculum, where topics are revisited multiple times throughout the year; or even a strand curriculum, where old topics are constantly interwoven into new topics. However, the effectiveness of these planning overhauls has not been rigorously tested. Instead, teachers could introduce spacing by providing students with opportunities to practise skills and recall of information from previous topics by giving lagged homework – homework set on material from previous lessons, rather than the current lesson.

Q **What are the most important study skills that students need to know?**

 Paul: What I often tell teachers is to take a look at what Barak Rosenshine wrote in his ten principles of instruction such as starting the lesson or revision session with a review of previous learning. Of course we know that prior knowledge is necessary, or it's important, but how many teachers for example start a biology lesson with three minutes of 'What do we remember about the heart?' before they start. Those are very simple, graspable techniques that Barak Rosenshine gives and every teacher should be acquainted with those ten principles. They've helped me quite a lot.

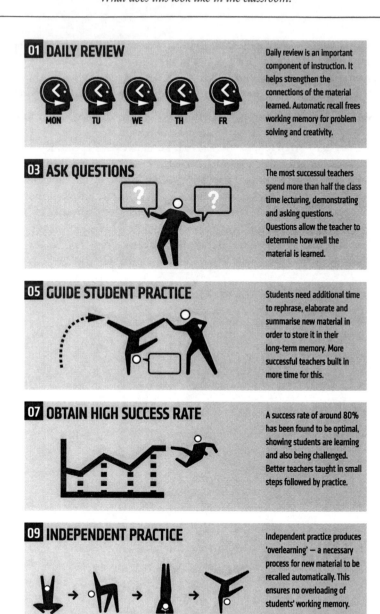

01 DAILY REVIEW

MON TU WE TH FR

Daily review is an important component of instruction. It helps strengthen the connections of the material learned. Automatic recall frees working memory for problem solving and creativity.

03 ASK QUESTIONS

The most successul teachers spend more than half the class time lecturing, demonstrating and asking questions. Questions allow the teacher to determine how well the material is learned.

05 GUIDE STUDENT PRACTICE

Students need additional time to rephrase, elaborate and summarise new material in order to store it in their long-term memory. More successful teachers built in more time for this.

07 OBTAIN HIGH SUCCESS RATE

A success rate of around 80% has been found to be optimal, showing students are learning and also being challenged. Better teachers taught in small steps followed by practice.

09 INDEPENDENT PRACTICE

Independent practice produces 'overlearning' — a necessary process for new material to be recalled automatically. This ensures no overloading of students' working memory.

Rosenshine, B., 'Principles of Instruction', *American Educator*, Spring 2012 (illustrations by Oliver Caviglioli)

02 NEW MATERIALS IN SMALL STEPS

Our working memory is small, only handling a few bits of information at once. Avoid its overload — present new material in small steps and proceed only when first steps are mastered.

04 PROVIDE MODELS

Students need cognitive support to help them learn how to solve problems. Modelling, worked examples and teacher thinking out loud help clarify the specific steps involved.

06 CHECK STUDENT UNDERSTANDING

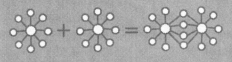

Less successful teachers merely ask "Are there any questions?" No questions are taken to mean no problems. False. By contrast, more successful teachers check on all students.

08 SCAFFOLDS FOR DIFFICULT TASKS

Scaffolds are temporary supports to assist learning. They can include modelling, teacher thinking aloud, cue cards and checklists. Scaffolds are part of cognitive apprenticeship.

10 WEEKLY & MONTHLY REVIEW

WEEK 1 WEEK 2 WEEK 3 WEEK 4 WEEK 5 WEEK 6 WEEK 7 WEEK 8

The effort involved in recalling recently-learned material embeds it in long-term memory. And the more this happens, the easier it is to connect new material to such prior knowledge.

Yana: We talk about six strategies on our website (learningscientists.org): spaced practice, retrieval practice, interleaving, elaboration, concrete examples, and dual coding. However, they are not all equal in terms of impact and evidence base. By far the most important strategies are spaced practice (spacing out studying the same information over time, *ie*, not cramming); and retrieval practice (practising bringing information to mind, rather than rereading information over and over again, or doing a shallow task such as copying out notes). Those are the two most important study skills that students need to know. After they have mastered those skills, they can integrate the others – for example, the principle of dual coding states that combining visual information and words is more helpful to memory than only using one or the other. To take advantage of this principle, students can draw as well as writing what they know from memory (retrieval practice).

Content by Yana Weinstein (University of Massachusetts Lowell) & Megan Smith (Rhode Island College) | Illustrations by Oliver Caviglioli (teachinghow2s.com/cogsci)
Funding provided by the APS Fund for Teaching and Public Understanding of Psychological Science

Most of my students leave exam revision to the last week. How can I encourage them to avoid this?

 Paul: One of the ways is not to make a final exam that important. You might want to use partial exams as being more important. As teachers we have this idea that we should, for example, have three partial exams worth 10% and the final exam is worth 70%. Why? If the final exam is nothing more than the summation of all of the previous, and this not more important than the three, then why not have all of the separate exams have the same amount of weight as the final exam? Also, why is the final exam often little more than a regurgitation of the knowledge needed in the three previous exams they have already done with a little more to cover the period between the third exam and the final? If you make your final examination worth 70% and the others ones worth 5 or 10% towards the final grade, then you're only encouraging pupils to do mass practice the night before the big exam, and they will do just that.

The second thing is to train students that it's better to space their study/reviewing rather than work for hours the night before the exam, and that's something that's more about changing their mindset, and I don't mean in the Carol Dweckian idea of mindset, but changing their way of thinking about how they have to study because they've never learned to study in that way. That's one of the problems with education: the further you get in education, the more stayed you become in your habits. Take rereading or highlighting. Most research shows that both are not very effective, but teachers and parents have brought these approaches over to their pupils/children and they faithfully use them while resisting approaches that have been proven to work.

By the way, the second important thing to do is to realise that a curriculum is not just a mass of separate courses. It's important for teachers to also coordinate their actions with each other so that they don't programme the curriculum so that interference results. For example, if I want my students to start studying Friday, Monday and Wednesday for the test on Friday, but two of my colleagues give a test on Wednesday or on Thursday, then there's a snowball's chance in hell that they're going to study for my examination in a spaced way if there are two other examinations that are going to be on those days. It requires quite a lot of coordination across the teachers in the school – a school-wide curriculum plan – because otherwise they're crossing each other's paths. We say in Dutch that they get into each other's travel routes or shipping lanes. (The Dutch have a tendency to have sayings that are nautical in nature.) But basically what it means is they get in each other's way.

Yana: This is really hard – not just for students, but also for people in general (including adults!). It is hard to schedule out studying when a test is not imminent, and then stick to that schedule. Teachers can encourage this in two ways. First, they can integrate spacing into their own teaching practice by providing opportunities in the classroom or in homework for students to revisit previous material. Second, particularly with older students, teachers can help their students plan and actualise spaced studying. This can be achieved by having students keep a log of what they do every hour of every day for a couple of weeks. Then, students review that log with their teachers, and find times that might work for spaced studying. For the next week or so, students try to stick to that plan, and log when they do actually sit down to study, and what they manage to achieve during that time. Afterwards – and this step is very important – teachers sit down with students and discuss what worked, what didn't, and what aspect of their plan they need to tweak in order to make it more realistic. Perhaps they need to change the time of day they are planning on studying, or set more realistic goals. Building in a reward structure could help, too.

Q **Is there any evidence to suggest working on whiteboards/using something visual improves memory?**

Paul: The research on dual coding is useful here. I wrote a blog called 'Double Barrelled Learning'[29] in which I presented evidence which showed that it works but only if you do it right. It's the creating of strong memory traces that improves the memory. If you just present something with pictures, students might remember the picture but possibly not the principle behind it. So it's the combination of two memory traces: an iconic trace and a semantic trace.

THE AMOUNT OF INFORMATION THAT CAN BE PROCESSED USING BOTH AUDITORY AND VISUAL CHANNELS SHOULD EXCEED THE PROCESSING CAPACITY OF A SINGLE CHANNEL.

THE MODALITY EFFECT IS USUALLY STRONGER FOR MEASURES OF TRANSFER RATHER THAN RETENTION.

AUDITORY CHANNEL → ← VISUAL CHANNEL

---

29. https://3starlearningexperiences.wordpress.com/2017/05/30/double-barrelled-learning-for-young-old

The semantic trace might be oral but it also might be written, and it's important that those things don't negatively interact with each other, which is often the case with the redundancy effect in which you read your slide, which increases cognitive load because you're asking the same working memory to semantically decode two different signals at the same time, not to mention that the learner may read in a different tempo than your recitation, thus causing interference!

Allen Paivio said in his dual coding theory that you have different memory stores. The theory assumes that we have two specific yet connected cognitive subsystems. One subsystem is specialised in representing and processing nonverbal objects/events (*ie* imagery), and the other subsystem is specialised in dealing with language and that these are additive. So what you're doing is you're increasing the size of your working memory in which you make connections between the image and its meaning. Again, research on that shows that in certain situations it works and in certain situations it doesn't. For example, having a triangle and angles and lengths on one page and then the discussion of it on the next page leads to a problem with spatial split-attention (that is, a lack of spatial contiguity) because you have to look back and forth from one page to the other and that increases the mental effort that you have to expend, which in turn makes it harder to learn. Eventually you'll learn it, but it just makes it harder if you don't have both things on one page or, even better, embedded in one and the same image.

 Yana: This relates back to the 'dual coding' principle. In general, if students are exposed to information in both visual (pictures) and verbal (words) format, they stand a higher chance of remembering it later. It's not exactly about 'improving memory', but it can help provide students with a clue to help them reconstruct the memory later. As mentioned above, the visual information should be relevant to what's being taught, otherwise it will only serve as a distraction.

There is also some research on whether moving (animated) images, such as videos, are better or worse than static images (*ie* pictures). The results there are mixed: generally, static images are better than complex videos, but there is some evidence that 'evolving' images (*ie* those that would be created if you drew on a whiteboard) can be good, too. My suggestion would be not to overthink it – include relevant images, draw on the whiteboard if you find it effortless and relevant (I find that I can sketch things spontaneously after teaching them many times over the course of a few years), and remember to keep it relevant.

 How can I help students to commit things to long-term memory?

 Paul: One way is to make use of dual-coding and retrieval practice; that is strengthening the storage as we just discussed and then encouraging certain types of repetitive retrieval. What you want to do is two things. First, you want to strengthen the storage. You can do that with images and words to strengthen the storage in long-term memory. Second, you want to do things which strengthen the memory traces by having students retrieve it more often and in different ways because the more memory traces and the more often the memory traces are used, the more strength they develop. Examples of retrieval techniques are flashcards, low-stakes quizzes, free recall exercises such as writing synopses or summaries, end-of-chapter questions, *etc*. Your brain is not like a muscle, but in this case, doing something more often, and in multiple ways helps.

A confounding factor is that if you choose to do something, it must be something that the students can do. One method of retrieval practice is having pupils make a synopsis or summary of something. What I found, however, is that most pupils haven't properly learned to write a synopsis or a summary. Thus, while retrieving something from what you've read to summarise it can be a very strong tool, if you haven't learned to use that tool – that is, you haven't learned how to summarise something properly – it doesn't have the effect that it should. You see that in quite a lot of research in which people make use of summaries as a retrieval tool and conclude that it doesn't work. But I've looked at research and done research in which we look at the summaries of the students, and you see that they can't summarise. So if they can't summarise, then writing a summary won't help.

So, if you use a technique with students to strengthen the trace of something in their long-term memory, you have to make sure that they can properly make use of that tool and thus you must teach them to do it if necessary. Otherwise, it's of no value and it's just a waste of their time that they could have possibly spent on studying the materials in another way, which may have led to a stronger memory trace.

Yana: I think the question isn't so much about 'long-term memory', but about deeper encoding. Technically, if students haven't committed something to long-term memory, they've literally forgotten it less than a minute later than it was presented. If this is what the question is asking, then I would recommend leveraging test expectancy effects. That is, when students expect to be tested at any time during a class, they are likely to make more effort to encode the information. If the question is more about long-term learning/deep encoding, then I would recommend strategies that make students think about the meaning and real-life applications of the material they are studying as much as possible.

I find that pupils often forget what they've learned in the previous lesson. How can I ensure they remember things from one lesson to the next?

Paul: Start each lesson like Barak Rosenshine recommends, reviewing what they did the day before. It's that simple. Review it. Before you start on something new, review the old. It doesn't mean you have to spend another 45-minute session on it. You can do it in three to five minutes, but then in the end it's more effective and efficient than having them either not learn things or forget them. So review it. Bring it back into their memory. And the next day bring it back. It becomes like a rolling snowball, constantly growing. Come in and ask them, 'Now, remember yesterday we were talking about the difference between Macbeth's soliloquy and Lady Macbeth's soliloquy and why one was … Can you think of other differences?' Or you can give a very short quiz about the two soliloquies. And how long does that take? One minute, two minutes of the lesson? But how many teachers start each lesson with a review of what was done the day before or a short quiz? And if you do that, then they can't forget it because it's there again. It's prior knowledge. You've now both refreshed their prior knowledge so that they can learn more and, via retrieval practice, strengthened the memory trace.

It's simple. It's really not rocket science as far as I'm concerned. Unless you're teaching rocket science.

Yana: This one's easy! Give them a starter quiz. Once they get used to the routine of needing to remember information from one class at the beginning of the next, they will adapt by trying to keep the information fresh in between classes. In addition, the retrieval practice in and of itself will cause additional learning.

I understand the concept of interleaving, but can this work intra-lesson? Is there a limit to how mixed up things can be in order to improve learning?

Paul: Yes there is a limit, of course. Things have to be related to each other; otherwise, we get into the problem of the limitations of working memory. I call it variability of practice in my book *Ten Steps to Complex Learning* which I co-wrote with Jeroen van Merriënboer. The idea with interleaving with variability of practice is that when you learn, you don't practise one skill until it's learned and then go on to the other, but rather mix the practice by switching from one thing to another. It takes a little bit longer to learn each of the individual skills, but the transferability is incredibly increased. It's called the *transfer paradox*. Getting back to your question on limits, we have to keep the activities within the limits of what the working memory can handle. If the things they have to interleave haven't been encapsulated in long-term memory or haven't been chunked in groups rather than separate units, then you increase the load on the working memory to more than it can actually handle. This will have a serious impact on learning.

Yana: The concept of interleaving has actually only been studied on a fine grain – that is, interleaving practice of different types of problems/skills during a finite study session. Interleaving refers to the finding that if you're trying to learn how to do something like solving problems, it is better to switch between different problem types rather than doing lots of similar problems in a row. The idea of mixing this up between lessons is not actually interleaving – that's more related to spacing. However, there is a lot we don't know about interleaving – what types of things should be interleaved for maximum impact? How often should students switch between topics when interleaving? I'm currently writing a grant to address some of these questions in children aged 10 through 16 learning maths.

Q **What strategies do you recommend to improve recall of information that was learned at the start of a course?**

Paul: It's basic practice. It's repeating at the beginning of the day, of the week, of the month. Constantly ensure that the prior knowledge is activated, that things that are ostensibly within long-term memory are retrieved, making new use of the things to have it be stored in other ways. All of the things that you can do to strengthen the memory or retrieval trace is what you can do to, as you say it, improve retrieval of that information.

When I was 16 I was working at the postal service in the United States and I had to learn on the route that I was on which buildings that were in which zip codes/postal codes. I did that using flashcards. Constantly going, 'Yeah, okay, 10023, is there 30 West 60th Street?' and vice versa – first the code and then the address and then the other way around. What you're doing looks like simple repetition, but what you're actually doing is making use of the testing effect. You're constantly retrieving what you have learned from memory, making the trace stronger, making it easier to recall.

The more you require the students to retrieve what they've already learned and the more you make use of techniques that will strengthen the storage and retrieval, the better it will be recalled. Recall of information, testing effect, spacing practice – it's not very hard.

Yana: I would recommend including multiple opportunities to review/practise retrieval on information that was presented at the start of a course, because that information needs to be remembered for the longest. It's also important to identify the key knowledge one needs in order to succeed in the course, and give students frequent opportunities to practise recalling that information.

7

CLASSROOM TALK AND QUESTIONING

CHAPTER

DOUG LEMOV & MARTIN ROBINSON

> THERE IS A GENERAL CONSENSUS HOWEVER THAT A CENTRAL MECHANISM IN EFFECTIVE CLASSROOM TALK IS GOOD USE OF QUESTIONING.

> NUTHALL'S RESEARCH GLEANED TWO IMPORTANT CONCLUSIONS; LEARNING IS HIGHLY INDIVIDUAL AND INVOLVES A PROGRESSIVE CHANGE IN WHAT A STUDENT KNOWS OR CAN DO.

> BY MODELLING A REVERENCE AND PASSION FOR SUBJECT, INSISTING ON HIGH STANDARDS IN TERMS OF BEHAVIOUR AND INTELLECTUAL CURIOSITY, AND BY FOSTERING PRODUCTIVE RELATIONSHIPS 'AUTHENTIC' TEACHERS ARE ABLE TO MODEL THE KINDS OF CLASSROOM BEHAVIOURS THAT THEY WOULD HOPE THE STUDENTS WOULD BEGIN TO EXHIBIT THEMSELVES.

> THE KIND OF TALK THAT HAPPENS IN A CLASSROOM LARGELY DETERMINES THE KIND OF LEARNING THAT TAKES PLACE AND DEVELOPING AN ARMOURY OF TOOLS TO FACILITATE THAT TALK SHOULD BE AT THE TOP OF EVERY TEACHER'S LIST WHETHER THAT BE LEARNING HOW TO SCAFFOLD LEARNING WITH EFFECTIVE EXPLANATIONS AND WORKED EXAMPLES OR SETTING UP THE KINDS OF FRUITFUL CONVERSATIONS THAT LEAD TO GENUINE LEARNING.

'But what I mean is, lots of time you don't know what interests you most till you start talking about something that doesn't interest you most'

J D Salinger, The Catcher in the Rye

Of all the debates in education one of the most contentious is the amount of time teachers should spend talking versus the amount of time students should spend talking. Research in this field is notoriously difficult as it is very difficult to grasp the import of spoken word with all its complexities and nuances. But in the 1990s, some important work was done by Graham Nuthall, who was able to use a unique method of data collection involving recording individual students in an authentic classroom setting to shed light on what he describes in the title of his seminal book as *The Hidden Lives of Learners*.

For Nuthall, 'three worlds' exist in the classroom. Firstly, there is the public world that is largely managed by the teacher and features easily visible lesson activities and routines. Secondly, there is the 'semi-private world of ongoing peer relationships'[30] in which students foster and maintain social roles in the classroom. (Crucially, transgressing the rules of this world can have worse consequences than transgressing the teacher's world.) Lastly, there is the private world of the student's own mind where learning actually takes place and self-beliefs and attitudes play a pivotal role. Nuthall's research gleaned two important conclusions; learning is highly individual and involves a progressive change in what a student knows or can do. These key points and the contexts in which they occur are highly complex ecosystems in a constant state of flux which illustrate why research on what actually goes on in the classroom is so difficult.

The most recent large scale study on classroom talk carried out by the Cambridge Primary Review Trust and the University of York[31] and funded by the EEF found that 'dialogic teaching', where teachers were trained on strategies which enabled pupils to 'reason, discuss, argue and explain rather than merely respond, in order to develop higher order thinking and articulacy', found that on average, students gained an additional two months' learning compared to groups who did not receive the intervention. However, some researchers have claimed that one of the central mechanisms of facilitating dialogic teaching, group work, can have a negative impact on learning in primary classrooms:

---

30. Nuthall, G. (2007) *The Hidden Lives of Learners*, NZCER Press, p.84
31. https://educationendowmentfoundation.org.uk/our-work/projects/dialogic-teaching/

There is robust evidence that sitting in groups has detrimental effects on attention. For individual task work, which features prominently in UK primary classrooms, other seating arrangements support much higher rates of attention and engagement, especially among those who find it difficult to concentrate when sitting in groups.[32] (Hastings, N. & Chantrey Wood, K., 2002)

There is a general consensus, however, that a central mechanism in effective classroom talk is good use of questioning. Broadly we can think of two types of questioning: closed questions, where teachers ask a question with a relatively straightforward answer such as, 'In the novel, did George shoot Lennie?'; and open questions which typically elicit longer responses and where students need to reflect and use more complex reasoning such as, 'Was George justified in shooting Lennie?' Barak Rosenshine claims in his 'Principles of Instruction' that good teachers should ask a large number of questions and claims that this will 'help students practice new information and connect new material to their prior learning'.[33] Although there is an implied hierarchy with closed and open questioning, both play an important role in the overall learning process as Andy Tharby and Shaun Allinson note:

> Before we move students on to open questions, we need to know if they have got the necessary surface knowledge. This is when closed questions are so important – for checking to see if they know their stuff. If they do not, there is no point in moving on to deeper concepts. (Allison S. and Tharby A, *Making Every Lesson Count*, p.201)

However, as several questions from our teachers pointed out, how do you deal with the student who rarely answers questions in class? And conversely, how do you deal with the student who wants to answer *every* question? Several techniques adapted from AFL principles include a 'hands down' policy where all students are expected to have an answer ready to any questions they might answer in the classroom which addresses the issue of the same pupils always putting their hands up. Doug Lemov refers to a variant on this process as 'cold calling' which he sees as a positive form of accountability and argues that 'students should always be ready to share their thoughts and participate' and that 'to be in class is to be a part of the conversation'.[34]

Despite the fact that a range of strategies can prove effective in general terms, it's clear that effective classroom talk is highly contingent on a range of factors

---

32. www.leeds.ac.uk/educol/documents/00002181.htm
33. www.aft.org/sites/default/files/periodicals/Rosenshine.pdf
34. http://teachlikeachampion.com/blog/cold-call-inclusive

that have to do with a positive class atmosphere and strong relationships between all participants. Robin Alexander distinguishes five central elements of effective classroom talk as being 'collective, reciprocal, supportive, cumulative and purposeful'[35], and fostering that climate of supportive and purposeful talk is at the heart of good teaching. More recent research claims that much of this has to do with what they describe as teacher 'authenticity':

> Teachers are perceived as authentic when they know what they are talking about and can translate subject matter to the students' knowledge level (expertise). Second, authentic teachers are passionate about what they teach (passion). Third, authentic teachers give students the feeling that each student and each class is different (uniqueness). Finally, authentic teachers aren't friends with their students but have an interest in them (distance). By describing these student perceptions, this study helps us to understand and build better relations between students and teachers.[36] (De Bruyckere & Kirschner, 2016, p.3)

By modelling a reverence and passion for subject, insisting on high standards in terms of behaviour and intellectual curiosity, and by fostering productive relationships, 'authentic' teachers are able to model the kinds of classroom behaviours that they would hope the students would begin to exhibit themselves. The kind of talk that happens in a classroom largely determines the kind of learning that takes place and developing an armoury of tools to facilitate that talk should be at the top of every teacher's list whether that be learning how to scaffold learning with effective explanations and worked examples or setting up the kinds of fruitful conversations that lead to genuine learning.

Doug Lemov is the author of the international bestseller *Teach Like a Champion*, and *Teach Like a Champion 2.0*. He is the co-author with TLAC team colleagues of *Practice Perfect, Reading Reconsidered: A Practical Guide to Rigorous Literacy Instruction*, and *Teach Like a Champion Field Guide 2.0*. and is a managing director of Uncommon Schools. Martin Robinson spent 20 years as a teacher in London state schools, as an Assistant Headteacher, an Advanced Skills Teacher, a Head of Faculty, a Head of Department, and a teacher of Drama and English. His bestselling book, *Trivium 21c: Preparing Young People for the Future with Lessons from the Past*, published in 2013 to critical acclaim, draws lessons from the ancient arts of the trivium to examine how both progressive & traditional pedagogies can be relevant to contemporary schooling.

---

35. Alexander, R. (2004) 'Towards Dialogic Teaching', *Rethinking Classroom Talk*, p.8 (4th Ed, March 2008)
36. www.tandfonline.com/doi/pdf/10.1080/2331186X.2016.1247609

CLASSROOM TALK AND QUESTIONING

DL

I THINK WE ALL NEED TO LISTEN BETTER AND ANY GOOD DISCUSSION IS DRIVEN AT LEAST AS MUCH BY HOW MUCH PEOPLE ARE LISTENING AS HOW WELL THEY'RE TALKING.

DL

WE SHOULD NOT TAKE A HAND WITHIN THE FIRST TWO SECONDS, BECAUSE HOW MANY REALLY CEREBRAL QUESTIONS CAN YOU ANSWER WITHIN TWO SECONDS?

DL

LOTS OF TIMES TEACHERS STRUGGLE WITH THE FOLLOW UP, BECAUSE THEY HAVEN'T THOUGHT THROUGH WHERE THEY WANT TO GO AND WHAT THE ULTIMATE GOAL IS IN THE ANSWER TO THE QUESTION.

DL

I WANT A BALANCE OF DIFFERENT TYPES OF QUESTIONS INCLUDING RETRIEVAL PRACTISE, WHICH IS FREQUENTLY OVERLOOKED BY TEACHERS.

MR

I WOULD OPEN UP WHAT I CALL THE DIALECTIC ARGUMENT, SO YOU'RE ALWAYS LOOKING FOR ARGUMENTS AND LOOKING FOR CONTROVERSIES AND LOOKING FOR CONFLICTS WHERE YOU CAN...YOU'RE ENGAGING, NOT IN MERE OPINION, BUT IN EDUCATED, THOUGHTFUL DISCOURSE.

MR

THEY'RE NOT RELUCTANT. THERE'S A REASON WHY THEY CAN'T TALK. YOU'VE GOT TO GIVE THEM A VOICE. YOU'VE GOT TO GIVE THEM THE SPACE TO HAVE A VOICE, BUT YOU'VE GOT TO GIVE THEM SOMETHING TO SAY AS WELL.

MR

YOU GET THE SAFE SPACE, WHICH SHOULD BE THAT ANYTHING CAN BE TALKED ABOUT IN THE CLASSROOM AND IT'S SAFE TO DO SO, RATHER THAN, IT SHOULD BE A SAFE SPACE NOT TO BE UPSET IN THE CLASSROOM.

Q Modern teaching practice typically emphasises student-active techniques rather than teacher-didactic methods. In the case of academically complex or technical material, I find the quality of student-led activities to be highly variable. Is group work really better than teacher instruction?

Doug: My sense is that didactic instruction is unfairly maligned and necessary to good instruction. Those maligning it often do so by describing it in caricature: 60 minutes of boring teacher lecture without pause and nary a question from any of the students. Why does it have to be 'boring'? Why can't there be questions of or by the teacher? These caricatures remind me that any technique in the classroom can be done terribly – group work as easily as lecture. A more important question to me is how to balance approaches. Teacher-driven dissemination of material is critical at times. It's one of the best ways to share knowledge, and not only is knowledge critical to learning in and of itself, but it's the driver of rigour during more interactive applied activities.

So if you want to have a discussion in groups or via teacher-guided questioning, the rigour of those activities will likely correlate to how much knowledge the participants have, and didactic instruction is one of the best ways to provide that. So I see more synergy than competition between didactic instruction and any form of application. The other thing that I would say is that I feel like group work is only one of several ways to do applied thinking in the classroom. Writing is one of my favourites and probably more rigorous in many cases. So I would be careful not to assume that group work is the only way to have an applied, active experience.

I also find the term 'group work' a little bit problematic. If there are 30 of us in the classroom, is that not a group if we're all doing an activity together? More important than whether I am sending people off into four different corners of the classroom is the question of whether I am asking students to process and apply their understanding in rigorous ways that yield insight and/or drive it into long-term memory. Group size is not an especially useful proxy for whether that is happening. So on net I'd say that 1) there's synergy between applied autonomous thinking and didactic teaching, and 2) I would not conflate group work with rigorous applied thinking tasks.

Martin: Obviously in certain subjects, group work is an intrinsic part of the subject and some subjects don't necessarily lend themselves to group work. I would say that group work can be part of most subjects, but what people usually do is introduce it far too early. Don't do it if kids don't really know what they're talking about and also don't do it when there isn't any need for group work whatsoever. If it's busy work in a classroom and filling in time, doing group work can be damaging to the learning process. Student-led 'group-work' activities which aren't specific, which aren't thought through, which aren't part of a longer-term need in a subject area, are a complete waste of time.

Q **My concern about group work is that some pupils dominate the discussion and others don't contribute at all. What can I do to address this?**

Doug: I think it's the right concern. So here are a couple of things that I've seen teachers do in the classroom to spread the thinking across all students in a more balanced and rigorous way.

One of the most useful things is to precede a discussion with writing. If I ask a series of questions beforehand, preliminary questions that cause students to reflect on the material, then a) everyone in the class answers the questions, b) what they bring to the group work will be version 2.0 of their thinking since they'll have already thought the question through, and c) they'll be more likely to want to participate. So the first thing I would do would be to precede my discussion with a written task that I require everyone to complete.

But here's one other idea for teachers who do 'Turn and Talks' and 'Pair Shares' and other ways to do conversations in small groups of two or three. We call it 'managed turns' and the idea is that just because you break up a conversation into small groups does not imply that everyone is participating equally. Perhaps there's one student who talks all the time, who probably needs to listen more, and one student who's very passive, who settles right into listening. Students sometimes fall into a role out of habit – but the habit does not always conform to their need. So let's say you asked, 'How is Jonas changing in this chapter? Discussion in with your partners please'; to 'manage turns' you might add '...wall side start, window side, be ready to respond'. With the understanding that this meant the student in every pair who was sitting nearer the wall would start the conversation. Next time, the student closer to the window would start. This makes sure that everyone participates, both as a talker and as a listener.

In larger groups I think that an idea called 'managing the meta' is useful. It's giving kids feedback on their conversation dynamics *as they're doing it*. So if I'm asking my pupils to discuss a topic, I might watch for a little while and say, 'Pause. Carl just made a really interesting point there about the reasons for American involvement in Vietnam, but no one responded to it. I've heard several new points but I think we need to make sure we respond to Carl's point before we go on.' In other words, it's teaching students how to develop and react to one another's ideas so that they can stay a little bit more on-point and productive.

I also could give feedback individually. So if I have a student who's dominating, I might say, 'Discussion is equal parts listening and talking. Make sure you're doing as much listening as talking. I'll evaluate you today on how well you take notes on what your peers say.'

Overall though, I think this is a very smart question, because most teachers equate talking with participation. It strikes me as a uniquely American mindset: I'm not doing anything unless I'm talking. Honestly, I think we all need to listen better and any good discussion is driven at least as much by how much people are listening as how well they're talking. Listening is as important a thing to build into the fabric of the classroom as talking.

One last technique I've learned from teachers to address this challenge is called 'Habits of Discussion', which is a way of teaching students sentence frames, to help them engage more productively in discussions. So the simplest form is to socialise students to begin a comment in a discussion with a phrase like, say, 'I agree with what Robin said, but I'd like to give another example'. Or, 'I saw it differently from Robin...'. By teaching students phrases to frame an answer like that, you enable them to be able to have a conversation that causes them to build listening skills. It becomes a habit, a way to build participation skills. Because if students aren't participating well, the most likely reason is no one has taught them how to.

Martin: You need to get to a point where everyone knows what they're talking about. You can set it up in certain ways. I'll give you an example of this from drama. I would start off with solo work, so every pupil is on their own, and then move to pair work, and I'm making sure that every child is working equally in the pair. If they don't, we go back to solo work for everyone. Even if one pupil breaks the rules, everyone goes back to the start. So solo work, pair work, and when the pair work's working, then I would move that into two pairs together. That was the process, solo/pair/small group – all involved; anyone not – back to solo, then pair, *etc* until they're all used to doing it. Fours would become eights, eights became sixteens; in the end I'd have a group of 32, so they'd be working together on one task, which was that they had to put together a play in an afternoon. They all had to work on it and that was a central aim of my teaching, I had to cajole them into collaborating constructively. It took about two years to get to that point. After this task they were ready to go off into their groups for their group project exams and they knew that the expectation was that every kid had to contribute.

I also did this thing when I started teaching a class, I'd put in some archetypes: 'You can either be a leader, a supporter, a sponge, or a disruptor. Those are the four character types. Disruptors are a complete waste of time. What they do is make sure everyone in their group is completely disrupted or other groups are. A sponge just sits there, does whatever they're told, and is a complete waste of space. A supporter always agrees enthusiastically with someone, but doesn't come up with any ideas. A leader really leads the group, but the trouble with leaders is that they can dominate the group and take it too far, have Napoleonic tendencies and want the play to be all about their own glory so the actual archetype you want to be is a leader-supporter, where you lead a group and you support whoever's leading at any particular time and you move around those things; like a flock of birds flying through the sky, a change of direction always entails a different leader.' That, along with the fact that I wasn't expecting linear development but expecting groups to come up with an interesting array of fragments, helped this process; the clear aim was not a finished product but interesting 'framed moments' that could be achieved and later built upon or discarded. We like hard work and messiness. That's what we want from everyone. My idea was to get kids to that point.

Q **If I want to improve my questioning style, what three bits of advice would give me?**

Doug: Sometimes the most mundane things are the most important. For example, it's important to be clear about the 'means of participation' you expect; when you ask a question, how do you want your students to answer? Is it okay if they call out the answers? Should they raise their hands? Are you cold calling? I often see a teacher ask a question and *not* be clear on what means of participation she desires from students. The result might be so three kids calling out the answers – the same three kids over and over. This skews participation obviously. And if she wanted to leave time so her students thought more deeply about the question, so she didn't get the first off-the-top-of-your-head answer, she can't do that if students are calling out. In other words, the teacher hasn't been clear that she wants students to raise their hands and the issues start from there. So establishing 'means of participation' is incredibly important if we want to signal that our questions deserve cerebral, thought-through responses – if only because it allows us to use Wait Time, the idea that we should not take a hand within the first two seconds. How many really cerebral questions can you expect after two seconds?

A second thing that's really important is to prepare key questions in advance. Script the language you'll use before the lesson and then answer the questions yourself. When you answer the question yourself beforehand, you recognise what an exemplar should look like and where you want to go with the follow up. Lots of times teachers struggle with the follow up, because they haven't thought through where they want to go and what the ultimate goal is in the answer to the question. You also often recognise what will be difficult for students about answering the question, which again helps you with follow up questions, or spotting flaws in the actual question. If you struggle to answer it yourself, of course, your kids will too.

Number three is to remember the importance of retrieval practice. Lots of times, we want to rush to ask what we think of as the deepest question possible. 'Is Dr King right that injustice against one is a threat to justice for all?' That's a great question to get to at the end of a discussion. But I can answer that question even if I haven't really understood Martin Luther King's letter from Birmingham jail. So it's useful to start with maybe some retrieval questions to reinforce knowledge in the text. 'Where was Dr. King when he was writing? Who was he writing to when he wrote the letter? What were the three major principles in his argument?' Just let's make sure we've got the facts and then maybe build that knowledge base into long-term memory a little bit before jumping to the broader questions.

I want a balance of different types of questions including retrieval practice, which is frequently overlooked by teachers.

Can I throw in one more? Teachers sometimes think about questions as tools for discovering an answer, and I think that applying an answer is just as rigorous if not more rigorous. The place that I see this most is with learning vocabulary. People will say, 'What do you think destitute means based on how it appears in this sentence? Can anyone guess what destitute means? Have you ever heard that word before?' If students don't know much about the word destitute, they're trying to guess what it means. Then you end up with a B minus definition, because it's derived from students who provide it based on lack of knowledge. Much better to say, 'Destitute means utterly without resources, especially those necessary to survival. Let's play with this word a little bit. What are some things you could be without and feel destitute? How is destitute different from just 'poor', say? Could a wealthy person be destitute? How?' The work here is in using the word as opposed to just trying to 'discover' (but really guess at) its meaning. The idea of applied practice is at least as rigorous but less often used.

Martin: Questioning, do not do 'pounce and bounce' or lollypop sticks or anything like that. You ask questions of kids who you think need to be questioned at any particular point. You're really testing out what they know and what they don't know, looking for depth of knowledge, and also it is about creating some sort of atmosphere in which kids can ask each other questions that are interesting. This is what you want, over years you want this class of novices to become a classroom full of curious, interested and interesting students. So you're modelling interesting questioning. Don't just ask one question and then 'bounce' to another pupil. Go for probing.

I used to do this thing where I'd say, 'One of you is in *the* chair.' They never knew who was in the chair; I pretended it was random, but of course it wasn't. The chair is the person who's going to get asked a huge number of questions in a particular moment when the *chair* was revealed. I'd be asking them about Chekhov, for instance, and I'd be talking about his style, the scenes of the play, characters, whatever it happened to be, and then keep asking this one person further and further. Then we'd involve others and they'd ask questions of each other. Again, solo to pair, to group, asking one, them questioning each other, then opening up to the whole class. It's how I would build a Socratic seminar atmosphere. It basically started with this idea of probing, seeing how deep you can go with the questioning. When they don't know, you just let up or look for another way of asking a question. Also, don't take it that just because they're giving the right answer, they actually know what they're talking about. Keep returning to the same points in different ways.

Q How can I get pupils who are used to talking informally (*eg* in slang) to be able to adopt the register required for success in exams and beyond?

Doug: I just want to say that I love this question. I love when teachers think this way. A useful move might be to write out and practise the prompts you would use to ask a student to upgrade their language. 'Good point. Can you put that in the language of the physicist?' Or, 'What you described is one of the key points of modern physics and now I want you to try to put it in scientific language.' If I've practised saying that beforehand, I'll be comfortable responding that way during a lesson. I think that's a beautiful moment when you say, 'Your idea's strong now. I want you to upgrade it with more precise language or more professional language.'

You can aid students by putting a list of technical tier three vocabulary on the wall in your classroom so kids can constantly see it, refer to it and use it. You could take an answer and look at the wall and say, 'See if you can upgrade that.' You're pushing pupils to constantly bring these words into their discourse. You might add a bit of challenge, 'Who can restate Carl's response and use the word, 'heliotropic'?' I think that is a game changer to do that.

Martin: Tell them it's not suitable. Perhaps mention the three different styles; the low style, the medium style, and the grand style. The grand style is for oratory to a large crowd, so think Martin Luther King. The low style is 'down with the kids', talking with your gang, so that's the sort of playground thing. In the classroom, I'd say the medium style, so not a low style, not the grand style, but in between the two. Tell them they've absolutely got to adopt a formal style in this classroom space. You don't need them to do grand style, 'I have a dream, sir'. You don't want to get to that point, though it does have its place, but you want them to talk in subject-specific language, in an appropriate register, and to talk in a way that can be understood. Clarity. And, so long as they're aware of the need for good rhetoric, classroom talk can help learning, thinking, arguing and writing. So don't let them get away with second-rate chatter.

Q How can I make sure that classroom discussion is rich rather than superficial?

Doug: Another great question. A simple thing: write the topic on the board. Kids lose sight of what the question was in the course of the discussion and it meanders. Putting the question on the board is an easy way to remind them, 'Here's what we're talking about.' I think there's a degree to which the 'outside the box' comment gets valorised. 'Oh, that's so outside the box.' But what we really want is a very insightful 'inside the box' comment first. So first I have to help them define with the box is. I think meta feedback, again, is really helpful here. 'He made an excellent point, let's respond before we move on to a new topic as we're straying from our objective.' Remind them there is a shared purpose in this conversation.

Then, maybe underneath your description of the topic, write key points on the board. We're all prisoners of working memory. We forget the things that people say in a conversation. They come up with great phrases and we want to be able to refer back to them and use them and make the conversation rich and deep, as opposed to constantly dancing onto a new topic. If I write down the key touch-points on the board, people can refer back to them. 'Oh, earlier, Robin said that this reminded him of what Napoleon said at Waterloo.' I want that point to endure, to be a central part of the conversation. What we would call this at our schools, 'charting it', helps students sustain ideas and keep them alive throughout discussion.

 Martin: A teacher takes a class from, in most cases, not knowing much or anything, to knowing a lot more. You have to ensure that the discussion is about building on knowledge and not a celebration and sharing of ignorance. You model the need for knowledge, and it's through your questioning of them, through a whole class discussion, where you can celebrate the power of knowing stuff. It's a discursive classroom. It's a conversational classroom, and it's done through whole-class teaching: the teacher holds the conversations, models, questioning, contemplating, and later you move into pairs discussing and feeding back. And you listen to pairs discussing – the whole class do too, you suddenly say everyone be quite apart from Jamal and Jane – you two continue your conversation, and you interject when things go awry or show how enthused you are, intellectually, when things are going great. You need to be aware that you are teaching the great art of conversation and argument within your discipline.

You make sure that it moves on with knowledge and discussion, knowledge and discussion, knowledge and discussion, so they're learning things, questioning things, talking about things, and you're questioning them, talking about things with them. It's interactive in that sense, so it's not a teacher talking at kids for five hours. You are building up the oracy (that's a horrible term), or the oratory of your kids, by getting them to talk right from early stages about what they're learning, but if they don't know anything, there's no point to it.

It's all about making the conversation rich and rewarding. I would open up what I call the dialectic argument, so you're always looking for arguments and looking for controversies and looking for conflicts where you can. Build up their knowledge of the great arguments in your discipline, so they actually have something meaty to talk about. If you're doing Antigone, you get right into the story, the argument between Creon and Antigone. You address it and you think about it and you look at from different angles and get really involved in discussing, not from your point of view, but trying to understand from the characters' points of view where they're coming from. You're engaging, not in mere opinion, but in educated, thoughtful discourse.

Q How do you deal with students who are reluctant to answer any question in a lesson?

Doug: My favourite approach is to have them write first, and then pre-call or cold call them. I might ask 'Why did Napoleon decide to attack on the morning of June 18th at Waterloo? 30 seconds, write down your response. Go.' Then I'd walk around and circulate, looking over my reluctant student's shoulder, perhaps, and say, 'That's very insightful. I'm going to cold call you to start.' Or, 'I may ask you to start, be ready.' Then the student knows that he has something worthy to say and is prepared for the fact that it's coming to him. Obviously, I would want to build into the fabric of the classroom the idea of cold calling, which is 'I may call on you whether or not you raised your hand.' I would probably want to describe to students at the outset why I do that and what the rules are. Something like, 'In my class I do something called cold calling. I call on students whether or not they've raised their hand. It's because it's my responsibility to understand what you know and what you don't know at any point in the lesson. I take that seriously. And sometimes I just want to hear from you in particular. I want to understand what you're thinking in this moment. So I may call on you. Know that I do it out of respect. As long as you can get us started and add something to the conversation, you're doing your job, even if you have to say, 'I don't fully understand the question and may need some help'. That's fine.'

The only answer I cannot accept from my students is, 'I don't know,' or a shrug, as that's a minimal effort thing. If a student really refuses to even try I'm going to have a conversation with them after class. Maybe there will be some consequences or he and I will have a sit down. But for the most part, I think if I can frame it positively and say, 'Any form of positive participation is a starting point here', then I think I can get it going.

One last idea – a great cold call question for a student who's reluctant is, 'Can you read the question for us, please, Robin?' Then the answer's right in front of the student. There's no way to get it wrong. I think that makes it very hard not to participate, because then I can draw my student in from there with further conversations.

 Martin: Ask them. They should know, so if they don't know and they're reluctant to answer, you've got to ask them, 'Do you know what we're talking about? Do you not know this?' If they say they don't know it, then that's fine. That's their get out. If they keep not knowing, that's a concern, but I can almost guarantee over a course of a few weeks you will find a way in for everyone. They've got to know what they're talking about, and they have to all take part. Make that your bottom line. You've got to find out the reason why they're reluctant. But they've got to know that the expectation is on them to take part.

In Drama, I had a pupil who was a school-refuser: he never came into school, well he came in for a few weeks and then started to refuse, but he turned up to my lessons. He wasn't able to speak at all, but instead of using that as an excuse, I used that as a thing for him. I did it through mime, to start with, and he started to speak from that. He knew he would have to speak at some point. I think this is what he *wanted* from the class. Why else turn up for the one subject that will challenge you so much? This was my underlying principle for all kids, they're not reluctant. There's a reason why they can't talk. You've got to give them a voice. You've got to give them the space to have a voice, but you've got to give them something to say as well. That's usually the problem, they haven't got anything to say, so that's why they need to know what they're talking about. You've got to educate them. Give Caliban his voice:

Be not afeard. The isle is full of noises,

Sounds, and sweet airs that give delight and hurt not.

Sometimes a thousand twangling instruments

Will hum about mine ears, and sometime voices

That, if I then had waked after long sleep,

Will make me sleep again. And then, in dreaming,

The clouds methought would open and show riches

Ready to drop upon me, that when I waked

I cried to dream again.

 What are the advantages of a 'hands-down' policy?

 Doug: Can I just distinguish between cold call and hands down? Because I prefer the former strongly. Cold calling, to me, means calling on any student in the classroom whether or not their hand is in the air. The advantages are, I can adjust my pacing in my classroom more easily instead of saying, 'Let's go over last night's homework. Who's got an answer to number two? I'm seeing the same three hands. I'd really like to hear from the boys in the back. Do I have to remind you that participation is graded?' All that sort of pleading that teachers do, you can just throw that out and say, 'Great. Let's go over the homework from last night. Number two, what did you get, Carl?' So it's useful for pacing, and useful for checking for understanding, useful for building an accountability loop of, you might be asked to participate at any point in class, so be engaged. So that's why I love cold call.

But cold call allows students to raise their hands. In fact I want them to raise their hands and to say, 'I want to speak, and I'd like to participate'. I think raising hands is great data. It's very different if I see 12 hands in the air, and then I cold call someone versus no one raises their hands and then I have to think about, 'Do I cold call someone? Do I turn and talk here? Do I have the right first? Why can't they answer?'

So there are some occasions where I might deliberately choose a hands down cold call, and say, 'I will not take hands now' – maybe the day before an exam when I really want to review and I want to signal everyone has to be ready, kind of like a final quiz – but, for the most part, I prefer cold calling when students are allowed to raise their hand.

 Martin: The teacher should be in charge of who's going to make a contribution. Part of what you're trying to do is find out what they know and what they don't, so you need to be in charge of who's answering questions, because you need to find out what people know and how much they know of it.

There's also an advantage of a 'hands-up sometimes' policy as well, because sometimes someone wants to make a really interesting and useful contribution. So I wouldn't have a blanket ban on hands-up either, especially later on in the process, where you've got perhaps a good, thoughtful class who are all part of the conversation, can actually have conversation, and have learnt how to have conversations. Then there's no point in you stopping people contributing when they've got something to say. At that point, the teacher, perhaps, is more of a facilitator of conversation, rather than a didactic sage on the stage, but that's a very advanced point that you've got to, with kids really knowing what they're talking about and really understanding how a conversational classroom can work. In fact, at this point, they might have learnt how to contribute without the need for putting their hand up, but just knowing when they can contribute.

I'm a sixth form politics teacher. Should certain topics be off-limits and should there be a 'safe-space' in classroom discussion?

Martin: You have to have certain topics off-limits, for child protection reasons *etc*. You don't want a child telling too much about themselves or their opinions that might get them or others into too much trouble outside of the class. I think this is to do with context, to do with knowing the kids and knowing what they're playing at – it might be bullying by any other name. They might be doing something more sinister, rather than not, but I don't think it should be a hard and fast rule. I don't think you should say race should never be talked about, gender, sex should never be talked about, or whatever. I don't think there's anything off-limits in that way, but you've got to be very wary of certain kids who are using it as bullying. I get the same thing with restorative justice. If you're using it and you haven't really got any idea of what's behind the issues, it can be bullying by any other name. It can actually just add to the victims' problems. Basically, my answer is, there should be no topics off-limits at all, but only if you know your kids and only if you know exactly what those little tensions in that classroom are all about, because sometimes it's a good way to have bullying by proxy.

So therefore you get the safe space, which should be that anything can be talked about in the classroom and it's safe to do so, rather than, it should be a safe space not to be upset in the classroom. That's a different thing altogether. It should be a challenging space, but it should be safe to discuss whatever you want to discuss. So if someone there is using it as bullying sanctioned by a teacher then that is not a safe space for that discussion to take place in. Those safe spaces, I'm against them. Topics being off-limits, I'm against that. I'm trying to say that there is another way of seeing this, which you've got to be very sensitive about as a teacher and know what's going on, because I've seen it when it hasn't been handled well.

Q **I've been told I shouldn't talk for more than ten minutes in a lesson. What's your opinion on this?**

Doug: That seems absurd. I don't know how teacher talk became a bad word. Should you break up long sequences of you talking with questions, application or reflection? Sure, most of the time. Are there times when should you try to make it engaging if you're going to talk for a long time? Sure, but that's more about the tools that you use to make times when you're talking beneficial. Are there also times when a lecture can be spell-binding? Immensely beneficial? Good practice for times in your life when you will have to learn in such a setting? Yes to all of those as well. I think establishing a rule of 'never talk more than ten minutes' is a way of suggesting that a teacher talking is a deeply unworthy thing – something done out of desperation, the last redoubt. I think it's important that teachers focus instead on how to do teacher talk well and how to balance talking with other approaches and activities. There are lots of ways to do that. But a rule like that – and the notion that teacher talk is a bad thing – is absurd.

Martin: Nonsense. Number one, are you going to sit there with a clock and then as soon as you get to your ten minutes never speak again? You're coming up with the best point ever and you've got to stop. Is that cumulative, or at any one time? Kids should be getting used to listening to people talking for a bit longer and a bit longer, reading stories, telling them 'stuff'. I think the worst thing would be someone talking very tediously or without much character in their voice, a monotonal droning-on with nothing interesting being said, for a whole lesson. That's what people, I think, are trying to avoid, and they put down this arbitrary ten minutes. Ten minutes, twenty minutes, half an hour of somebody doing something really, really interesting, really well-told, really thoughtful, really life-changing, you wouldn't stop them doing that, would you? Or would you? Why would you?! It's an arbitrary number, it's nonsense. It doesn't mean anything.

When structuring a group-work task, how do I ensure that students are held accountable?

Doug: This is a very good question because group work tasks are inherently challenging from an accountability standpoint. But again, I think writing is your friend both before and especially afterwards. The best way to hold someone accountable after group work task is to say, 'Now, process everything. Describe what you've learned in writing.' Or even better have them write beforehand, and then afterwards say, 'Now that you've done this activity, rewrite what you wrote beforehand and describe how your ideas have changed, because that makes you accountable not just for having ideas after the group work, but for describing how the group work changed or improved your thinking.' Sandwich it with writing on the front end or the back end.

Martin: Again, this is subject-specific, perhaps. I used to say that you're as strong as your weakest link, so beware whoever is letting the group down at any point. They've got to be told to get back into it and keep things going. So you hold students accountable for the quality of everyone's work in their group. In terms of the finished work, you're always checking on it as they're making it and just going there and saying, 'Right, how's it going?' Then you question each pupil. You don't just get feedback from one person. And if you find that one child doesn't know what the hell is going on, you chastise the group.

You have an idea of who the weakest link in the group is. That's the person you ask the most questions of. They all start to realise, actually, they've all got to know what's going on. So always ask the person who you think is the least likely to answer the questions well, or to know what's going on, the most difficult questions. In the end, you don't have weak people in the group.

8
CHAPTER

LEARNING MYTHS

DAVID DIDAU & PEDRO de BRUYCKERE

" THERE ARE TWO CORE REASONS FOR THE ORIGIN AND EVOLUTION OF A LEARNING MYTH. THE FIRST IS THAT INITIATIVES AND INTERVENTIONS ARE SUGGESTED FROM AREAS THAT HAVE NO BASIS IN EVIDENCE WHATSOEVER.

" A POPULAR RIFF HERE IS THE FALLACY THAT THE 21ST CENTURY IS SOMEHOW FUNDAMENTALLY DIFFERENT FROM ALL OTHER CENTURIES AND REQUIRES EDUCATION TO BE COMPLETELY REINVENTED TO ADAPT TO THE NEW PARADIGM.

" THE SECOND, MORE INFLUENTIAL, TYPE OF MYTH STEMS FROM INITIATIVES THAT ARE LAUNCHED ON THE BACK OF VERY POORLY CONDUCTED RESEARCH.

" MYTHS PERSIST THROUGH SIMPLE REPETITION, AND— COUNTER-INTUITIVELY- ALSO WHEN SCEPTICS PROVIDE EVIDENCE TO SHOW THAT THEY ARE FALLACIES.

" OTHER PROFESSIONS ARE ABLE TO USE RESEARCH SO THAT THEIR PRACTITIONERS ARE ABLE TO STAND ON THE SHOULDERS OF GIANTS AND MOVE FORWARD. WE NEED TO DO THE SAME.

*'Science must begin with myths, and with the
criticism of myths'*

Karl Popper

*'There is something feeble and a little contemptible
about a man who cannot face the perils of life without
the help of comfortable myths'*

Bertrand Russell

In the heat of the space race in the 1960s, NASA worked feverishly to solve a problem that was dogging their Apollo programme. In zero-gravity conditions, ink doesn't flow in pens. So, millions of dollars were pumped into producing a nitrogen-pressurised pen that would work. What did the Soviets do in response? They used a pencil.

This is a great anecdote, but sadly it is a myth. It's true that a pen was developed to counter the gravity problem but the cost was far less and was due not to NASA but an entrepreneur who sold his product to both the Americans and the Soviets. He probably deserves a lot more credit than he gets from the development of this myth, which has gained currency because it speaks to the value of simple, common sense over wastefulness and bureaucratic idiocy.

Myths are powerful things that many people want to believe in. They may be harmless – an extension of fiction that can fire the imagination. However, learning myths are a much more dangerous breed because they undermine education. What causes them? The answers tells us a lot about the current state of our profession. There are two core reasons for the origin and evolution of a learning myth. The first is that initiatives and interventions are suggested from areas that have no basis in evidence whatsoever. These can be driven by ideology (political as much as educational) and/or moral panics which demand action. The proponents themselves will likely have little experience of delivering education, but they will have access to a bully pulpit (and are probably avid watchers of TED talks). A popular riff here is the fallacy that the 21st century is somehow fundamentally different from all other centuries and requires education to be completely reinvented to adapt to the new paradigm. If you want a good example of this, the much-derided article by Caitlin Moran in *The Times*[37] sets out exactly this case. Although this kind of tub-thumping tends to grab the headlines, it is actually the lesser of two evils when it comes to learning myths.

The second, more influential, type of myth stems from initiatives that are launched on the back of very poorly conducted research. Education is not alone in suffering from that most dangerous of phrases, 'Research shows that…'. Indeed it may, but was it properly conducted? Was the data analysed accurately? The problem of weak research is tackled by Gorard, See and Siddiqui in *The Trial of Evidence-Based Education*. They argue that:

> These anecdotal, third hand, observational and commercially or politically motivated kinds of evidence may appear useful, and could be occasionally effective. They are more often confused, poorly understood, distorted, unbalanced, and unwarranted. Perhaps most importantly, these kinds of evidence are at least as likely to cause harm as they are to do any good, and mostly they will just waste effort, time and money that could have been used to make the lives of each cohort of participants in education better. This sounds and indeed is unethical.[38]

This does not mean that teachers and school leaders should shy away from being evidence-informed in their practice. Instead, it is a clarion call to be precisely that, so the chaff and the wheat can be separated and only sound conclusions that emerge from research findings can be turned into interventions and strategies.

We are some way from this, and in the meantime we have to deal with many myths which have taken root, occupying precious teacher time and devaluing the learning experience of pupils. Myths persist through simple repetition, and – counter-intuitively – also when sceptics provide evidence to show that they *are* fallacies.[39] As a result, interventions come and go in an ever-revolving door which has expanded workloads, bred cynicism, and gradually depleted morale in teaching. A common refrain from experienced teachers is that trends come and go; if you stick around long enough you can see everything go full circle, from best practice to heresy and back again. Marking is vital, marking is a waste of time, marking needs to be done three-fold, marking is out again. Must this be

37. Moran, C (2017) 'Why I should run our schools', *The Times*, www.thetimes.co.uk/article/caitlin-moran-why-i-should-be-education-secretary-9llh939r2
38. Gorard, S., See, B. and Siddiqui, N. (2017) *The Trials of Evidence-based Education*, Milton: Taylor and Francis, pp.3-4
39. De Bruyckere, P., Kirschner, P. and Hulshof, C. (2005) *Urban Myths about Learning and Education*, Academic Press.

so? Not if we use research effectively in the context in which we teach. After all, doctors don't say things like, 'Leeches were all the rage, then they were out, but I see we're starting to use them again.' Other professions are able to use research so that their practitioners are able to stand on the shoulders of giants and move forward. We need to do the same.

The optimistic note that we can strike here is that myth-busting has been a prominent feature of recent education history. In the past two decades there has been a much greater application of research to practice, and although there is some distance to go it does seem that we can test out different strategies and avoid the ones that lead us up an educational garden path. One of the most significant websites that all teachers should spend time perusing is the Education Endowment Foundation's Teaching and Learning Toolkit.[40] This shows three clear things about different teaching methods and resources: their cost implication; the amount of research that has been done to test their efficacy; and their impact measured in months of progress gained over a given school year. The fightback is on.

In addition to this, there are three important books which should be available in all school CPD libraries. Daisy Christodoulou was the first to break ground in 2014 with her *Seven Myths About Education*. This tackles seven powerful myths, including the aforementioned belief that 'the 21st century changes everything'. The following year saw David Didau produce *What If Everything You Knew About Education Was Wrong?* and also *Urban Myths About Learning And Education* by Pedro De Bruyckere, Paul A Kirschner and Casper D Hulshof. In an important passage in her book, Daisy Christodoulou uses the term 'educational formalism' because:

...many of these myths work on the assumption that form is more important than substance. If I had to come up with an intellectual trend that underpins them, then I would choose postmodernism ... Postmodernism is sceptical about the value of truth and knowledge, and many of these myths have at their heart a deep scepticism about the value of knowledge.[41]

Given the changes in political discourse the world saw in 2016, this battleground is even more important than it was when this was written in 2014.

As you will read in the coming chapter, there are plenty of poorly-supported theories and strategies that have been applied – and still apply – without

40. https://educationendowmentfoundation.org.uk/resources/teaching-learning-toolkit accessed 5/7/2017
41. Christodoulou, D. (2014) *Seven myths about education*, Routledge.

questioning the evidence base for them. You will no doubt recognise many, and perhaps all, of the ones discussed here. Distressingly, it is far from a comprehensive list. Our interviewees are both well versed in the minefields of learning myths. Pedro de Bruyckere taught Dutch, history and geography before becoming an educational scientist, and as well as being a co-author of *Urban Myths About Learning and Education* is also a frequent blogger and teacher-trainer. David Didau has been writing the highly influential blog *The Learning Spy* since 2011. He has called for a spirit of enquiry in pedagogy in his book *What if Everything you Knew About Education Was Wrong?* He asks teachers to keep an open mind about their craft, even questioning their own intuition that has served them well for so many years. The work done by Pedro and David can be used as a first line of defence so that any strategy or intervention introduced by an enthusiastic school leader (or pedalled by a consultant) is questioned seriously before asking teachers to waste precious time reinventing the wheel.

> **DD** THERE IS SOME EVIDENCE THAT PUPILS LEARN BETTER IN GROUPS, AND THERE'S ALSO EVIDENCE THAT THEY DON'T.

> **PdB** SO 21ST CENTURY SKILLS ARE ACTUALLY OFTEN 8TH OR 18TH CENTURY SKILLS WITH A DASH OF DIGITAL ADDED.

LEARNING MYTHS

CREATE · EVALUATE · ANALYSE · APPLY · UNDERSTAND · REMEMBER

CHAPTER 8

DAVID DIDAU

PEDRO de BRUYCKERE

> **PdB** THERE ARE SOME MYTHS CONCERNING THE TAXONOMY... THE TRIANGLE DOES NOT APPEAR ANYWHERE IN EITHER TAXONOMY. THE TRIANGULAR REPRESENTATION WAS QUITE LIKELY DESIGNED BY SOMEONE AS PART OF A PRESENTATION MADE TO EDUCATIONAL PRACTITIONERS.

> **DD** SIR KEN HAS DONE VERY WELL OUT OF BANGING HIS CREATIVITY DRUM. THE TROUBLE IS, IN CLAIMING THAT SCHOOLS KILL CREATIVITY HE IS PERHAPS GUILTY OF A TOUCH TOO MUCH CREATIVITY HIMSELF.

> **DD** GARDNER'S ARGUMENT IS A CLASSIC CLOSED CIRCLE: I'M RIGHT BECAUSE I HAVE A LOT OF DATA WHICH SAYS I'M RIGHT. HOW DOES HE KNOW THE DATA'S CORRECT? BECAUSE HE'S GOT A LOT OF IT.

> **PdB** THE FIRST LAW OF KRANZBERG SAYS "TECHNOLOGY IS NEITHER GOOD NOR BAD, BUT IT'S ALSO NEVER NEUTRAL."

> **PdB** AS PASHLER ET AL. HAS SHOWN THERE IS NO SOLID EVIDENCE FOR ANY DISTINCTION IN LEARNING STYLES YET. STILL A BIT OF AN ISSUE, THIS WOULDN'T BE THAT IMPORTANT IF TAKING LEARNING STYLES INTO ACCOUNT WOULD BENEFIT TEACHING.

What does the evidence suggest about using Bloom's Taxonomy in the classroom?

 David: As most teachers probably know, all learning is supposed to look pretty much like this:[42]

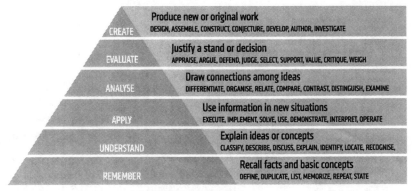

CREATE	**Produce new or original work** DESIGN, ASSEMBLE, CONSTRUCT, CONJECTURE, DEVELOP, AUTHOR, INVESTIGATE
EVALUATE	**Justify a stand or decision** APPRAISE, ARGUE, DEFEND, JUDGE, SELECT, SUPPORT, VALUE, CRITIQUE, WEIGH
ANALYSE	**Draw connections among ideas** DIFFERENTIATE, ORGANISE, RELATE, COMPARE, CONTRAST, DISTINGUISH, EXAMINE
APPLY	**Use information in new situations** EXECUTE, IMPLEMENT, SOLVE, USE, DEMONSTRATE, INTERPRET, OPERATE
UNDERSTAND	**Explain ideas or concepts** CLASSIFY, DESCRIBE, DISCUSS, EXPLAIN, IDENTIFY, LOCATE, RECOGNISE,
REMEMBER	**Recall facts and basic concepts** DEFINE, DUPLICATE, LIST, MEMORIZE, REPEAT, STATE

Vanderbilt University Center for Teaching

Knowledge is the dull, quotidian base of the triangle and at its apex we have the wondrous 'higher order thinking skills': creativity, evaluation, analysis *etc.* Quite how things came to be viewed this way is not entirely clear.

The educational psychologist, Benjamin Bloom, who developed the first iteration of his taxonomy in 1956, saw knowledge as the basis, the foundation, of all thinking, not as a category of thinking skill but as 'the necessary precondition for putting these skills and abilities into practice'. This is presumably why the designers of the diagram placed knowledge at the base of the triangle and gave it an area larger than all the other areas.[43]

It's worth knowing that Bloom's taxonomy wasn't based on empirical evidence of how learning takes place or on a scientifically validated model of how cognition occurs, it was just what Bloom reckoned.

So, while there is no evidence to suggest that teachers should use Bloom's taxonomy in the classroom, whether it's useful depends on how you interpret it. If you see the objective of a lesson as being to get students to demonstrate the 'higher order' skills and in so doing brush aside the

---

42. https://cft.vanderbilt.edu/guides-sub-pages/blooms-taxonomy/
43. Precisely who this person or people might have been is unclear. All we know is that it certainly wasn't Bloom.

foundational knowledge that makes such thinking possible, then you're going to come a cropper. If however you interpret it as a reminder to build students' thinking on a firm base, then you should be fine.

How do we know this? Well, the consensus from cognitive psychology is that skills such as critical thinking and problems solving do not exist in the absence of factual knowledge; in order to think, you have to have something to think *about*.

 Pedro: This is actually one of the most often asked questions that we received since Paul, Casper and I wrote our book on educational myths. But it's a difficult question to answer. A taxonomy is a model to be put on reality, acknowledging that no model ever will be perfect. So it's not a question if the model is backed by evidence, rather if it suits practice best. But there are some myths concerning the taxonomy. You often find adapted, incorrect versions of the model. Recently Lorin Anderson who revised the original taxonomy with Bloom pointed this out in a reaction on the blog of Larry Ferlazzo:

1. The triangle does not appear anywhere in either Taxonomy. The triangular representation was quite likely designed by someone as part of a presentation made to educational practitioners (*eg* teachers, administrators). I believe that the triangular representation was developed in order to indicate that, in the original Taxonomy, the six categories formed a cumulative hierarchy. That is, it was believed by the authors of the original Taxonomy that mastery of each lower category was necessary before moving to the next higher category. For example, you have to comprehend something before you can apply it.

THE COGNITIVE PROCESS DIMENSION

THE KNOWLEDGE DIMENSION	Remember	Understand	Apply	Analyse	Evaluate	Create
Factual Knowledge	List	Summarise	Classify	Order	Rank	Combine
Conceptual Knowledge	Describe	Interpret	Experiment	Explain	Assess	Plan
Procedural Knowledge	Tabulate	Predict	Calculate	Differentiate	Conclude	Compose
MetaCognitive Knowledge	Appropriate Use	Execute	Construct	Achieve	Action	Actualise

2. The triangular representation of the revised Taxonomy is particularly inappropriate for several reasons. First, the revised Taxonomy contains

two dimensions, not one. The authors believed that knowledge was sufficiently important to be a separate dimension. They also believed there were different types or forms of knowledge: factual, conceptual, procedural, and metacognitive. Second, the nouns in the original Taxonomy were replaced by verbs, In this process, remember replaced knowledge at the lowest 'level' of the second dimension, termed 'cognitive processes'. If you read the text of the original Taxonomy, the equation of 'knowledge' with 'recall' and 'recognition' is quite evident. Remember was followed by understand, apply, analyze, evaluate, and create. Third, the categories (verbs) in the cognitive process dimension did NOT form a cumulative hierarchy. Rather, they were considered to be 'tools in a toolbox'. Thus, it was possible (and often quite useful) to apply in order to understand or to evaluate as you apply.

Q **Sir Ken Robinson's TED talk claims that schools kill creativity. Is he right?**

David: Sir Ken has done very well out of banging his creativity drum. The trouble is, in claiming that schools kill creativity he is perhaps guilty of a touch too much creativity himself.

In order to know whether schools are killing creativity we have to be able to measure it. This is trickier than you might think. In the 1960s, J P Guilford came up with an interesting proxy for measuring creativity – 'divergent thinking': the idea that there are multiple solutions to any problem. He devised a number of tests to quantify divergent thinking including the 1967 Alternative Uses Test which asked participants to suggest as many alternative uses as they are able for everyday objects including toothpicks, bricks and paper clips.

In 1968, George Land conducted a research study to test the creativity of 1600 children ranging in ages from three to five years old. This was the same creativity test he devised for NASA to help select innovative engineers and scientists, sometimes referred to as 'the paper clip test' in which participants have to come up with as many different uses for a paper clip as they can think of. Most people are able to come up with 10-15 uses. People who are good at divergent thinking come up with around 200.

Ken refers to this test in his talk and tells us that when very young children are tested they score very highly, coming up with all sorts of fabulous possible ways of using everyday items, but then, after they been through school, they do far less well and can only think of a few uses. This is true, as far as it goes. Land's longitudinal study found 98% of children at age five were assessed as having genius levels of divergent thinking. Five years later, when they were aged eight to ten years, those at genius level had dropped to 30%. By the time they were 15, the average score was just 12%. Adults taking the same test tend to score around 2%. Creativity guru Ken Robinson argues that the main intervention these children have had is a conveyor belt education that tells them, 'There's only one answer. It's at the back. And don't look. That's called cheating.'

Ken's argument is that the process of having to conform to the 'factory model' of schooling has crushed children's spirits and made them dull, plodding drones. Despite the fact that a great many of the most creative people who've ever lived – including Robinson – have been products of the school system, the real problem with Land's analysis is that simply giving us percentages tells us nothing about the quality of the answers the children provided. It is possible that adults think of fewer uses for a paper clip because they have the ability to filter out nonsense answers. Students naturally possess a relatively limited set of schemata, and thus their ability to be creative (to combine schemata from different domains to generate interesting variations) is also fairly limited. What probably impresses us as adults is the uninhibited way children make productions based on these limited schemata. Princesses are painted, doctors and nurses are role-played, cardboard robots are constructed without embarrassment, and these unselected productions are usually (and quite naturally) rewarded by praise and attention.

However, as we get older we begin to identify more with our peers and, even if our parents still encourage us, our creativity starts to undergo more internal selection before production. Over time we come to understand that the first thoughts that pop into our heads are rarely true expressions of genius, and the nature of our creativity starts to expand and change. As we learn more, the schemata available to us expands, and we become more discerning about what represents quality.

We need to be a bit more critical of what it means for children to be creative. True creativity is about overcoming barriers and constraints. The more children know about the world, the greater the depth with which they understand the subjects they learn about, the more likely they are to come up with ideas that have utility.

Rather than haranguing teachers and students with their lack of creativity, Ken and other creativity gurus would be better off sharing messages endorsed by psychological studies into what it means to be creative.

Teachers should teach students that creativity is not always desirable. Sometimes it is better to follow tried and tested procedures. Asking students to be creative without support is likely to lead to cognitive overload. Instead, design well-structured tasks with clear constraints for them to overcome. A creative approach to problem solving requires experience and expertise. Students need to be given an experience of success before being expected to approach tasks independently. We would do better to teach students how to be creative within subject areas by modelling subject-specific processes and explaining how to apply what they have learned in similar contexts. Then, once students have a firm grasp of the foundational knowledge in the subject areas they are studying, only then should we get them to question and critique what they have learned.

 Pedro: This was the most often asked question, that's why we added this myth to our book when we translated our work to English. First question: does the paperclip experiment that Robinson mentions exist? Answer: Yes, it does, it is called the Torrence Creativity Test. Second question: does it show that a six-year-old has the same creative abilities as a genius? Answer: yes, it does. But as Keith Sawyer shows in his work on creativity from 2012, this test uses a very narrow definition of creativity. Most of the other tests show that children become more creative while getting older. This is because creativity needs knowledge. Now, one of the places where children receive new knowledge is school. The question should have been 'Does school foster creativity enough?'. If Sir Ken would have answered that question, the answer would probably have been yes. If you look at the work by, for example, Anne Bamford, who wrote *The Wow Factor*, the answer would probably be 'no'.

Q **What evidence is there to suggest that displaying the learning objectives at the beginning of each lesson aids pupil learning?**

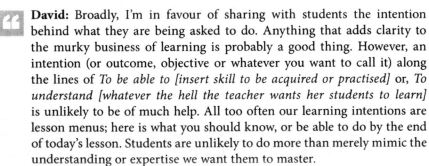 **David:** Broadly, I'm in favour of sharing with students the intention behind what they are being asked to do. Anything that adds clarity to the murky business of learning is probably a good thing. However, an intention (or outcome, objective or whatever you want to call it) along the lines of *To be able to [insert skill to be acquired or practised]* or, *To understand [whatever the hell the teacher wants her students to learn]* is unlikely to be of much help. All too often our learning intentions are lesson menus; here is what you should know, or be able to do by the end of today's lesson. Students are unlikely to do more than merely mimic the understanding or expertise we want them to master.

If instead we were to share our intention for students to master difficult concepts, then we could tell them that it might take them weeks to wrap their heads around such troublesome knowledge. We could remind them that in this lesson they are making progress towards a goal and that there is no expectation for them to 'get it' in the next hour or even the next week. Lessons may be the unit of delivery but that doesn't mean they ought to be the unit of planning or assessment.

Learning does not follow a neat, linear trajectory; it's liminal. Students not only need to spend time in that confusing, frustrating in-between space, they need to know how important it is to stay there for as long as need be. If learning intentions rush or limit this experience then they might be doing more harm than good. To a teacher, labouring under the curse of knowledge, the meaning behind our intentions is clear. But to students, standing at the threshold, not knowing the things we take so much for granted, our stated lesson outcomes are often impossibly vague.

Consider this example:

Learning objective: To understand the influences that affect personal economic choices.

Success criteria: I can:

1. explain how limited resources create the need for choices

2. identify costs and benefits of a choice

3. identify and evaluate incentives

4. analyse choices and predict consequences

This may be clear to an expert, but to a novice it's a checklist of barely understood ideas that will lead only to shallow mimicry.

 Pedro: This is a typical element of what has been called a cognitive theory on learning. The influence of behaviourists on education was in part the introduction of learning objectives; cognitive-inspired educationalists added the idea of displaying the learning objectives at the beginning of each lesson. I see two reasons to do this. First of all it is all about transparency in assessment. Knowing the goals on which you will be assessed is important for learners and is one of the main focuses of what is called the docimology, the science of assessment. Secondly – as Ramsden described in his 1992 book on teaching in higher education –

for many students the assessment *is* the curriculum. I know that a lot of my students in teacher training write their learning objectives as the last element in their preparation, and they write them only because we ask them to. This is a pity. I try to explain to them over and over again that when done properly, learning objectives are the tail that wags the dog. It shows you the end of the line, making clear how to get there.

Q Why have my sixth form sets who use exercise books and pens been 45% quicker as they work through course material than those who use laptops?

David: Erm? Not sure about this.

There is evidence that taking notes electronically leads to poorer recall than handwritten notes. The benefits of handwritten over typed notes include better immediate recall as well as improved retention after two weeks. In addition, students who take handwritten notes are more like to remember facts but also to have better future understanding of the topic. Fascinatingly, it doesn't even matter whether you ever look at these notes – the simple act of making them appears to be beneficial.

Why might this be? One problem is that most people can type faster than they can write. Although this makes typing easier it results in notes which are much more likely to be accurate verbatim reports of what a speaker has said. Because handwriting is slower, we are forced to interpret and paraphrase what a speaker says instead of simply producing a transcript. This act of synthesis leads to better semantic processing which means that schematic changes to long-term memory are likely to be taking place as notes are taken. Typing, because it demands less of us, results in less change to long-term memory.

Pedro: There is no clear answer why this is the case with your pupils. I can see many different reasons why this could be. Maybe they are less fluent with technology, maybe they were doing other stuff in the meantime or maybe the software was slow. Still, there is a lot to say both pro and contra using technology.

First of all, for taking notes, paper still beats technology. This has nothing to do with technology, but is because when you write by hand, you write less down than when you type it on a keyboard. So you need to select what you write down, and this thinking is good for remembering. We also know that technology can be very distracting and multitasking is very bad for learning. There is a 2016 MIT study that showed that in a traditional approach to teaching even students who could only use software related to the course they were being taught underperformed to the group that didn't use any technology at all. But this study doesn't mean that there couldn't be good reasons to use technology in the classroom. In a 2014 experiment on 'Personalised review', personalised spaced repetition based on algorithms was shown to outperform massed spaced repetition by a mile. But to make these algorithms possible, students did need to make the exercises on a device.

Kranzberg's first Law of Technology says 'technology is neither good nor bad, but it's also never neutral'. For education and for teachers this means that it's not about being for or against technology but knowing when your classroom should be a hotspot and when a coldspot.

Q What is the evidence for multiple intelligences?

 David: In 1983, Howard Gardner came up with his theory of multiple intelligences. Basically he said that instead of there being one general intelligence there were lots of different types of intelligence: logical-mathematical, linguistic, musical, intra- and extra-personal and so on. He claimed that while someone might have a low linguistic intelligence they might do very well in, say, naturalistic intelligence. This is a seductive idea, but one which is conceptually confused and for which there is little support. Gardener never tested his theory or conducted any studies. It was just a hunch. A popular and enduring hunch to be sure, but one of which even Gardener himself said in 2016, 'I readily admit that the theory is no longer current.'[44]

Of course, he's not quite ready to entirely abandon his theory. While he admits that he never carried out any experiments designed to test his theory, he's not willing to accept that it lacks empirical support. He says, 'The theory is not experimental in the traditional sense … but it is strictly empirical, drawing on hundreds of findings from half-a-dozen fields of science.'[45] I'm not at all sure this is good enough. Just because you've got a lot of data, it doesn't mean that you understand what it's telling you. One of the central pillars of science is that, because it's all too easy to prove yourself right, to really test your claims you have to try to disprove, or falsify them.

44. Gardner, H. (2016) https://howardgardner01.files.wordpress.com/2016/11/scientists-making-a-difference_gardner.pdf
45. Ibid

Gardner's argument is a classic closed circle: I'm right because I have a lot of data which says I'm right. How does he know the data's correct? Because he's got a lot of it. A closed circle argument is one where there is no possibility of convincing an opponent that they might be wrong. They are right because they're right.

And really, so what if he's right? What difference can it make to teachers to discover that some children are musical and others are sporty? How would this change what teachers do in classrooms? Just because someone has 'naturalistic intelligence' does this mean they need to be taught maths differently? As we saw with learning styles, matching instruction to children's preferences can only narrow their experience. As Gardner himself admits, if he'd steered clear from the word 'intelligence' no one would have given his idea a second glance. It's uncontroversial to say different people have different talents, but the evidence into intelligence research makes clear that being good at one of the battery of subtests encountered in an IQ test will tend to mean you're likely to be good at all of them. Intelligence seems to be general rather than distributed amongst different abilities.

Pedro: In our book on urban myths about learning and education we don't call multiple intelligences a myth, we do say it's nuanced to say the least. First of all: why aren't we calling it a myth? Well, it's no myth that people are different, so as a kind of philosophy, this thinking isn't that wrong. But MI does have issues. Even Howard Gardner himself repeatedly stated that people often treat his intelligences as learning styles and that this is wrong. But in 2016 it got a bit worse. In an essay replying to the question, 'Reflecting on your life, what has been your greatest accomplishment so far and why?', Gardner said some very interesting things. First, on why he used the concept of intelligences: 'I termed the resulting categories 'intelligences' rather than talents. In so doing I challenged those psychologists who believed that they owned the word 'intelligence' and had a monopoly on its definition and measurement. If I had written about human talents, rather than intelligences, I probably would not have been asked to contribute to this volume.' Yes, but in the concept of intelligence there is a notion of prediction. His theory doesn't have this notion.

Secondly, on how empirical his theory is: 'Nor, indeed, have I carried out experiments designed to test the theory. This has led some critics to declare that my theory is not empirical. That charge is baloney! The theory is not experimental in the traditional sense (as was my earlier work with brain-damaged patients); but it is strictly empirical, drawing on hundreds of findings from half-a-dozen fields of science.'

But there is an even more important third quote from his 2016 essay: 'At the same time, I readily admit that the theory is no longer current. Several fields of knowledge have advanced significantly since the early 1980s. Any reinvigoration of the theory would require a survey similar to the one that colleagues and I carried out thirty-five years ago. Whether or not I ever carry out such an update, I encourage others to do so. And that is because I am no longer wedded to the particular list of intelligences that I initially developed.'

 Should I consider different pupil learning styles when planning lessons?

 David: Another beguiling educational myth is that if teachers match their instruction to children's preferred style of learning then they will learn more. If you think this is true, you're not alone. Sadly it's not. If you have evidence to the contrary you could claim $5000 from Will at Work. Here's how:

1. Take 60 or so children and give each child a learning styles questionnaire. (There are about 60 or so to choose from but it really doesn't matter which one you go for.)

2. Randomly allocate the children to one of two groups. The first group will be the experimental group, the second will be the control.

3. You can teach the students anything you like as long as it's the same topic for both groups. In the experimental group, instruction must be matched to students' preferred learning style, in the control it's business as usual.

4. Give children an assessment of how well they have learned the content they've been taught. If the experimental group significantly outperform the control group, the cash is as good as yours.

The trouble is, no one has yet been able to demonstrate that 'meshing' instruction with students' preferences makes any difference.

The fact that we have preferences is undeniable. It may well be that some people prefer to learn visually, aurally or kinaesthetically, but just because we have a preference doesn't mean we can't learn in other ways. My preference is to learn whilst drinking an espresso but clearly I can, if pressed, do without.

It makes more sense to match instruction to the content you want to teach. If you want students to learn about the course of the river Nile, everyone, no matter their preference, will learn this best if shown a picture. If you want students to learn how to make a backhand return in tennis, then it's no good just showing them a video or explaining it to them, they have to have a go.

Pedro: To put it bluntly: no. It's one of the most popular myths in education. There are two reasons why learning styles are a bad idea in education. As Pashler *et al* have shown there is no solid evidence for any distinction in learning styles yet. Still a bit of an issue, this wouldn't be that important if taking learning styles into account would benefit teaching. But secondly, the effect size of learning styles in, for example, the work by John Hattie is very low (.14, not in the first edition of his book). But if you are still not convinced, maybe you can try to win the $5000 Learning Styles Challenge that Will at Work has put out based on the work by Pashler *et al.* If any person or group creates a real-world learning intervention that takes learning styles into account and proves that such an intervention produces better learning results than a non-learning-styles intervention, they'll be awarded $5000! Good luck!

In an age of Google, do students need to retain knowledge less than in the days before the internet?

David: The internet is ace. A world of information is available at the click of a mouse and we can find out pretty much anything we want to know. This results in absurdities like, 'knowledge isn't all that important because you can always look up whatever you need to know on the internet'. People really do seem to believe this. This lazy, uncritical thinking has been trotted out in recent months by Caitlin Moran[46] and George Monbiot[47], but the most egregious examples of this fallacy tend to come from physics professor turned edu-preneur, Sugata Mitra, who is on record as having said, 'Knowing is obsolete. People often think I'm saying

46. Moran, C (2017) 'Why I should run our schools', *The Times*, www.thetimes.co.uk/article/caitlin-moran-why-i-should-be-education-secretary-9llh939r2

47. Monbiot, G. (2017) 'In an age of robots, schools are teaching our children to be redundant', *The Guardian*, www.theguardian.com/commentisfree/2017/feb/15/robots-schools-teaching-children-redundant-testing-learn-future

that knowledge is obsolete, which I'm not. I'm saying putting knowledge in your head – that's obsolete, because you can know anything when you need to know it via the internet.'[48]

Persuasive as this argument can seem, it ignores the fact that a lot of tacit, procedural knowledge – stuff we're not consciously aware of thinking *about* – is what we think *with*. Our minds are full of different kinds of knowledge and it's what we know that, as much as anything else, makes us who we are. Our ability to think, reason, problem-solve, create and collaborate are all entirely dependent on what we know. In order to think we have to have something to both think *with* and *about*. If you don't know lots of useful, powerful and interesting stuff then you'll struggle to be useful, powerful or interesting.

Anything we are dependent on looking up we are unable to think with. 'Thinking with' and 'thinking about' are different ways of handling knowledge but both depend on having the stuff in our heads. If you only know where to look something up, that's the extent of your thinking. You hold it in your head long enough to complete a task and then let it go. If we don't value the knowledge of how to send photos to friends sufficiently to want to memorise it, that's fair enough, but what you look up only makes sense when it's integrated with all that you already know. *Only* being able to look things up is an impoverishing experience. Knowledge is only knowledge if it lives inside us.

Not only that, it takes knowledge to gain knowledge; the more you know, the more you will learn. If you don't know very much about, say, osmosis, looking it up isn't going to help much because you won't understand most of what you find.

 Pedro: There is a big difference between information and knowledge. You'll find information on the internet while you'll need knowledge to know if the information is correct. For example, as Sparrow and her colleagues have shown, it is true that we rely more on technology as a kind of extended memory, just as we started doing with paper since we first knew how to write. But this doesn't mean we don't need to teach knowledge anymore. There was a big issue lately because of the results displayed by Google when you asked the search engine if the Holocaust really did happen. We can teach our pupils to check several sources as

48. Cadwalladr, C. (2015) 'The 'granny cloud': the network of volunteers helping poorer children learn', *The Guardian*, www.theguardian.com/education/2015/aug/02/sugata-mitra-school-in-the-cloud accessed 27 April 2017

a skill, but if the sources they check are all bad and they don't have the knowledge to verify, well, we are pretty much doomed. A second reason that I need to mention is that we need knowledge to be creative as we need to know stuff to make new associations between elements.

 I've been told that pupils learn best when in groups. What is the evidence for this claim?

 David: Way back in 1913, French agricultural engineer Maximilien Ringelmann discovered something rather surprising: the productivity of a group decreases as its size increases. If we pull a rope all by ourselves we tend to pull our hardest but as soon as others pop up to help us out we slacken off. Even though they are likely to be unaware of this slackening of effort, everyone pulls a bit less hard. The bigger the group, the greater the tendency for *social loafing*. The Ringelmann Effect suggests that when we're part of a group we believe every other member is doing the hard work. We can take it easy because our lack of effort won't be exposed.

Unconsciously, we rely on those around us to pull out the stops to get the job done. This phenomenon is well known to teachers. It ought to be reasonable to expect a group of four pupils to produce four times as much work collectively as they would produce alone. In fact they tend to produce less together than they might alone. Not only that, but working in groups actually makes us less creative. In particular, 'brain-storming' (or 'thought-showering' if you prefer the more politically correct synonym) actually limits our capacity to come up with interesting ideas.

There *is* some evidence that pupils learn better in groups, and there's also evidence that they don't. Most of the supporting evidence for group work uses an experimental design which sets the group condition against just a control. As almost everything can be shown to work, especially if you set up your experiment the right way, this doesn't tell us much. Where we have 'horse race' style experiments which pit more than one intervention against each other, explicit, whole class instruction does better.

Getting groups to work effectively is hard because of the tendency for social loafing. Researchers like Bob Slavin have found that by setting up conditions where there is group responsibility but individual accountability works best, but then is it worth going to all this trouble? Most of the time teachers will be better off getting students to take part in whole-class instruction before working individually.

So why bother at all? Well, first, group work lends itself to some subjects more than others. Drama or PE without group work would be absurd. But do we need children to faff about in groups in other subjects? Maybe not. Secondly, all teachers will have encountered pupils who struggle to answer questions and come up with ideas. Left to their own devices they sit, head on desk and dream of being somewhere better. We know that simply getting them to discuss some possibilities with the student sitting next to them can be sufficient to jolly them along. Maybe they haven't become more creative – maybe this just gives them less of an excuse for doing nothing? Who cares: it gets them working. I'm sure we can all cite thousands of examples from our own lives of occasions when a simple conversation with a friend or colleague opened up new possibilities or pointed us in previously unexplored directions. The point of collaboration is that it opens us to the ideas of others. But then, so does reading books.

 Pedro: It is true that collaborative working has a big effect size in John Hattie's visible learning, but again this is an average and there are many different forms of group work. For example, the jigsaw approach seems to be quite effective. For people who don't know this approach, Katrina Schwartz summarises it as follows: 'In a jigsaw activity students are reading new information, discussing it with others who have read the same thing to extend their understanding, and then moving to new groups where they teach peers about what they read and learn new information from group members.' At the same time there are other examples of learning in group that aren't that clear cut in having a positive effect. Take problem-based learning. This happens in a group, can be great for training skills when students already have the basic knowledge needed, but is really bad for learning that basis knowledge, as a 2017 review by Michael Schneider & Franzis Preckel again demonstrated.

So, yes pupils can learn better in groups, but it depends on how, when and to what purpose they do. Again it is important that the teacher uses these approaches wisely.

 Can you teach critical thinking and if so, how?

David: My position on this is summarised in these three propositions:

1. Knowledge is both what we think *with* and *about*.

2. We cannot think with or about something we don't know.

3.   The more we know about something, the more sophisticated our thinking.

Critical thinking depends on knowledge; we are what we know. You can't think about something you don't know. Try it for a moment. The best you can do is to ask, 'What don't I know?', but even that is something you know. What we think about are concepts, ideas, experiences and facts, nothing but facts. We can think about the capital of Chad or the length of the Nile. We can think about our favourite colour or what we'd like for our birthday. We can think about anything we know at least something about, but this can be a shallow, unfulfilling experience. The more things we know, the more detail we possess, the more links and connections we can make. Seeing these links is insight; making these connections is creative. What you know is like intellectual Velcro; new stuff sticks to it, so, the more you know, the more you learn. The more you learn, the more you are.

But all this propositional knowledge is just the tip of an unimaginably enormous iceberg. Although you probably can't explain it, you know how to balance. You know how to recognise thousands of different human faces. You might not know you know this, but if you're reading this you know the relationships between the 44 phonemes and over 170 graphemes that make up the English alphabetic code. These aren't things most people think about, but we use them to think *with* all the time.

All skills require knowledge, and thinking, in whatever form it takes, is procedural knowledge. There's no such thing as a generic ability to be analytical or creative; you can only analyse some *thing* or be creative in a particular field. To understand this we need to deconstruct the idea of skills. Instead of seeing skills as somehow separate from knowledge it's more useful to view knowledge and its application as inseparably intertwined and mutually interdependent.

To become an expert in a domain you must have something to think critically about *and* practise thinking critically. But, sadly, this will not make you more expert in any other but the most closely related domains. You have to think critically *about* the facts you have learned; this is part of the domain. Knowledge is both necessary *and* sufficient; there is nothing else. Expertise requires domain-specific knowledge, which *obviously* is more than just a bunch of facts. So, you *can* teach critical thinking within a subject domain but not as a transferable generic skill.

Pedro: This maybe isn't a million-dollar question, but in times where fake news is making the – ahem – news, it seems critical thinking is more important than ever. First of all, what you need is enough knowledge to be able to think critically. Being critical without knowing what you are talking about, is not being critical but being an annoyance. But can it be taught? A 2017 study by North Carolina State University researchers finds that teaching critical thinking skills in a humanities course significantly reduces student beliefs in 'pseudoscience' that is unsupported by facts, which is nice, and a 2014 study by Dennis Fung showed that when used effectively group work can boost critical thinking.

 ## Should schools be geared towards 21st century skills?

 David: Not if you believe in social justice. It's difficult to ignore the appealing certainty that the times in which we are alive are unique and fundamentally different from any that have gone before. The most cited reason for this is the fact that the internet has changed everything.

Technology has been transforming education for as long as either have been in existence. Language, arguably the most crucial technological advancement in human history, moved education from mere mimicry and emulation into the realms of cultural transmission; as we became able to express abstractions so we could teach our offspring about the interior world of thought beyond the concrete reality we experienced directly.

Today we're told that on average human knowledge doubles in just over a year. Some estimates suggest that, soon, what we collectively know is set to double every twelve hours. No wonder so many have been persuaded that there is no longer a need to learn facts as what we know will quickly be superseded and, after all, we can always just look up whatever we need to know on the internet.

In response to the apparent obsolescence of knowledge, some schools have started to reinvent themselves as places where children learn transferable skills which would allow them to navigate the shifting, uncertain world of the future. Maybe the traditional curriculum of school subjects has had its day, as tech guru Sugata Mitra claims. Maybe all we have to do is teach kids how to use Google and they will magically teach themselves all they need to know. After all, most of what schools teach is a waste of time, it seems. According to Mitra, the Chinese and Americans 'don't bother about grammar at all'. Children don't need to know how to spell, and 'the less arithmetic you do in your head, the better'.

There is nothing more philistine, more impoverished than reducing the curriculum to the little that's visible through the narrow lens of children's current interest and passing fancies. How do they know what they might need to know? And in any case, do we really want to educate the next generation merely in what we think they will need?

Of course the future is uncertain, unknowable, so how best can we prepare students for it? Well, perhaps we should stop delivering rapidly outdated facts and instead teach students the skills they will need to thrive in the 21st century. And what are these futuristic skills? Typically they are considered to include critical thinking, problem-solving, communication, collaboration and creativity. Wonderful things, all of them – but attempting to substitute them wholesale for a more traditional school curriculum comes with problems.

Are these really '21st century' skills? Or, in fact, hasn't this stuff always been pretty important? And if it *was* important for Socrates to think critically, Julius Caesar to solve problems, Shakespeare to communicate, Leonardo da Vinci to be creative and the builders of the Great Wall of China to collaborate – how on earth did they achieve what they did without a specific, 21st century learning curriculum? The point is, these skills are innate human characteristics. We all, to a greater or lesser degree, use them all the time. How could we not? Of course, we can encourage children to be more creative, critical and collaborative, but can we actually teach these things as subjects in their own right?

How, exactly, do you teach someone to communicate or solve problems in more sophisticated ways? *What* is it we want students to communicate? What sorts of things do we want them to create? What do we want to collaborate on? The problem with attempting to teach a generic skill like critical thinking is that you must have something to think critically about; if you know nothing about quantum physics no amount of training in critical thinking is going to help you come up with much on the subject that is very profound. Likewise, to be truly creative we need to know a lot about the form or discipline we're trying to be creative in. Skills divorced from a body of knowledge are bland to the point of meaninglessness. In fact, these so-called 21st century skills are in fact biologically primary evolutionary adaptations. We are innately creative. We solve problems as a matter of course and collaboration comes to us naturally. What makes people appear to struggle with these innate attributes is that we want them to use them to manipulate biologically secondary, abstract knowledge.

Anyone can collaborate on a playground game, but to collaborate on finding a cure for cancer you would need a lot of highly specialised expertise. The only thing that makes these innate skills desirable in the 21st century is the academic content on which they depend.

 Pedro: There are two aspects in this question. First of all: is there such a thing as 21st century skills? I would argue no, because most of the elements were already needed in the 18th century and when Sarah Adams made a comparison between the 21st century skills and the *septem artes liberales*, the seven liberal arts, she found many similarities. So 21st century skills are actually often 8th or 18th century skills with a dash of digital added. This brings us to the second question: should school be gearing towards these goals? I do think so; as Biesta describes, schools have three tasks: qualification, socialization, subjectification. So besides the importance of personal development (a blunt translation of subjectification) we also need to prepare our children to participate in our society and teach them to live together. It would be wrong to think that gearing towards these goals would mean that we should abandon other elements of the curriculum as they are often needed for these goals.

> AN INCREMENTAL APPROACH FOLLOWED BY EVIDENCE-BASED TEACHER TRAINING TO EXPAND YOUR SYSTEM IS THE MOST LIKELY ROUTE TO SUCCESS.

> THE ROOT-PROBLEM IS NOT CLEAR-CUT. IT MAY NOT BE THE TECHNOLOGY ITSELF, BUT HOW WE USE IT.

> IN YOUR CLASSROOM, HOW CAN TECHNOLOGY SUPPORT LEARNING RATHER THAN CREATING A DISTRACTION?

> TEACHERS NEED TO BE INFORMED ABOUT THE OPTIONS, TRAINED IN HOW TO USE THE SOFTWARE AND THE HARDWARE, AND SUPPORTED AS THEY BEGIN TO USE IT IN THE CLASSROOM. THE DELIVERY OF THIS TRAINING NEEDS TO BE RESEARCH-INFORMED ON HOW STUDENTS WILL LEARN, RATHER THAN TECH-INFORMED ABOUT HOW IT RUNS.

> ONE OF THE BEST THINGS THAT TECHNOLOGY CAN DO IS REDUCE TEACHER WORKLOAD AND STRESS. THAT ALONE WILL IMPROVE THE QUALITY OF LEARNING IN THE CLASSROOM AS MORE TIME CAN BE SPEND ON PLANNING LESSONS.

If you were to design the school of the future, what would it look like? This is a great question to start a whole-school discussion on digital philosophy and strategy. We say this not as a general thought, but because that's what Cary Matsuoka, a school district superintendent in California, did with the schools in his area in 2012. It worked wonders. Rather than implement a top-down system of technology use, he preferred a bottom-up approach where his schools could decide what was best for themselves. He explains that 'any time you control things from the top, you get compliance, where people just go through the motions'. He goes on, 'We wanted to say: "Here's the model. Come up with your version of it and go test it".[49] Interestingly, the system that was tested and honed showed that not every student needed their own device. This was not only cost-effective, but also improved teaching and learning by getting schools to think carefully about optimal impact of a rotation policy.

This example stands in stark contrast to perhaps the biggest EdTech debacle to date, in the same state. In 2013, Los Angeles splashed out an eye-watering $1.3 billion on giving every child an iPad. Apple partnered with Pearson and the top-down strategy was rolled out all at once. Within two years, all but two schools had given up on this. There are many key lessons to learn here, but the contrasting examples of what Matsuoka did and what LA did point to two that are vital. Firstly, consider vision as the starting point and *then* think of solutions. Once you've done this, test what you're doing via a pilot rather than a blanket launch. This can not only save a lot of money but also – crucially – prevent the squandering of valuable teacher time on initiatives that pretty much never work on a massive scale. An incremental approach followed by evidence-based teacher training to expand your system is the most likely route to success.

This might explain why major studies into the efficacy of technology have been very pessimistic. The OECD published a substantial study in 2015 which came to this dire conclusion:

> This analysis shows that the reality in our schools lags considerably behind the promise of technology. In 2012, 96% of 15-year-old students in OECD countries reported that they have a computer at home, but only 72% reported that they use a desktop, laptop, or tablet computer at school, and in some countries fewer than one in two students reported doing so. And even where computers are used in the classroom, their impact on student performance is mixed at best. Students who use computers moderately in school tend to have somewhat better learning outcomes than students who use computers

---

49. www.wired.com/2015/05/los-angeles-edtech

comparatively rarely. But students who use computers very frequently in school do a lot worse in most learning outcomes, even after accounting for social background and student demographics.[50]

It would be easy (perhaps lazy) to draw the conclusion that technology is therefore more hindrance than help for learning. Yet the same report acknowledges that the root-problem is not clear-cut. It may not be the technology itself, but how we use it:

> One interpretation of all this is that building deep, conceptual understanding and higher-order thinking requires intensive teacher-student interactions, and technology sometimes distracts from this valuable human engagement. Another interpretation is that we have not yet become good enough at the kind of pedagogies that make the most of technology; that adding 21st-century technologies to 20th-century teaching practices will just dilute the effectiveness of teaching.

> If students use smartphones to copy and paste prefabricated answers to questions, it is unlikely to help them to become smarter. If we want students to become smarter than a smartphone, we need to think harder about the pedagogies we are using to teach them. Technology can amplify great teaching but great technology cannot replace poor teaching.[51]

The final sentence highlights that research on use of EdTech is vital for several reasons. Primarily, we need to consider how students actually learn (a consistent theme and core aim of this book). Once teachers have a secure understanding of cognitive processes then we can ask the salient question, 'How can technology enhance these processes?' This is a question that every teacher needs to ask themselves. In your classroom, how can technology support learning rather than creating a distraction?

Secondly, professional learning is key because this is an area where pupils are likely to have more understanding of the field than teachers, making it a unique area (we certainly hope that wouldn't be the case with, say, assessment). Teachers need to be informed about the options, trained in how to use the software and the hardware, and supported as they begin to use it in the classroom. The delivery of this training needs to be research-informed on how students will learn, rather than tech-informed about how it runs. This is a strategic error

---

50. OECD (2015) 'Students, Computers and Learning: Making the Connection', PISA, OECD Publishing, p.3
51. Ibid

that is all too common in schools. For example, knowledge of the myth about multi-tasking tackled in chapter 8 would help inform practice about how to make sure that students use laptops for a specific task with clear guidance rather than having it generally open in front of them when not needed, and losing focus. Something else to keep in mind is that all people (young and old) use technology for both entertainment and practical purposes. Leaders therefore need to create a culture where children know that tech must be used for working purposes when in school, and only for social and entertainment purposes outside of this. Never forget how hard it is for young people to appreciate this distinction and self-regulate accordingly.

Although they may not be reading this, people who work for tech firms should also strongly consider reading research about how children learn before developing software and hardware. They are as guilty as anyone else in education when it comes to generating fads. This is where schools can play a really important role. If tech firms come to schools for guidance on what to develop and how to make an impact, make sure they are connected with solid research about how children learn. Also, remind them that one of the best things that technology can do is reduce teacher workload and stress. That alone will improve the quality of learning in the classroom as more time can be spent on planning lessons. If technology is unreliable or inefficient then it fails in this core objective.

Our interviewees are both classroom practitioners who are well-versed in what works and what doesn't. Dr Neelam Parmar is Director of E-Learning at Ashford School in Kent and has significant experience as an EdTech consultant. José Picardo is Assistant Principal at Surbiton High School and writes for the *TES*. He is co-author of *Educate 1-to-1* (2014) and has a new book, *Using Technology In The Classroom* (2017). Their answers to the questions show both the extent of misconceptions about the uses of technology in the classroom, and the range of practical advice that will steer you in the right direction. Download the following pages to your long-term memory...

TECHNOLOGY

JOSE PICARDO

NEELAM PARMAR

CHAPTER 5

NP

TURN IT UN...WOULD ACTUALLY BE A REALLY GOOD TOOL TO BRING DOWN INTO GCSE AND SIXTH FORM YEARS SO THAT THE OLDER STUDENTS CAN ENSURE THAT THE WORK THEY ARE HANDING IN IS ORIGINAL AND REFERENCED CORRECTLY.

NP

I THINK IT IS NECESSARY TO USE TECHNOLOGY IN TEACHING ONLY WHEN IT COMPLEMENTS, REDEFINES OR MAKES PURPOSEFUL THE LESSON TO ENRICH LEARNING WITH STUDENTS.

NP

MANY SCHOOL WIRELESS NETWORK SOLUTIONS ARE NOT CURRENTLY DESIGNED TO HANDLE THE AMOUNT OF ACTIVITY AND NUMBER OF DEVICES THAT WILL BE USING UP BANDWIDTH IN BYOD ENVIRONMENTS.

NP

STUDENTS DO NOT LIKE TO BE DISCONNECTED LONGER THAN 30 MINUTES.

JP

SOCIAL MEDIA HAS ADDED AN EXTRA LAYER OF EXTRA COMPLEXITY THAT MANY SCHOOLS ARE FINDING DIFFICULT TO ACCEPT. YET THIS IS THE REALITY IN WHICH WE LIVE.

JP

PATHOLOGISING TECHNOLOGY USE SERVES NO PRACTICAL PURPOSE AND OBFUSCATES THE MORE IMPORTANT QUESTION THAT WE SHOULD BE ASKING: HOW IS TECHNOLOGY USEFUL?

JP

THE NOTION THAT GREAT TEACHING AND THE EFFECTIVE USE OF TECHNOLOGY TO SUPPORT LEARNING ARE SOMEHOW MUTUALLY EXCLUSIVE IS ULTIMATELY PERNICIOUS.

JP

WHERE TECHNOLOGY USE IS FOCUSED ON ACADEMIC PURPOSES, TEACHERS DON'T RELINQUISH CONTROL OVER TO TECHNOLOGY

Would you ban mobile phones in schools?

 José: If I answered no, some would think that I am in favour of unfettered access to mobile phones at any time during the school day. This is not quite the case. Although I would not ban the presence of mobile phones in schools, I would not allow students to use them in lessons unless they are instructed to by a teacher for a specific purpose. In my view, and with the benefit of experience, it is possible to develop and apply rewards and sanctions policies that focus on promoting the appropriate use of mobile devices. This should be every school's first port of call. Having said that, I am also mindful that an outright ban may be the most appropriate course of action in certain contexts, where, for example, poor behaviour is the number one challenge for the school.

 Neelam: No, I would not ban mobile phones in secondary schools. To ban mobile phones and 'expect' students to not bring them into school is naïve. I appreciate that some schools struggle with mobile phones in a classroom where it can be disruptive; however, in such cases, an explicit school policy on the possible consequences of such actions needs to be addressed. If the school uses the mobile phone as part of their BYOD strategy, I would encourage students to put their phones on the desk, along with their resources, *ie* books, pens, pencils, calculator, *etc*.

Whether the mobile phone is part of the BYOD programme or not, an outright ban on all mobile phones for older students is unrealistic. Indeed, to do so will only encourage students to lie and become deceptive.

Note: I would ask students in the primary years to leave their mobile phones at Reception during the school day (if the child owns one and brings it to school, as per the request of the parent).

 How can I guard against plagiarism when the internet has increased opportunities for pupils to be academically dishonest?

 José: The facile riposte is that plagiarism has always been an issue. Long before the internet, students copied from their dusty encyclopaedia or their library books. But this dismissal does not acknowledge or address the ease with which we all can feel seduced to pass other people's work as our own with a quick copy and paste. It would be tempting but fatuous to focus solely on what negative aspects the arrival of the internet has heightened without also considering the huge positive impact in terms of access to curriculum resources that it brings. From this perspective, a strong programme of digital citizenship and literacy (What are copyright and intellectual property? What do these concepts mean in a world where file-sharing is habitual?) that teaches students honesty, agency and to avoid using other people's work without acknowledgement is preferable to constant policing. Another advantage of such a programme would be to encourage students to become critical consumers of internet-sourced information. Arguably it is uncritical consumption of information – not plagiarism – that is the biggest problem facing old and young people alike in the age of fake news and social media-enabled echo chambers.

Neelam: Plagiarism is not new. It has been here before even the internet was even introduced. However, with the copious amount of information available online, it is easier for students to plagiarise and get away with it.

Most universities use a software called TurnitIn which can identify when a student has submitted work that is plagiarised. This would actually be a really good tool to bring down into GCSE and sixth form years so that the older students can ensure that the work they are handing in is original and referenced correctly. Another tool is to Google suspicious-sounding sentences which can highlight sentences that have been lifted out from online resources of student essays.

I would look at this as an opportunity to educate students to ensure honesty when they are producing their papers and insist on protecting academic integrity. This would be an ideal time to teach proper citation methods and discuss with students what is considered fair use and what is stealing.

How far do I need to be a digital spy in order to check that my pupils are using technology positively and not for things like bullying?

José: Pastoral care in schools encompasses so much more today than it did ten years ago. Social media has added an extra layer of extra complexity that many schools are finding difficult to accept. Yet this is the reality in which we live. Yes, social media can be used by bullies and for other nefarious motives. But social media can also bring hope, joy and satisfaction just as easily. Schools need to step up and educate the whole child, not just in maths, English and science, but also how to flourish and thrive in the society in which we live and not in an alternative reality in which the internet doesn't exist. Only then will students be equipped with the knowledge and skills to change that society for the better. Traditional interpretations of the problem of opportunity cost in our curricula often lead to focusing exclusively on curricular knowledge in the hope or belief that good citizenship would develop by unconscious assimilation, as the natural outcome of acquiring curricular knowledge in an academically rigorous environment. As a consequence, increasingly strict bans and sanctions proliferate in place of a truly supportive pastoral provision, one which tackles the behaviour, not the technology. As Steven Pinker once observed, wherever human behaviour is the problem, human behaviour is also the solution.

 Neelam: I am not sure the term 'digital spy' is appropriate in this context. I am currently the digital safeguarding lead in Ashford School and I believe it is important to keep your students safe. They are ultimately in our care during school hours and it is our responsibility to keep them safe from harm to achieve their well-being at all times.

A school's wi-fi filters should be controlled and able to filter out any inappropriate websites or links. Additionally, an email alert should be in place such that when inappropriate content or links are accessed, an email can be pinged to the designated safeguard lead who can follow it up with the child. As part of the school online agreement user policy (AUP), students should be aware that the school has access to read their emails or view their internet history, if the need arises. This is particularly useful in cases of cyberbullying when a trail of history can be accessed.

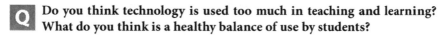 **Do you think technology is used too much in teaching and learning? What do you think is a healthy balance of use by students?**

José: I hope I can be forgiven for suggesting this is not a very good question on two counts. First is the implied assumption that there is a limit after which, if exceeded, technology is somehow bad for teaching and learning. Second is the implication that, to remain healthy, there needs to be a cap on how much technology we use. This approach biases our evaluation of the advantages or disadvantages of the use of technology by assigning intrinsic characteristics to technology – in this case harmfulness – and leads us to an ultimately fallacious argument about whether technology should be used at all. Since the notion that technology can support teaching and learning when used effectively is quite rightly not in dispute, instead the question should have sought to ascertain how teachers can use technology to support teaching and learning and how students can benefit from screen time by focusing on controlling, not the length of time students spend on their different devices, but, as Professor Livingstone of LSE suggests, how they spend that time. Pathologising technology use serves no practical purpose and obfuscates the more important question that we should be asking: how is technology useful?

Neelam: I think there are some schools where students are spending more time using technology and less time actually learning. I think it is necessary to use technology in teaching only when it complements, redefines or makes purposeful the lesson to enrich learning with students. While it is important to acquire technology-related skills, I think there is still much value in 'good teaching' and 'setting high expectations' for your students in order to make the lasting difference. The use of technology in learning is just the icing on the cake.

There are some schools that have managed to strike a very good balance with the use of educational technology. Teachers are using EdTech to enrich their pedagogical practices to better facilitate their marking, feedback and assessment or to facilitate content curation and flipped learning for their students.

See the Ashford Technology for Teaching Toolkit below.

Key Core Generic Applications School Wide – Technology for Teaching ToolKit

To facilitate marking, feedback and assessment	To facilitate content curation and delivery	To facilitate flipped learning (+ video casting)
Socrative	See Saw (Pre-Prep)	Explain Everything
Kahoot	Showbie (PS)	0365 Powerpoint Mix
0365 Forms	Firefly (SS)	Ashford Youtube
	(0365 One Note/Class Notebook – EduTeams).	

In return, students are able to use the technology to access their information and learn anytime, anywhere and anyhow. This is quite a powerful concept as it personalises a student's learning style. However, while the use of technology has the power to bring together students to communicate and collaborate virtually, it can never fully replace the face-to-face interaction that is offered by their teachers. There is just not an app for that.

 Do computers help long-term factual recall compared to paper?

 José: My assumption is that the question refers to the known fact that handwriting notes leads to better retention than typing the same notes on a computer. The question once again leads us down the rabbit hole to

another fallacious argument about whether technology should be used at all, as if typing is all that having a computer or mobile device available to you would allow you to achieve. If this assumption is correct, then, by focusing on the narrow point about handwriting, the question ignores how computers can be used to receive timely feedback, deliver curated content, promote the interleaving of topics and distributed learning, provide opportunities for retrieval practice, or redesign and improve the quality of the work teachers set. The notion that great teaching and the effective use of technology to support learning are somehow mutually exclusive is ultimately pernicious, as it stops us on our tracks from developing professionally by learning to incorporate whichever technology is appropriate to serve a given pedagogical purpose.

 Neelam: Computers – or some applications that are available – can aid in long-term factual recall. However, this is not to say that it is better or worse than using paper. The Quizlet app is a reflection of the flashcard paper-based approach and one that is used quite regularly with our MFL/EAL students who use it to help with memory recall. Students find it easier to use Quizlet with some teacher-based ready-made resources that they can use within an interactive game-like simulation to aid learning.

However, in research conducted by Pam A Mueller and Daniel M Oppenheimer at UCLA, findings indicate that putting pen to paper offers students a better grasp of understanding of what they have just learned and absorbed during a lesson', *versus* their peers who took notes on their mobile devices.[52] The scientists found that students who took handwritten notes scored higher on a test a week later, compared with those who typed in their notes. The results from the two experiments suggest that taking notes with pen to paper instead of on a laptop or mobile device leads to higher quality thinking and that the process of writing is a better strategy for storing and internalizing ideas, which encourages a person to express information in their own words.

 As a head of department, what advice would you give me on drafting a department policy on the use of technology in the classroom?

 José: If you're starting with 'The answer is technology ... what is the question again?', then you're almost certainly heading down the wrong path. Conversely, if you dismiss technology altogether as a distraction or a hindrance to learning, then you almost certainly don't have good

---

52. http://journals.sagepub.com/doi/abs/10.1177/0956797614524581

enough knowledge or understanding about technology in the context of teaching and learning to be able to think critically about technology adoption or avoidance in that context. In either case, being reflective and informing yourself about research findings and other teachers' practice is the best antidote against bad practice. When it comes to applying technology, give some thought to how the application of technology can support learning (access to content, enabling effective use of dual coding, facilitating retrieval practice, *etc*) and include recommendations in your schemes of work and programmes of study as to what technology could be used when and how. Be explicit in outlining how technology could be used to support learning but avoid being prescriptive. Give teachers the freedom to opt in or out. And above all, remember: technology use is only a gimmick if you make it one.

 Neelam: My advice here would be that you should ensure that you spend a good amount of time in this area to make sure that you have all the relevant policies in place and that there are no gaps in design. When developing a policy, it is good to consider all your stakeholders involved, from the SLT team to teachers and governors, and give importance to both student and parent voice. The role of student engagement when writing and developing online safety policies and practices is paramount.

Most schools should look to have one main ICT or technology-based policy covering areas of the scope of the technology policy, the roles and responsibilities of the designated leads/staff and areas of e-safety, mobile devices, social media, internet filtering, technical security along with all the necessary AUPs as required for the school. This policy needs to be read by all staff.

We have taken this one step further and also include a half-A4 summary of the *key* policy points below which we encourage staff, students and parents to read and sign online via our learning management systems.

- AUP ICT usage for pupils

- AUP ICT usage for staff

- AUP of Cameras and Hand Held Devices

- AUP of Mobile phones for pupils

- AUP of Mobile Phones for staff

There is also good value in adding a flowchart to showcase how any incidents of misuse of technology are actioned so that processes are already set in place when a problem arises.

 My school has a 'bring your own device' policy. How can I make best use of this?

 José: In a mixed-device environment, the common denominator is access to online resources. On the one hand, I would organise my departmental resources so that they could be accessed online and shared digitally by teachers and pupils (with different level of access). This ubiquitous access to curated content can facilitate self-regulation and other metacognitive strategies that have been shown to benefit learning. The mere presence of technology does not generate better learning, but how the teachers adapt their practice slightly to harness the presence of devices for a positive impact that matters. On the other hand, I would also investigate ways in which I could review assessment. For example, technology allows us to create banks of low-stakes tests that self-mark (reducing teacher workload) and that can be used by teachers to evaluate progress and inform their practice and by students as a learning aid (frequent retrieval practice). There is a plethora of tools and online resources that allow you to create reusable quizzes, flashcards, tests and assessments.

Neelam: BYOD is a great way for schools to incorporate the use of mobile technology in teaching and learning as a cost-effective solution. While there have been some schools that have integrated BYOD with no problems, there have been others who have struggled with a multitude of issues.

From an IT perspective, I would say that there are three main areas to think about when considering going BYOD:

1. Ensure your school wireless network can cope with a multitude of users because if not, it can easily become overloaded and crash. Many school wireless network solutions are not currently designed to handle the amount of activity and number of devices that will be using up bandwidth in BYOD environments. So ensure that your IT infrastructure can cope with a significant number of devices otherwise the whole BYOD strategy will fail.

2. Keeping children safe on your internet filters is a big challenge. While your school may have restrictions on the types of sites the students can access using your wi-fi filters, children are curious and will find a way to skirt around the system to get to what they

want. Most of the time, they just want to push the boundaries to see if they can, without any malicious intentions.

With a BYOD strategy in place, it is paramount to keep up to date with your security filters and incorporate sophisticated tech so that the IT team are able to view what is being used on their network, which sites/apps are accessed and which applications students are using based on their roles and permissions.

3. With a multitude of devices onsite will come a whole range of issues and problems with the devices. It becomes very difficult for teachers and/or IT staff to have solutions for them all. My advice here will be to set up a BYOD policy to state exactly what IT support will be offered and what is not. Ultimately, it is the responsibility of the student to get their devices fixed and serviced.

From a teaching and learning perspective, students will have their own personal apps and technology that they use fluently within their own devices. Teachers will have to begin to trust their students' own innovation and initiative when assigning project tasks and delivery.

How can I help my students minimise the distraction that can be caused by their tech?

José: Technically, it is possible to use filters and device managers that can help to focus students' interaction with technology, but this is most effectively achieved when accompanied by the provision of the academic resources required by students to put tech to work for learning. Allowing students to bring devices to school but not altering the way in which teachers assess learning or deliver content is a recipe for distraction. Numerous studies have shown that, when this is the case, no improvement in learning takes place. In this scenario, you would be better off avoiding devices altogether. If, however, you provide reasons and means for students to engage with technology for academic purposes, the result is that said technology ceases to be viewed and used solely as a tool for leisure, as it would otherwise be the case. In contexts where technology use is focused on academic purposes, teachers don't relinquish control over to technology; instead they control how the technology is used. This way, technology does not stand in opposition to learning; it supports it, while students develop agency and learn effective ways to manage their distractions, which is a key skill in this day and age.

Neelam: I advise all students to create technology breaks when they study.

By this, I mean putting your phone/mobile device/tech away for a full 30 minutes. At this point, all technology is turned off including TV and music (although I understand some children study better with music). If they cannot last five minutes and are looking as though they will have a nervous breakdown, they can start with five minutes first, catch up with their tech, another 10 minutes and so on until they can slowly increase the time, moving up to 15 and then 30 minutes.

Research has found that students do not like to be disconnected longer than 30 minutes. The reason for this is that children live in a constantly connected world. They suffer from fear of missing out (FOMO) and would rather multi-task than not know what they are missing out on.

I'm a self-confessed Luddite but would like to use more technology. What's the best way to get more engaged with it?

José: Being a self-confessed Luddite is not an intellectually robust position to take. It's a bit like confessing proudly that you're terrible at maths, what a lark, or that, isn't it funny, you're terrible at spelling or grammar. Nobody should feel they can self-confess to such illiteracy and expect sympathy. Having said that, it is possible to avoid using a lot of technology as a teacher in the classroom but encourage your students to be its primary users. This way, even if you feel you've not yet caught up with technology yourself, you can allow your students to take advantage of its benefits while you reflect on your practice. Content delivery, tests and quizzes are all pedagogically sound ways for your students to use technology. As a self-confessed Luddite who doesn't really understand how technology can be used to support learning you could be prone to using technology as a gimmick, undermining your teaching and cheating your students out of learning. This generates a vicious circle in which your attitude is supported by your experience. Luckily for us all, as with many other self-confessed admissions of inadequacy, greater knowledge is the cure.

Neelam: Initially, I would suggest you find an area of your teaching practices that you would like to improve. This could be anything from improving feedback for students to reducing the amount of printing or even the dire need to photocopy worksheets that students paste into their workbooks. While this may not impact directly on the students' learning at first, this will help the teacher see the value of using technology in a positive manner.

For example, I had a teacher who just could not bear the idea of photocopying another worksheet so one day she decided that she had had enough, and if technology was the answer to some of these types of problems, she was going to try it out. Unbeknown to me, she decided to AirDrop photos of her maths homework/worksheets to her students' devices after each lesson. This worked really well and she managed to get rid of printing homework for her students. The children were happy to accommodate to this new way of working and if anything preferred it to the copious amounts of paper they originally received.

We were then able to take this further by introducing Showbie, the virtual classroom platform, in which resources, materials, homework, feedback, marking and assessment can also be stored and shared between participants in one area. This meant that she would now have a history of the sequence of tasks and activities that was assigned to the class over the year.

The students find working in this way much easier and more productive. They receive faster and richer feedback (voice based) and never have an excuse for not having resources, materials or tasks at hand. Teachers appreciate this new tool as it has streamlined all their teaching workflows in one place and it always works.

 What are the most useful apps for learning?

 José: The notion that technology is intrinsically good or bad for learning is one which I strongly dispute. It is how technology is used that produces good or bad outcomes. This applies to apps too. There are numerous apps that can support learning in the school context, but only if its use is guided expertly by a teacher. Delegating teaching to a computer or an app does not generally result in improved outcomes. However, there are many apps that, when used appropriately, can support good practice in teaching and learning by enhancing that which we know works in the school context: the provision of effective, timely feedback (Showbie); the fostering of self-regulation (Calendar, Homework Apps) and metacognition (Explain Everything); or access to frequent retrieval practice tests and quizzes (Quizlet), just to name a few. But the wisest thing for any aspiring user of technology to remember is this: there is no app for great teaching.

Neelam: This is a difficult question to answer because there are so many valuable apps out there in the market. If I were to break down this question into two bits, there are apps that are beneficial in a teaching environment (see the Toolkit on p.194) and those that are helpful in learning (see below). However, there is a crossover between the two areas and some of the teaching apps above such as Kahoot or Explain Everything are just as beneficial to a learner.

So to answer the question as simply as I can and to showcase what we at Ashford School use to enrich learning, please see below:

Prep	Senior School (plus Prep)	Generic
TT Rockstars – timetables	Explain Everything	All the Office 365 apps – Microsoft package plus Forms, One Drive, OneNote and ClassNotebook.
Duo Lingo – Green Screen	Showbie app	
Math Fight – Fraction app	Quizlet app	
See-Saw to Showbie app	Periodic app	
Google Maps	Wolfram Alpha	
Morpho	GeoAlgebra	
Book Creator	GCSE Pod	
Pic Collage	Firefly app	
Yakit	Mendeley	
Duo Lingo	Twitter, BBC, Linkedin	
iMovie	Popplett	
Garageband	Pinterest	
Kindle	Notes app	
GarageBand		
QR Reader		
Nearpod		

> INDEPENDENT LEARNING MIGHT BE A DESIRED OUTCOME BUT PARADOXICALLY, IT MAY NOT BE THE BEST WAY TO ACHIEVE THAT OUTCOME. FOR NOVICES IN PARTICULAR, INDEPENDENCE DOES NOT SEEM TO BE THE BEST WAY TO BECOME INDEPENDENT.

> IT STANDS TO REASON THAT IN ORDER TO ACHIEVE SOMETHING INDEPENDENTLY, WE NEED TO BE MOTIVATED TO DO IT BUT IF MOTIVATION IS SEEN NOT AS A CAUSE BUT RATHER AS A CONSEQUENCE OF ACHIEVEMENT (WILIAM, 2011) THEN FOR WANT OF A BETTER PHRASE, EXPLICITLY DOING THE THING THAT YOU WANT TO ACHIEVE MIGHT NOT BE THE BEST WAY TO ACHIEVE THAT THING.

> IF STUDENTS DO NOT HAVE SOPHISTICATED SCHEMAS OF KNOWLEDGE ABOUT A PARTICULAR AREA THEN IT IS VERY HARD FOR THEM TO TRULY WORK INDEPENDENTLY IN THAT PARTICULAR AREA. THIS CAN RESULT IN SHALLOW TASKS AS THE ACTIVITY IS MATCHED TO WHAT THE STUDENT KNOWS.

> IN A VERY REAL SENSE, STUDENTS CANNOT THINK CRITICALLY ABOUT THINGS THEY DO NOT KNOW.

'How wonderful that we have met with a paradox. Now we have some hope of making progress.'

Niels Bohr

The Independent learning paradox

Independent learning is probably one of the most common aims in school development plans. Most educators would want to see students leaving school with a robust ability to self-regulate, to plan and see through long-term projects and an enhanced ability to cope with challenge and adversity. However, as we have seen in this book, one of the more consistent findings of research on learning is just how counterintuitive it is.

Firstly, consider motivation, a key component of independence. It stands to reason that in order to achieve something independently, we need to be motivated to do it; but as we saw in chapter 5, if motivation is seen not as a cause but rather as a *consequence* of achievement,then for want of a better phrase, *explicitly doing the thing that you want to achieve might not be the best way to achieve that thing.* In other words, independent learning might be a desired outcome, but paradoxically, it may not be the best way to achieve that outcome.

Secondly, consider the most common vehicle of independent learning: minimally guided instruction. This often takes the form of low levels of teacher talk, students working in groups independently on projects and problem-solving, and, increasingly, technology being used to enable what is often referred to as 'personalised learning'. Now again, many would probably agree that these are desired outcomes but there is evidence to suggest that for students, using these approaches to get to the 'sunlit uplands' of independent learning might not be optimal:

> Two bodies of research reveal the weakness of partially and minimally guided approaches: research comparing pedagogies and research on how people learn. The past half century of empirical research has provided overwhelming and unambiguous evidence that, for everyone but experts, partial guidance during instruction is significantly less effective and efficient than full guidance.[53]

As chapter 6 showed, this can be accounted for in no small measure by the limitations of working memory. If students do not have sophisticated schemas

---

53. Clark, R., Kirschner, P. and Sweller, J. (2012) 'Putting Students on the Path to Learning', *American Educator*, p.7 www.aft.org/sites/default/files/periodicals/Clark.pdf

of knowledge about a particular area then it is very hard for them to truly work independently in that particular area. This can result in shallow tasks as the activity is matched to what the student knows. As Daisy Christodoulou notes, in English writing lessons this can manifest itself in less than ideal ways: 'The only way for independent learning to be practicable is for pupils to work with knowledge they already know; that is, to write letters about school uniforms or their local area.'[54.] For novices, independence does not seem to be the best way to become independent.

Generic v domain-specific skills

Independent learning is often referred to as generic skills that can be applied in a range of contexts. However, there is considerable evidence that many of these skills are domain-specific and highly dependent on the context in which students are working (Neber and Schommer-Aikins, 2002). For example, one pupil might display a high degree of motivation and self-regulation in biology but not in French and *vice versa*. Of course, critical thinking is an essential part of a student's mental equipment. However, it cannot be detached from context. Teaching students generic 'thinking skills' separately from the rest of their curriculum is often a less than optimal approach, as Daniel Willingham notes:

> If you remind a student to "look at an issue from multiple perspectives" often enough, he will learn that he ought to do so, but if he doesn't know much about an issue, he *can't* think about it from multiple perspectives ... critical thinking (as well as scientific thinking and other domain-based thinking) is not a skill. There is not a set of critical thinking skills that can be acquired and deployed regardless of context.[55]

In a very real sense, students cannot think critically about things they do not know. Thinking critically about the French Revolution, for example, means knowing about the social inequality heightened by an unequal system of taxation, the harvest failures that led to food shortages and the legacy of Enlightenment ideals that gave rise to revolutionary fervour against the *Ancien Régime*. Without sufficient knowledge of all of these factors, it's very difficult to think critically abt the causes of the French Revolution without resorting to guesswork and misapprehension. As Willingham writes: 'Thought processes are intertwined with what is being thought about.' Students need to be given real and significant things from the world to think with and about, if teachers want to influence how they do that thinking.

---

54. Christodoulou, D. (2014) *Seven myths about education,* Routledge, p.37
55. www.tandfonline.com/doi/abs/10.3200/AEPR.109.4.21-32

Independent Learning: a continuum not a spectrum

Independent learning is something that can develop over time; as the expertise of the learner increases so the teacher can reduce the extent of guidance that is being offered. It would be lovely if it happened in a nice, linear process that is predictable and smooth. Sadly, this isn't the case. This is because independent learning looks different at different stages, and develops as a continuum rather than having the nature of a spectrum.

> The dynamic of the continuum is a shift in responsibility between learner and teacher, so that by degrees the learner assumes greater responsibility for directing his or her own learning and negotiating strategies and processes with the teacher. For movement to take place along the continuum, together with the transfer of responsibility there must be a development of independent learning skills by the child.[56]

How do we get students to make these shifts in responsibility? This is a difficult step and will certainly involve a degree of mental stress (and possibly emotional stress) for the pupil. It's what Robert Bjork styles 'desirable difficulties', meaning that learning is pitched at an optimal level so that the pupil is able to generate an answer using acquired knowledge, without the level of challenge being beyond them. The curious thing about this stage is that acquisition of knowledge actually sees a slowing down effect – a period of cognitive struggle – that then leads to better long-term retention. We actually want to keep students in this phase for as long as we can so that the quality of retention and later performance is improved. This is how steps are made along the continuum, and being able to slow things down at the right moment is crucial to progress. A good maxim for this process comes from the excellent book *Make it Stick*: 'When learning is easy, it is often superficial and soon forgotten.'[57]

What we have done with this section is pose the same simple question to all of the people interviewed in this book: 'What does independent learning look like in the classroom?' This is, therefore, the most in-depth single question in this book. What you will see from the answers that follow is that the process required to reach independence is counter-intuitive; the desired independence is the means rather than the end. Independence is something that is achieved and exercised by experts, and our students will have a long way to go to reach this level of ability. What we do as teachers along the way is vital, and requires

56. Meyer, W. R. (2010) 'Independent Learning: a literature review and new project', p.12
57. Brown, P., Roediger III, H. and McDaniel, A. (2014) *Make it Stick*, Harvard University Press, p.226

a lot of scaffolding. It is therefore a long process – as Martin Robinson states, it may take a good five to six years. We also face difficulties in measuring this because, as Dianne Murphy notes, for true independence to exist it must be outside the classroom, when we are not there. This remains the holy grail for educators, and is worthy of substantial discussion as a teaching body. Is there a culture of learning that can foster independence?

INDEPENDENT LEARNING

CHAPTER 10

❝ AQ

WITH THESE RESEARCH INSIGHTS IN MIND, OUR STUDENTS SELF-TESTING (MAYBE IT IS BY USING FLASHCARDS, OR RECONSTRUCTING THEIR NOTES GRAPHIC ORGANISER STYLE) OR QUIZZING THEMSELVES IS PROBABLY WHAT EFFECTIVE INDEPENDENT LEARNING LOOKS LIKE.

❝ DD

NEGLECTING TO SCAFFOLD THROWS PUPILS IN AT THE DEEP END BEFORE THEY'RE READY TO SWIM.

❝ LC

IF CHILDREN ARE GOING TO GET ON WITH INDEPENDENT WORK, IT IS IMPORTANT THAT THIS IS BUILT UP IN SMALL STEPS, GIVING CHILDREN THE CHANCE TO DEVELOP THE SKILLS REQUIRED TO SELF-DIRECT.

❝ DC

I THINK INDEPENDENT LEARNING IS IN SOME WAYS THE ULTIMATE AIM OF EDUCATION, BUT THAT DOESN'T MEAN IT SHOULD MAKE UP THE METHOD.

❝ DL

FOR ME THE MOST IMPORTANT PART OF INDEPENDENT LEARNING IS WRITING; IT'S THE COIN OF THE REALM.

❝ DM

TO SOME EXTENT "INDEPENDENT LEARNING IN THE CLASSROOM" IS A CONTRADICTION.

❝ MR

WHAT IT'S ABOUT IS GIVING STRUCTURE, GIVING RITUALS, GIVING WAYS OF DOING, WAYS OF SEEING, WAYS OF THINKING, WAYS OF ARGUING, WAYS OF DEBATING, WAYS OF READING, WAYS OF WRITING.

Q Do teachers have the support to apply pedagogical methods that will increase the opportunities for independence? Above all, do school leaders have the patience to allow for the long process that all of this entails? We hope the following answers will light the touch paper on such discussions, and we welcome feedback on what our readers think about it. A lot of work needs to be done for this to be more effectively embedded across the profession.

Alex Quigley: As a school leader and teacher I've spent years looking at lessons and seeking out learning. I used to think that my students being busy simply equated with lots of learning happening, or that a well-placed plenary cured all ills. Now I recognise that observing learning in the classroom is devilishly hard and that the best job I can do is spot learning proxies occurring over time.

Q So what proxies make for effective independent learning?

Well, a lot of effective independent learning is the act of reading and finding out more about a given topic, so a student who asks pertinent questions and reveals answers in their verbal contributions in class is likely exhibiting the results of effective independent learning. If they are good at asking questions and engaging thoughtfully in debate and dialogue then they are likely exhibiting the hard thinking that best characterises independent learning.

We know from the vast research synthesised by Dunlosky *et al*[58] that effective independent learning often looks a little different from what our students *think* works. With these research insights in mind, our students self-testing (maybe it is by using flashcards, or reconstructing their notes graphic organiser style) or quizzing themselves is probably what effective independent learning looks like.

Ultimately, we should stop looking to *see* independent learning and instead aim to foster really effective study habits that students carry with them everywhere and change more fundamentally how they think.

Daisy Christodoulou: My worry and my concern with independent learning is that independent learning for me is an aim and it isn't always necessarily mastered. I think independent learning is in some ways the

58. Dunlosky, J., Rawson, K. A., Marsh, E. J., Nathan, M. J., & Willingham, D. T. (2013) 'Improving students' learning with effective learning techniques: promising directions from cognitive and educational psychology', *Psychological Science in the Public Interest,* 14(1), pp.4–58.

ultimate aim of education, but that doesn't mean it should make up the method. I think we can get in a bit of a paradox in that we can end up with pupils sort of always being told that they are independent learners and actually never developed the skills and knowledge they need to be independent learners. So I think people do need some guidance particularly when starting out on a topic and particularly when they're novices, then they really need some guidance to help them avoid the common misconceptions.

I think the paradox is that the things that make you a good independent learner don't necessarily look like independent learning. If I look at, say, a Primary class where a pupil is good in phonics, that's a really teacher-led activity, it's highly interactive, so the pupils are responding and you're recording the response over time. It doesn't really look that independent, but I would argue the pupils are learning a skill that will enable them to learn independently for life, because they're learning how to do context.

Similarly, the earlier parts of the English mastery unit on *A Midsummer Night's Dream* involve quite a lot of teacher-led call and response work on who loves who at which point, what's the relationship between the characters, and that doesn't look very independent at those moments. The pupils are responding to what their teacher has put in there, but by the end of that unit those pupils are able to talk independently about how at the end of *A Midsummer Night's Dream* Demetrius has lost his feelings because he's not in love with the woman he loved at the start of the play and the love potion has changed his reality. At the end of that unit those pupils have quite independent discussions about whether it's better to be happy and living a lie or whether it's best to be unhappy but know the truth. They have quite independent discussions with each other and with the teacher about those, so I would argue such independent discussion and independent learning is predicated on a lot of the teacher-led instruction that's done in previous lessons.

Sometimes when teachers and other people come in and see them having those great discussions or they read the work they've written, they see that and they think, 'Wow, that's amazing. How do I get my pupils to be like that?', but sometimes what it takes to get the pupils to that level looks quite different from what their final output looks like.

 David Didau: The difficulty here is that some schools have confused the means with the end. We all want students to go off into the world and flourish – or at the very least, we want them to be able to take their exams without us having to cheat – but if we try to make our students more independent by forcing them to work without instruction, then we are more likely to make them dependent.

If we really want our students to be independent then we should start by explaining a new concept, its subject-specific vocabulary and how it connects to those things pupils have already learned. When this exposition is complete and pupils' basic understanding is secure, we then move on to demonstrating a model of how this concept might be applied and deconstructing the ways in which it was put together. Once these processes are clear, we can then move on to providing a scaffold to enable pupils to apply the knowledge they have learned. Then, when pupils have achieved a minimum standard of control over these processes, we can allow them, with clear guidance and feedback, to practise independently. And finally, when they have mastered the skill they have practised, it is time to connect new concepts and increased complexity; the cycle begins again.

It should be clear that no part of this sequence is really possible without any other part. If you've failed to explain the concept you wish pupils to learn, then they will be confused and quickly become lost. If you don't explicitly model how to apply this new knowledge, then the process will remain mysterious; some will pick it up but many won't. Neglecting to scaffold throws pupils in at the deep end before they're ready to swim. The arm bands offered by a competent teacher provide a much-needed feeling of safety and equip pupils with the ability to take risks within a safe environment. Not allowing pupils to practise prevents them from encoding the knowledge they've learned, and the opportunity to transfer concepts from working to long-term memory is missed.

This may seem obvious, but it doesn't reflect the way many teachers feel they are expected to teach. Or perhaps it does; in many schools it has become an expectation that each part of this cycle should be (briefly) included in one 50-60 minute lesson. The madness inherent in believing that learning takes place in neat, lesson-shaped chunks has resulted in the four-part lesson and the reluctant acceptance that if we want to please observers we must perform the Monkey Dance and conceal the (essential) parts of our teaching that certain people seem not to approve of. Skipping over the fundamental need to explain, model and scaffold in order to demonstrate the 'preferred' method of minimal teacher talk and independent learning for its own sake may have done more to damage children's education than any other single idea.

Dianne Murphy: To some extent 'independent learning in the classroom' is a contradiction. If learning is taking place in a classroom, it cannot be considered truly independent since the teacher is responsible for organising the learning environment. Truly independent learning is that which takes place apart from institutions and people to oversee the learning.

What we generally mean by independent learning is that students have enough confidence and capability to work for extended periods without prompting or help. To reach this level, students will:

- Have the required foundational skills and knowledge required for the task.

- Have passed through the stages of learning required for mastery (acquisition, accuracy, fluency, retention and generalisation).

- Have sufficient intrinsic motivation to attempt and persist at the task.

- Have a clear sense of the standard required for competency.

As teachers we often focus on the last two and then wonder why students struggle to be 'independent', when they have gaps in the pre-requisite knowledge or have not mastered the skills required by the task. Close analysis of what we want the student to learn and close assessment of their levels of competency are required in order to establish such 'independent' learning. (For more on these topics, see Engelmann, 1991; White and Haring, 1980; Alberto and Troutman, 1986; Kamee'nui & Simmons, 1990)

 Doug Lemov: For me the most important part of independent learning is writing; it's the coin of the realm. You don't really have an idea until you can write about it. Both because that's how you have to present your ideas at university and professional level and because the level of rigour is higher. So for me, any activity that ends with students writing independently about it allows them to distil and reflect on the idea. I don't think that's how most people define it. I think they define it as being without the teacher's direct oversight. But for me, writing is usually an independent activity. Being independent means being able to write it.

 Dylan Wiliam: Different people define independent learning in different ways. If you look at the self-regulated learning research, there are some people who say that this should only apply to something the child has already decided to learn; in other words, 'I want students to be able to learn independently in the things that they want to learn' but I think we need to go a bit further than that. In school, we need students to learn stuff that they don't necessarily want to learn. I think we also need to broaden it out. I think that's why Deci and Ryan's self-determination theory is quite useful. The idea is that we should get students to understand why it's important they get good at certain stuff, even if they don't enjoy it, even if they don't like it. It's important to their future success, so we need students to become effective managers of their own learning, even when they're learning things they don't particularly value and wouldn't choose to do, other than the fact that they need the qualification.

Then, I think we should share with our students what we're learning about how we learn, for example through the work of Bjork, Roediger and Karpicke, which is dealt with very effectively by Benedict Carey in his book *How We Learn*. In other words, we need to give our students a user manual for the brain. For example, many people have picked up on Angela Lee Duckworth's concept of grit and they're reinforcing to their students how important it is that students stick at stuff. That's true, but it's also important to realise that you might be stuck and the best thing to do might be to stop banging your head against a brick wall and go and take a walk. I think, for me, a good independent learner is somebody who knows about how the brain works, about the value of practice testing, about how when you're stuck, the best thing to do is take a break.

For example, most of us have had the experience of reading a page and realising that we haven't actually taken in any of the content. What I'm suggesting is that we should be talking to our students about these ideas – getting our students to consider, 'Am I learning this stuff? Is it going in? Am I reading this line and skimming over the page?' I think that sharing with our students what I sometimes describe as a 'user manual' for the brain would be valuable and could go a long way towards creating independent learners.

Now in all this, it is important to recognise that there are also huge differences in our students' abilities. Some of our students have brains that seem to absorb the kinds of things we value in school learning with relatively little effort, while others find it much more difficult. This is a fact about the world. It's not a pleasant fact. I wish that everybody had the same abilities to learn, but that's not what we observe. The important point is that every student learns the kinds of things that they need to do to maximise the effectiveness of their own learning efforts. Moreover, I think that we know enough about this to make it a coherent part of any school curriculum.

 Jill Berry: To me, independent learning is about learners taking responsibility and initiative, thinking for themselves, going beyond what is demanded of them and showing self-efficacy with respect to their education. If we can encourage this kind of approach among school-age children, then there is clearly a greater likelihood that they will continue on their learning journey well beyond school.

In the classroom we need to do what we can to foster this approach, so that students understand that the work we ask of them doesn't simply need to be completed to get the teacher off their back! It isn't about doing the minimum, getting by without too much effort and exertion. It's about having high aspirations that relate to our pride in a learning task well done. It's about being committed to doing our best because we find learning energising, fascinating, rewarding. We want to learn and we want to stretch ourselves and test what we are capable of. We want to grow as learners, and as people. We want to BE our best.

This, to me, is at the root of independent learning.

Lucy Crehan: In East Asia, there are timetabled lessons for independent study. In these lessons, children quietly get on with work they have been set by their teachers, and teachers use the opportunity to work with students one-on-one where they need it. Is independent learning a different thing? I don't think so. The practice and the application of what students have been taught in the lessons are part of the learning. In the lessons, it looks a little different. In top-performing countries ranging from Finland to Japan, I saw lessons in which the teacher would have a very clear idea of what she wanted the children to learn, with some carefully planned questions and activities to get children thinking. In Japan, the teacher would often start with a problem or question that got the children interested, and that they would be able to solve or answer by the end of the lesson. In Singapore, I saw a lesson in which the teacher set them a question which she wouldn't even answer at the end of the lesson, encouraging them to go home and think about it further.

What I did not see much of was children set independent, different work, that they were left to get on with by themselves during lessons. That is not to say that this would be a bad thing, just that I did not see much of it in countries that prepare their children well for tests in the application of reading, maths and science. Japan experimented with such an approach a little while ago, when they were concerned that their students were working too hard, and introduced a timetabled period in which students would work independently on a project of their choice. This worked well for the 'more able' children (in quotation marks because I don't believe this is a permanent feature of the child but a current state), but those who didn't have the skills to do this used the time to doodle or sleep, rather than doing anything productive. Perhaps the obvious conclusion to draw from this is that if children are going to get on with independent work, it is important that this is built up in small steps, giving children the chance to develop the skills required to self-direct.

Maggie Snowling: It's as much about personality and self-discipline as it is about learning ability. I think it's important because over the last couple of decades there's been an increasing amount of spoon-feeding in schools and indeed in universities where students want to be told what to do as opposed to, 'How can I be really interested in this subject and go out and learn independently and bring my own ideas and actually then excel?' In a university context, independent learning project work requires supervision, regular meetings with a supervisor or mentor who is overseeing the work. Probably that person should be looking at the plan, and monitoring regularly where the student is with the plan and discussing and actively critically appraising that work. In a school context I don't know how frequent that would be, but obviously that needs to be timetabled. Students that have difficulty with this are the sort of kids with either learning problems, or attentional problems. Procrastination is the worst problem with them.

Martin Robinson: At the beginning, it doesn't look like independent learning. It depends very much again on the subject area. Let's use the analogy of riding a bike. You're holding the saddle, they've got those stabilisers on, they've got a crash helmet on. They've got the support network shouting at them, 'You can do it, you can do it,' and all this stuff going on. So you've got them held very close. At the end, they're cycling by themselves on the road, looking after themselves and they've got to that point. Between those two pictures is the slow letting-go. It's a very slow letting-go, so it might take five years. Whatever you do, it doesn't look like throwing a kid into independent work with no structure whatsoever. What it's about is giving structure, giving rituals, giving ways of doing, ways of seeing, ways of thinking, ways of arguing, ways of debating, ways of reading, ways of writing. All these structures you're giving them, slowly, slowly letting them go on each, until you've built up the point where some of them are more independent than others, until you get to a point where they're all independent. Independence is a process, not looking in the classroom, saying 'Oh, they're all independent' I'm talking about a five-year process, six-year process.

Neelam Parmar: Independent learning, within the context of Educational Technology, is not dissimilar to the more traditional thinking for encouraging our learners to take charge of their own learning journey.

Independent learning is a process, a philosophy in which a learner acquires his/her knowledge by his/her own efforts and develops the ability over time to enquire and critically analyse information.

Based on the definition above, one of the prerequisites of independent learning is the ability for our students to work on their own, solve problems by themselves and complete tasks with minimal direction from the teacher. In an age where there is information readily on the internet, a teacher should be able to assign a task or specific project work, and be able to take a back seat in offering copious amount of information, while work alongside them as a facilitator, steering the content and providing extension, as necessary.

There is no doubt that we want our students to become independent learners who are motivated and responsible for their own learning. Listed below are a few examples of how best to utilise EdTech to help promote independent learning in the classroom:

1. Offer students flipped learning lessons so that they can carry on their studies and interests outside the classroom.

2. Encourage group work so that learners can work together and connect anywhere and anytime – particularly useful for when they are inspired and have a sudden stroke of genius.

3. Give students choices in how they wish to complete their tasks/ homework so that they can reflect on their interests and/or demonstrate their own skills and experiences, *eg* using Popplet to brainstorm, creating a video to illustrate their thought processes, running a podcast or blog *etc*.

Nick Rose: What independent learning looks like in the classroom starts with a great deal of scaffolding from the teacher, because independence isn't something that you can do straight off. Particularly in the kind of subject areas that we teach within schools, I'm particularly thinking in terms of science teaching.

I've seen what it doesn't look like. So for instance I once had to moderate a piece of BTEC course work on making uses of energy in the body and what this student had done which was clear from the real care in terms of the presentation and the initial effort that they'd put into it, that this was a really keen student, who really wanted to do well within a particular subject area, of course when it came to answering the question of what does energy look like when it is in the body, she clearly clicked on Google and found all sorts of alternative medicine sites that said things like 'energy is an invisible, spiritual substance that flows through chi channels in the body, which can be unblocked through acupuncture' and all these kinds of things whereas what the actual question wanted to know about was like respiration, ATP, and metabolism and aspects of biology.

So what independent learning doesn't look like is kids crammed around a computer looking things up on Google. It's a scaffolded process where the teacher provides a great deal of guidance and structure to begin with, and probably scaffolds with work examples and partial solutions, so that students are more capable of practising whatever their particular kind of learning is more independently on their own. Working towards independence may involve quite a lot of teacher guidance and scaffolding but eventually students will be able to practise all of the things independently on their own. You may have to see the teacher running around the room trying to explain it to 30 students individually because they all have a fairly strong idea of what they are trying to do within their independent practice.

Paul Kirschner: The only classroom in which independent learning really works is a classroom of experts who already know what they know, know what they don't know, and know what they need to know in order to solve the problem at hand. And by definition, that's not a student.

A student is by definition a novice. It's that simple. And that doesn't mean they're worth less or they are less, but they're a student and you have to instruct them properly. And at certain points give them the leeway to make use of what you've taught them without you constantly standing in front of the class and lecturing; a teacher that only stands in front of the classroom and lectures is a fish and chips shop instead of a three-star Michelin restaurant.

Instruction means making a holy trinity when it comes to teaching. It requires a certain amount of deep knowledge and skills by the teacher of the tools, techniques, and ingredients of the teaching trade just like it does for a chef with respect to cooking, so just as a chef makes tasty, good-looking and nutritious meals, a teacher makes an effective, efficient and enjoyable learning experience. They both make proper use of tools, techniques and ingredients in carrying out their professions.

 Pedro de Bruyckere: This is a tricky question to answer for two reasons. Firstly it is difficult to see when people are actually learning and secondly it's very difficult to define what independent means. Professor Coe already described different bad proxies for learning, explaining that your pupils being busy, engaged or motivated doesn't mean they are actually learning. But is a pupil who is working in silent on a task given by you working independently? Would the pupil be working if you hadn't asked him or her? I do think it's important that children and young people learn to learn independently. That they have an attitude to look things up or to ask stuff if they don't know. I really like the situation when their brains are getting short-circuited and they want to solve it by learning. But maybe the answer is simpler than I thought: whenever a child surprises you with insights that weren't your objective but that are great, it has learned independently.

Tom Bennett: Independent learning is something that is rightly prized as an indication that students are working at a high level of self-awareness, self-regulation, and motivation. Unfortunately, many people mistake this desired outcome for a process, and cause a good deal of damage to students' educations along the way. IL is something you hope students will eventually achieve. But attempting to stimulate it by excessively expecting students to be capable of it before they are ready is a mistake.

Learners – especially novice learners – require explicit, guided instruction as the primary method of pedagogy. And learners with only basic behavioural skills need to be similarly guided into useful and successful habits of behaviour that will maximise their classroom experiences. There is no point expecting a pupil with low self-control to behave simply because they are given the chance to act poorly or not. Rather, correct standards of behaviour must be clearly drawn, modelled, and then repeated, until they become habit. At this point, the pupil may be said to be ready for independent learning, safe in the knowledge that they will successfully manage the autonomy and choice that can both paralyse and intoxicate a less-disciplined mind.

The independent learner is a sign that successful teaching has taken place; it is not a vehicle to achieve itself.

ROBIN AND CARL INTRODUCE

11 CONCLUSION

CHAPTER

> AT ITS BEST, RESEARCH SHOULD ACT AS A BULWARK, A SEA-WALL AGAINST THE TIDAL WAVE OF EDU-GUFF THAT HAS SO OFTEN WASHED OVER OUR SCHOOLS.

> RESEARCH CAN NEVER TELL TEACHERS PRECISELY WHAT TO DO IN THE CLASSROOM; THERE ARE TOO MANY VARIABLES AND CHAOTIC ELEMENTS FOR IT TO BE SO PRESCRIPTIVE. HOWEVER IT CAN POINT TOWARD A SERIES OF 'BEST BETS' THAT MAY YIELD BETTER OUTCOMES THAN MERE HUNCHES OR FOLK WISDOM.

> TEACHERS DON'T NEED TO BE THE RESEARCHERS, THEY JUST NEED TO BE RESEARCH-INFORMED. TO DO THIS EFFECTIVELY IT DOES HELP ENORMOUSLY TO KNOW HOW TO CRITIQUE ANY PIECE OF RESEARCH, BY ASKING QUESTIONS LIKE WHAT BASELINE EVIDENCE EXISTS, AND WERE COUNTERFACTUALS EXPLORED?

> THE PEOPLE WHO SPEND THE MOST TIME DELIVERING LESSONS NEED TO HAVE A VOICE, AND AN OPPORTUNITY TO DEVELOP AS PROFESSIONALS. IF YOU CAN GIVE THEM BOTH OF THESE THINGS THE IMPACT ON PUPILS WILL BE TANGIBLE.

The Abilene Paradox or why schools do things nobody actually wants

On an indecently hot day in Texas, Professor Jerry B Harvey was visiting his wife's family when his father-in-law suggested that they visit a new restaurant in the town of Abilene, to which his wife exclaimed 'sounds like a great idea'. Harvey had reservations about this, however, as a 53-mile trip in a car with no air-conditioning sounded terrible to him, but not wanting to rock the boat he also claimed this to be a 'great idea' and asked his mother-in-law if she wanted to go. As she was now the only one in the group who had not yet expressed agreement with this 'great idea', she also exclaimed that they should go, and so they began their journey to Abilene. As Harvey explains, the trip was not a success:

> My predictions were fulfilled. The heat was brutal. Perspiration had cemented a fine layer of dust to our skin by the time we had arrived. The cafeteria's food could serve as a first-rate prop in an antacid commercial.

> Some four hours and 106 miles later, we returned to Coleman, hot and exhausted. We silently sat in front of the fan for a long time. Then to be sociable, I dishonestly said, 'It was a great trip wasn't it?' No one spoke.

After a while, his mother-in-law admitted that she never really wanted to go but only did so because she thought everyone else wanted to and didn't want to cause a fuss, to which his wife also protested that she never really wanted to go either which then lead to a blazing argument. Eventually his father-in-law broke a long silence by exclaiming, in a long Texas drawl, 'Listen, I never wanted to go to Abilene. I just thought you might be bored. You visit so seldom I wanted to be sure you enjoyed it. I would have preferred to play another game of dominoes and eat the leftovers in the icebox.' This experience led to Harvey coining the term 'the Abilene paradox' to explain a curious aspect of group dynamics in which the opposite of what everyone wants is tacitly created by the group who thinks they are agreeing with what everyone else wants.

The Abilene paradox lies in the fact that we have problems not with disagreement, but rather with agreement. It is characterised by groups of people in an organisation privately agreeing that one course of action makes sense but failing to properly communicate those ideas and then collectively stumbling to what they *think* is the right course of action or what everyone else wants.

Eventually an inaccurate picture of what to do emerges and, based on that, the organisation takes steps towards actions that nobody really wants and which are counterproductive to the ultimate aims of the organisation itself.

You can witness the Abilene paradox at work in many schools. Often this takes the form of convoluted marking policies which increase teacher workload to the point of exhaustion, copious collection of data which is then entered into various spreadsheets, behaviour policies that punish the teacher more than the student who misbehaves, or graded lesson observations where teachers abandon what they normally do to put on a one-off, all-singing, all-dancing lesson for the observer, because that's what they think the inspectors would want to see should they visit.

A lot of this can be accounted for by innate cognitive biases such as groupthink but it can also be exacerbated by either poor evidence (as in the case of learning styles) or a poor understanding and misappropriation of good evidence (as in the case of formative assessment) and from the kind of groupthink outlined above. But with the emergence of a solid base of evidence about the most effective ways of creating effective learning environments, we might just be able to defend ourselves from these kind of cognitive biases. At its best, research should act as a bulwark, a sea-wall against the tidal wave of edu-guff that has so often washed over our schools. If we are not adopting evidence to make decisions, then we are at risk of loading the entire staff onto the school mini-bus and heading off to Abilene.

What can research do for schools?
The gap between research and practice is well documented and has led to calls for teachers to actively become researchers but there is of course a world of difference between *doing* research and *using* research. A champion Formula 1 driver doesn't need to know the intimate workings of an engine in order to be a champion any more than an engineer needs to know how to drive the car. As Dan Willingham reminds us, there is a fundamental difference between what researchers do and what teachers do: 'Scientists seek to describe the world as it is. Educators, in contrast, don't seek to describe what happens, but to *make* something happen.'[59]

In trying to '*make* something happen' in the classroom, teachers need the best resources to hand that have been tried and tested, and yet erroneous beliefs about how students learn still abound and continue to have a profoundly detrimental effect on what happens in the classroom. Before the middle of the 19th century,

---

59. Willingham, D. (2017) *The Reading Mind*, Jossey-Bass, p.187

doctors believed that cholera was caused by various unseen agents including a mysterious miasma or 'night air' that could cause a whole range of things such as obesity simply from inhaling the smell of certain foods. In 1854 John Snow posited a link between cholera and contaminated water, a discovery that would save millions of lives and paved the way for a more evidence-based approach to healthcare. As chapter 8 highlighted, many beliefs about how learning happens have had more in common with miasma theory and should really have been consigned to the pedagogical dustbin of history long ago, yet they still persist.

Research can never tell teachers precisely what to do in the classroom; there are too many variables and chaotic elements for it to be so prescriptive. However it can point toward a series of 'best bets' that may yield better outcomes than mere hunches or folk wisdom. Effective teaching is, in many regards, a craft and may often look like a concert pianist in full flow, but there is still the need for a properly-tuned piano, years of honed practice and an advanced mental representation of the piece they are playing.

The theologian Martin Luther once described the elements of religious practice that were not necessary as being adiaphora. Everything else was unnecessary. This was not to say that it was bad, but nor was it good or essential, hence it was the flotsam and jetsam of religious observance. It won't damage your health, but it won't do you any good either.

What, then, counts as adiaphora in education? What do we not really need? We started with the contention that being research-informed as a teacher, in a research-informed school, should lead to a reduction in workload. There is no silver bullet for this chronic problem, otherwise someone would have fired it by now, but the symptoms of overload can be managed and reduced if the unnecessary aspects of education can be trimmed. What we want is a classroom which runs efficiently, not one that is bogged down with pedagogy and interventions which are adiaphoric. Let's identify the essentials of teaching based on knowledge of research which shows what works. Let's bring these elements in, and cast everything else out. In short, let's streamline the classroom.

The streamlined classroom

One of the things we have learned in writing this book is that an awful lot of what goes on in the classroom simply doesn't matter. The signal-to-noise ratio is often at a less-than-optimal level for effective learning, with many extraneous activities taking up valuable learning time in the name of demonstrating progress, whether that be burdensome marking strategies or the creation of time-consuming resources to 'engage' students. Many of these approaches not only have limited impact on learning but they can have a hugely detrimental impact on teacher workload and teacher wellbeing. There are many reasons for why this culture has emerged but a central one is the conflation between learning and performance. In a culture that audits itself in terms of lesson observations and league tables, a premium will be given to that which can be observed through performance as an indicator of progress, but as Robert and Elizabeth Bjork point out, this can be highly misleading:

> Performance is what we can observe and measure during instruction or training. Learning – that is, the more or less permanent change in knowledge or understanding that is the target of instruction – is something we must try to infer, and current performance can be a highly unreliable index of whether learning has occurred.[60]

As we saw in chapter 5, engagement is a very poor proxy for effective learning but one that often drives success criteria of effective learning. By the same token, summative assessment can also be a very poor proxy for learning and, as Dylan Wiliam pointed out in chapter 1, using value-added data at the level of the student is an almost meaningless exercise in determining progress. Many of the most effective agents of change in the classroom are, if not invisible, then very hard to observe. But what kinds of things should teachers focus on?

There is a lot of evidence to suggest that teachers should be pruning back what they do and focus instead on a more streamlined approach that is less about cutting things up and putting them in envelopes and more about creating a set of conditions in which students can make the kinds of changes that will result in durable, long-lasting knowledge that can be applied in a range of situations. As Kirschner, Sweller and Clark remind us, 'If nothing has changed in long-term memory, nothing has been learned.'[61] The following six principles of classroom teaching are a distillation of the journey we have been on writing this book, both from talking to experts in the relevant fields and reading a recommended body of research around those fields. It's important to say that these principles work synergistically – they interact together in a way that is often greater than the sum of their individual parts and should be viewed in that light.

---

60. Bjork, E. and Bjork, R. (2009) 'Making Things Hard on Yourself, But in a Good Way: Creating Desirable Difficulties to Enhance Learning', *Psychology and the Real World*, p.57
61. Kirschner, A. Sweller, J. and Clark, R. (2006) 'Why Minimal Guidance During Instruction Does Not Work: An Analysis of the Failure of Constructivist, Discovery, Problem-Based, Experiential, and Inquiry-Based Teaching', *Educational Psychologist*, 41(2), p.77

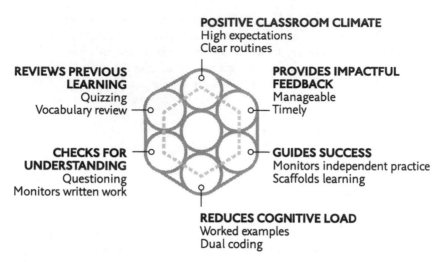

POSITIVE CLASSROOM CLIMATE
High expectations
Clear routines

REVIEWS PREVIOUS LEARNING
Quizzing
Vocabulary review

PROVIDES IMPACTFUL FEEDBACK
Manageable
Timely

CHECKS FOR UNDERSTANDING
Questioning
Monitors written work

GUIDES SUCCESS
Monitors independent practice
Scaffolds learning

REDUCES COGNITIVE LOAD
Worked examples
Dual coding

The streamlined classroom: 6 elements of effective classroom teaching

1. Review previous learning

One of the central findings from research on effective learning is that learners are exposed to new information a range of different times. For Graham Nuthall, students should encounter a new concept on at least three separate occasions in order to learn it properly. The beginning of a lesson is an excellent place to consolidate previous learning and create a sense of continuity. As Barak Rosenshine notes in his 10 principles of instruction, reviewing previous learning at the start of lessons can have a dramatic effect on learning:

> The most effective teachers in the studies of classroom instruction understood the importance of practice, and they began their lessons with a five- to eight-minute review of previously covered material. Some teachers reviewed vocabulary, formulae, events, or previously learned concepts. These teachers provided additional practice on facts and skills that were needed for recall to become automatic. Effective teacher activities also included reviewing the concepts and skills that were necessary to do the homework, having students correct each other's papers, and asking about points on which the students had difficulty or made errors. These reviews ensured that the students had a firm grasp of the skills and concepts that would be needed for the day's lesson.[62]

---

62. Rosenshine, B. (2012) 'Principles of Instruction', *American Educator*, p.16, www.aft.org//sites/default/files/periodicals/Rosenshine.pdf

2. Check for understanding

This is a deft skill and requires both a knowledge of your students and an understanding of common misconceptions. Various techniques can achieve this but probably the most useful tool in the box will be judicious questioning that is both open and closed in nature but, crucially, which informs what you will do next. Dylan Wiliam suggests that 'hinge-point questions' are of great use here:

> Firstly, it should take no longer than two minutes, and ideally less than one minute, for all students to respond to the questions; the idea is that the hinge-point question is a quick check on understanding, rather than a new piece of work in itself. Second, it must be possible for the teacher to view and interpret the responses from the class in 30 seconds (and ideally half that time).[63]

Marking student work is another effective way of checking understanding and as we saw in chapter 1, it doesn't need to be an onerous task. Some marking should simply function as a quick signpost to the teacher of how they should attenuate their teaching in response to what students have or have not learned.

3. Provides impactful feedback

Once a teacher gets into the habit of regularly checking for understanding, they are in a position to provide meaningful feedback. As we saw in chapter 1 from Dylan Wiliam, marking and feedback are not the same thing and a key aspect of a successful classroom is that feedback is given to improve the student and not the work:

> I think the important take-away here is that too many teachers focus on the purpose of feedback as changing or improving the work, whereas the major purpose of feedback should be to improve the student. If the feedback isn't helping the student to do a better task and a better job the *next time* they are doing a similar task, then it is probably going to be ineffective.

Whatever feedback we provide, it should enable students to reflect on where they have come from and where they need to go next. A teacher correcting misconceptions is an important element of this but is really just a starting point. Affording students the opportunity to consider their own progress against their peers and through the evaluation of exemplar work is another strong way to conceptualise improvement. If the teacher is working harder than the students in this process, then something has gone wrong. For students, feedback should be more like a mirror than a painted picture.

---

63. Wiliam, D. (2011) *Embedded Formative Assessment*, Solution Tree Press, p.101

4. Positive classroom climate

Of all the elements of a successful classroom, this is possibly the most important because without a positive classroom climate, most of the others are made impossible. Creating an environment where learning is not an aspiration but an expectation is the bedrock of any effective learning environment. As Tom Bennett notes in chapter 2:

> Designing and communicating clear, concrete routines to the class long in advance of any misbehaviour will minimise misbehaviour, because students will be aware of the classroom cultural norms. Driven home often enough, it can create tram lines for behaviour to default to. Instead of leaving behavioural choices to chance, the best strategy is for teachers to draw up exactly what is expected of their students from the beginning of the relationship.

Forging strong relationships where students have respect for not just the sanctity of the classroom but the privilege of learning about 'the best which has been thought and said in the world' is possibly the most important thing a teacher can do.

5. Guides success

As we saw in chapter 6, the limitations of working memory can be particularly problematic for novice learners and while there is good evidence that more expert learners can work independently, the vast majority of learners will need careful guidance to get to that place, especially when encountering new information:

> In one study, the more successful teachers of mathematics spent more time presenting new material and guiding practice. The more successful teachers used this extra time to provide additional explanations, give many examples, check for student understanding, and provide sufficient instruction so that the students could learn to work independently without difficulty. In contrast, the less successful teachers gave much shorter presentations and explanations, and then they passed out worksheets and told the students to work on the problems. Under these conditions the students made too many errors and had to be retaught the lesson.[64]

As discussed in the previous chapter, getting students to a place where they can work independently is a hugely desired outcome but perhaps not the best vehicle to get there. Providing worked examples and scaffolding is an integral part of enabling students to not just build the skills and knowledge they need

---

64. Rosenshine, B. (2012) 'Principles of Instruction', *American Educator*, p.16, www.aft.org//sites/default/files/periodicals/Rosenshine.pdf

to understand a difficult concept, but also the confidence to believe they can.

6. Reduces cognitive load

Cognitive load theory has been described as 'the single most important thing for teachers to know'.[65] As we saw in chapter 6, reducing the level of information to an optimal amount which does not overload or bore the student is crucial to effective learning. Once learners have built up schemas of knowledge that allow them to work on problems without exceeding their cognitive bandwidth, then they can work independently. Without it, their work might be in vain:

> If the learner has no relevant concepts or procedures in long term memory, the only thing to do is blindly search for solutions. Novices can engage in problem solving for extended periods and learn almost nothing.[66]

Presenting new information in small steps, providing worked examples and 'offering images and text at the same time so that the learner doesn't have to remember the one part while processing the other,'[67] are highly effective ways of reducing cognitive load and creating the optimal conditions for learning new material.

Next steps for teachers

This book is aimed at you, so we hope that if you've read this far you've found some useful things to enhance your practice. There is no such thing as a perfect teacher, so we can all look for ways to improve. There is definitely such a thing as an overburdened teacher (arguably a tautology), so ask yourself how you can streamline your classroom. It would be naïve for us to expect this can happen without a degree of conflict with the school leadership if they are wedded to aspects of obsolete practice. What you can do to defend your position, professionally, is to be up to date with the latest findings.

The best vehicle for this, at the time of writing, is Twitter. There is a lot of edu-nonsense on Twitter and some debates that do more to bring the profession into disrepute, but please don't let this put you off. You don't need to be an avid Tweeter, you don't need to throw hashtags all over the place, you just need to follow people who know educational research and share distilled versions of it through blogs and forums. If you're following the people we interviewed in this book, you're making a good start. For example, following Yana Weinstein

---

65. Wiliam, D., Twitter 26/01/17 https://twitter.com/dylanwiliam/status/824682504602943489

66. Clark, R., Kirschner, P. and Sweller, J. (2012) 'Putting Students on the Path to Learning', *American Educator*, p.7 www.aft.org/sites/default/files/periodicals/Clark.pdf, p.10

67. Kirschner, P. & Neelen, M. (2017)'Double Barrelled Learning For the Young and Old', https://3starlearningexperiences.wordpress.com/2017/05/30/double-barrelled-learning-for-young-old/

would give you access to the concise and highly informative blogs posts of the Learning Scientists. This is the type of professional development that makes a difference. The Teacher Development Trust has shown that one-off courses are largely a waste of time, and taking a day out of school (at the expense of the CPD budget) adds to planning, marking and creates cover for colleagues. Instead, read little and often. It's free, effective, and enjoyable. There may be a better vehicle than Twitter now or in the future, but this is a good place to start.

At the end of this book we have given a select reading list. This isn't a bibliography as such, but a list of books that you should consider reading. This is a growing market because a much greater proportion of educational writing is being done by teachers, for teachers. This is a hugely positive development because the books provide accessible, informative and manageable information that can be put to good use. Also, because reading a book takes longer than going on a one-day course, it allows for that most valuable of habits: reflection. If we spend time thinking deeply about our practice and pushing ourselves to be better at what we do, the outcomes will be better for us, our colleagues and our students. What we have found in organising the Telegraph Festival of Education is that teachers who know a lot about practice come to share their expertise and debate with fellow professionals. This 'to-and-fro' is much better than sitting in a hotel basement, copying down things from a flipchart. Try to take on professional learning that is proactive and allows you to debate your practice so that reflection is encouraged, and the insights you acquire are channelled into your classroom.

If you want to embark on research yourself, that's fine. However, it isn't necessary – teachers don't need to be the researchers, they just need to be research-informed. To do this effectively it does help enormously to know how to critique any piece of research, by asking questions like what baseline evidence exists, and were counterfactuals explored? Spending some time on this will reap dividends in the long term. It means that you can sift the weak, inflated arguments from the research that holds real weight.

Next steps for school leaders

We have said that this book is for classroom practitioners, so a question all school leaders should ask of themselves is whether their classroom experience is as sharp as it should be. You may be doing a little teaching, or perhaps none at all. There's a good chance that you observe more lessons than you teach. If this is the case, the first step is to review the research around observation and what we really learn from it. Rob Coe has argued that:

The evidence shows that when untrained observers are asked to judge the quality of a lesson, there is likely to be only modest agreement among them. Worse still, even if they do agree that what they see is good practice, it often actually isn't.[68]

Even if you are really confident that you know good teaching when you see it, you may be wrong. The evidence shows that judgement even between two trained observers of the same lesson is more likely to be in disagreement about the quality of the lesson. The variance increases substantially in judgements about 'inadequate' lessons. The invisible nature of learning and the poor proxies for it mean that any observer needs to be able to spot red herrings in a classroom. We strongly advise that you look at the range of recent research and writing on this so that observation is a powerful learning tool and not a weapon of mass school destruction.

Secondly, who is in charge of filtering research in your school? Is it the sole responsibility of a deputy head? Or is it down to the leadership team collectively? Are conversations about teaching and learning common to the culture of the school and can classroom practitioners – especially those on full timetables – influence the direction of policy? The people who spend the most time delivering lessons need to have a voice, and an opportunity to develop as professionals. If you can give them both of these things, the impact on pupils will be tangible.

Thirdly, any intervention, policy change or new strategy must always be vetted heavily by asking these questions:

1. What is the need for the change?

2. What are the potential benefits?

3. What is the evidence base for it?

4. What impact will it have on teacher workload?

5. What effect will it have on pupil learning?

6. Can a pilot be done before the initiative goes whole-school?

7. Who needs to be consulted to ensure successful implementation?

If any new idea makes it through these seven questions without coming unstuck then you may be making a very valuable contribution to pedagogy at your school. If you skip a step, or ignore the evidence, you will likely be doing more harm than good. What we have argued for is the need for a streamlined

---

68. www.cem.org/blog/414/

classroom. Can you look at the classrooms in your school and say that this is truly the case? Or are your staff carrying an unnecessary burden that is inhibiting the progress made by their pupils? Ask yourself what you can do to unbolt things to allow your staff to excel at what they do. Becoming a research-informed school is the best step to take to facilitate this.

APPENDIX

Suggested reading list

Books

Shaun Allison and Andy Tharby, *Make Every Lesson Count*

Brown, Roediger and McDaniel, *Make it Stick*

Benedict Carey, *How We Learn*

Daisy Christodoulou, *Seven Myths About Education*

David Didau, *What if everything you knew about education was wrong?*

John Hattie and Gregory Yates, *Visible Learning and the Science of How We Learn*

Graham Nuthall, *The Hidden Lives of Learners*

Dylan Wiliam, *Embedded formative assessment*

Dan Willingham, *Why Don't Students Like School?*

Useful free resources

Bjork, E. L., & Bjork, R. A. 'Making things hard on yourself, but in a good way: Creating desirable difficulties to enhance learning', in Gernsbacher, M.A. *et al* (Ed) *Psychology and the real world: Essays illustrating fundamental contributions to society*, New York: Worth Publishers (p56-64). Available at: https://teaching.yale-nus.edu.sg/wp-content/uploads/sites/25/2016/02/Making-Things-Hard-on-Yourself-but-in-a-Good-Way-2011.pdf

Coe, R., Aloisi, C., Higgins, S. and Elliot Major, L. 'What makes great teaching? Review of the underpinning research', Sutton Trust, October 2014. Available at: www.suttontrust.com/researcharchive/great-teaching/

Cordingley, P., Higgins, S., Greany, T., Buckler, N., Coles-Jordan, D., Crisp, B., Saunders, L., Coe, R. 'Developing Great Teaching: Lessons from the international reviews into effective professional development', Teacher Development Trust. Available at: http://tdtrust.org/about/dgt/

Deans for Impact 'The Science of Learning', Austin, TX: Deans for Impact. Available at: http://deansforimpact.org/pdfs/The_Science_of_Learning.pdf

Dunlosky, J. 'Strengthening the Student Toolbox: Study Strategies to Boost Learning', *American Educator*, 37(3), 12-21. Available at: www.aft.org/sites/default/files/periodicals/dunlosky.pdf

Marzano, R. J., Gaddy, B. B., & Dean, C. 'What Works in Classroom Instruction', Available at: www.at-udl.com/library_bkup/DATA/Misc%20PDF's/whatworks.pdf

Rosenshine, B. 'Principles of Instruction: Research based principles that all teachers should know', *American Educator*, Spring 2012. Available at: www.aft.org/pdfs/americaneducator/spring2012/Rosenshine.pdf

CPSIA information can be obtained
at www.ICGtesting.com
Printed in the USA
LVOW10s1954191117
556944LV00034B/312/P